CULTURE
AND
CONSUMPTION

CULTURE
AND
CONSUMPTION

New Approaches to the Symbolic
Character of Consumer Goods
and Activities

GRANT McCRACKEN

INDIANA UNIVERSITY PRESS
Bloomington and Indianapolis

First Midland Book Edition 1990

Permission to reprint the articles below was granted by their original publishers:

"Clothing as Language" (Chapter 4). Reprinted by permission of University Press of America, Inc.

"Meaning Manufacture and Movement in the World of Goods" (Chapter 5) was originally published as "Culture and Consumption: A Theoretical Account of the Structure and Movement of the Cultural Meaning of Consumer Goods," *Journal of Consumer Research* 13 (1 June 1986): 71–84. It has been partially rewritten. Reprinted by permission of the *Journal of Consumer Research*.

"Consumer Goods, Gender Construction, and a Rehabilitated Trickle-down Theory" (Chapter 6) was originally published as "The Trickle-Down Theory Rehabilitated" in *The Psychology of Fashion*, edited by Michael R. Solomon (Lexington, Mass.: Lexington Books, D. C. Heath and Company, copyright 1985, D. C. Heath and Company). Reprinted by permission of the publisher.

Manufactured in the United States of America

Library of Congress Cataloging-in-Publication Data

McCracken, Grant David, 1951–
  Culture and consumption.

  Bibliography: p.
  Includes index.
  1. Consumption (Economics)—History.   2. Culture—History.   3. Social values—History.   I. Title.
HC79.C6M385   1988   339.4'7   87–45394
ISBN 0-253-31526-3
ISBN 0-253-20628-6 (pbk.)

    5 6 7 94 93

To the memory of my grandfathers,
Joseph Allan McQuade (1896–1983)
and Elsworth Smith McCracken
(1889–1973)

Contents

ACKNOWLEDGMENTS

I wish to thank the following people for their contributions to this book: M. Vadasz, L. Michaels, A. Knight, V. Ayoub, N. Lesko, M. Sahlins, A. Fienup Riordan, S. McKinnon, J. Curry, M. Verdon, T. and V. Li, K. O. L. Burridge, R. Pollay, M. Sommers, J. Wardlaw, R. Belk, and D. Woolcott. Thanks are also due to the Killam Trust and the Social Science and Humanities Research Council of Canada for financial support of research reported here.

INTRODUCTION

This collection of essays has a single theme: the relationship between culture and consumption. By "culture" I mean the ideas and activities with which we construe and construct our world. By "consumption" I broaden the conventional definition to include the processes by which consumer goods and services are created, bought, and used. Culture and consumption have an unprecedented relationship in the modern world. No other time or place has seen these elements enter into a relationship of such intense mutuality. Never has the relationship between them been so deeply complicated.

The social sciences have been slow to see this relationship, and slower still to take stock of its significance. They have generally failed to see that consumption is a thoroughly cultural phenomenon. As the essays in this book seek to demonstrate, consumption is shaped, driven, and constrained at every point by cultural considerations. The system of design and production that creates consumer goods is an entirely cultural enterprise. The consumer goods on which the consumer lavishes time, attention, and income are charged with cultural meaning. Consumers use this meaning to entirely cultural purposes. They use the meaning of consumer goods to express cultural categories and principles, cultivate ideals, create and sustain lifestyles, construct notions of the self, and create (and survive) social change. Consumption is thoroughly cultural in character.

The reciprocal truth is, of course, that in Western developed societies culture is profoundly connected to and dependent on consumption. Without consumer goods, modern, developed societies would lose key instruments for the reproduction, representation, and manipulation of their culture. The worlds of design, product development, advertising, and fashion that create these goods are themselves important authors of our cultural universe. They work constantly to shape, transform, and vivify this universe. Without them the modern world would almost certainly come undone. The meaning of consumer goods and the meaning creation accomplished by consumer processes are important parts of the scaffolding of our present realities. Without consumer goods, certain acts of self-definition and collective definition in this culture would be impossible.

The idea that culture and consumption should be so mutually dependent comes as a surprise to us. It is indeed entirely contrary to a familiar truth. We "know" from popular opinion and social scientific study that our materialism is one of the things that is most wrong with our society, and one of the most significant causes of our modern difficulties. This familiar, and entirely wrongheaded, idea has helped keep us from seeing the cultural significance of consumption plainly.

The purpose of these essays is to begin to improve upon this impoverished view. It is to show that the goods that are so often identified as the unhappy, destructive preoccupation of a materialist society are in fact one of the chief instruments of its survival, one of the ways in which its order is created and maintained. Each of these essays was written to stand on its own, but all address the nature of the relationship between culture and consumption. All of them represent the effort of an anthropologist to determine just why we are so preoccupied with consumer goods, and what contribution they make to our novel culture and society.

The book is divided into three sections. The first section is historical and contains three chapters. The first two chapters examine the origins of the consumer society and trace its development from the sixteenth century to the present day. The third chapter treats the experience of a modern-day consumer whose pattern of consumption has strong pre-modern characteristics. The second section is theoretical in character. It examines the theoretical models available to us in the consideration of the relationship between culture and consumption. The "goods as language" model is rejected in one chapter and a new model that looks at the movement of cultural meaning is constructed in the next. The third section consists in four chapters, each of which examines a different use of consumer goods to accomplish social and cultural work. These chapters examine the use of goods to express new notions of gender, to protect cultural ideals, to maintain product and lifestyle consistencies, and to create and respond to social change.

Before reviewing these chapters in more detail, let me briefly comment on the scholarly foundations of this book. There are two contributing disciplines. One is anthropology, the field in which I was trained. The second is consumer behavior, the field in which I have taught and done research for the past four years. This book represents a kind of rapprochement of these two quite different disciplinary perspectives. A word on the nature of this rapprochement is perhaps in order.

Anthropology and the study of consumer behavior have been reluctant participants in the study of the relationship between culture and consumption. Neither has evidenced, until quite recently, an interest in examining the cultural aspects of consumption or the importance of consumption to culture. Happily, this is beginning to change. Developments within both fields are beginning to make the study of culture and consumption an imaginable, practicable activity.

In the field of consumer behavior, these developments are numerous. First, scholars have begun to broaden the definition of "consumer behavior." This emerging definition takes it beyond "purchase behavior" (i.e., what happens when the consumer reaches to the shelf to choose brand "x" or brand "y") to include all of the interaction between the good and the consumer before the moment of purchase and after it. Second, they have also begun to move beyond their long-standing preoccupation with the "decision-making process" to look at the role of other cognitive processes (especially symbolic ones) and the role of affect. Third, the field has displayed a new willingness to transcend the methodological individualism and microscosmic focus inherited from the field of psychology, and to consider the larger social and cultural systems and contexts of consumption. In a fully Durkheimian shift, the field is developing a macroscopic perspective that takes account of the supra-individual characteristics of consumption. Fourth, more scholars have begun to accept as legitimate topics for research ones that have no immediate relevance for the marketing community, and this marketing community has begun, in turn, to define the nature of its inquiry more broadly. In general terms, in this broadening of the field, consumption is now less often defined as a small slice of the individual's reality and more often approached as a range of diverse, systematic, embracing, and fully cultural phenomena.[1]

Anthropology has also seen a series of developments that has allowed it to take up the study of culture and consumption. First of all, it has begun to renew its interest in material culture, an essential development for the study of consumer goods. Second, it is beginning to shift away from its almost neurotic refusal to contemplate its own culture. Anthropology has traditionally felt an attraction for the alien and the marginal. Anthropologists have passed over opportunities to study their own culture, and especially the "mainstream" aspects of this culture, with mind-numbing regularity. (Interestingly, this has made novelists the most active and successful ethnographers at work in North America today.) Third, anthropology has developed the theories of culture, of meaning, and of symbolism that were needed to understand the cultural and communicative properties of consumer goods and behavior.

Fourth, still more recently anthropologists have begun to develop the theories of process and context that allow them to capture the dynamic character of consumption. Fifth, there is evidence that some members of the field are beginning to transcend the ideological suspicion that any treatment of the cultural properties of consumer goods is tantamount to participation in the free enterprise system. Sixth, some anthropologists are preparing to give up their elitist pretense that any examination of contemporary popular culture must be a form of intellectual slumming. Finally, and perhaps most important, they have begun to move beyond the peculiar notion that consumption can be dismissed as a nasty combination of self indulgence, greed, vanity, and irrationality that does not need or deserve systematic study.[2]

In its attempt to combine anthropology and consumer behavior, this book should be read much more as a "first go" than the "final word." It is distinctly *not* a judicious survey of the two fields that concludes in magisterial pronouncements and directives. Or, to change the metaphor, this is not a document in the nature of a report from a Royal Commission or a United Nations paper that bids unfamiliar and uneasy parties to the conference table and the contemplation of their mutual interests. More exactly, this is the work of a single, often quite nervous, individual who has spent the last few years smuggling concepts and data back and forth across a well-guarded border, keen to see what one field looks like in the context of the other. This treatment is then partial, experimental, and tentative. It is more a demonstration of possibilities than of certain truths. It means to begin the rapprochement. It does not pretend to accomplish it.

Let us look now at each of the chapters in turn. The first chapter investigates how Western society undertook its reckless new experiment with consumption. "The Making of Modern Consumption" draws on the explosion of scholarly activity that followed the appearance of the work of Braudel in the 1960s. It also draws on the author's own research into Elizabethan England. The chapter considers three episodes in this making of modern consumption. These took place in the sixteenth, eighteenth, and nineteenth centuries, and each reveals a new stage and a new set of forces in the creation of our modern consumer society. This study allows us to glimpse the extraordinary process by which we began by stages to recognize and exploit the meaningful, symbolic properties of consumer goods and make these the scaffolding of our implausible social life.

The second chapter, "Ever Dearer in Our Thoughts," narrows our attention from the broad sweep of Western societies to a single cultural institution within them. Here we examine the role of "patina" as a symbolic device. Before the eighteenth century, the rich were especially fond of patina. The fine surface that accumulated on their possessions as a result of oxidization and use was proof of their long-standing claim to high status. It was proof that they were "ancient" nobles, not newly minted ones. In this way, the ruling classes used the patina of goods as a status gatekeeper, a means of distinguishing aristocrats from arrivistes and pretenders. In the eighteenth century, however, the advent of the fashion system helped to eclipse patina, and thereafter this status strategy became the exclusive concern of only a very small and very particular group in society. This chapter is an attempt to tell the story of patina from the sixteenth century through to the modern day. In the process we will have occasion to discuss theories of status and symbolism from Goffman, Veblen, and Pierce.

The third chapter is entitled "Lois Roget: Curatorial Consumer in a Modern World," and it reports the experience of a modern individual whose consumption has several entirely pre-modern characteristics. This treatment of Lois Roget gives us the opportunity to reconstruct in intimate ethnographic detail certain aspects of consumption as a "lived reality" before the eighteenth century. In a sense, this chapter means to do for pre-industrial consumption what Peter Laslett's *The World We Have Lost* (1971) does for pre-industrial family life. It attempts to suggest some of the connections between culture and consumption before the dawn of modernity.

The fourth chapter, "Clothing as Language," looks at one of the ways we have traditionally come to think about the symbolic properties of our consumer goods. Academic and popular treatments have encouraged us to think of these things as a kind of "language." Certainly this is an improvement over the antique ideas with which we have considered (usually to condemn) consumer goods. But it is nevertheless still unsatisfactory. This chapter examines the attempts to suggest that the consumer good, clothing, is a "language." It argues that clothing is in fact quite unlike language and that indeed it communicates cultural meaning best when it departs from the syntagmatic principle on which language operates.

This fifth chapter, "Meaning Manufacture and Movement in the World of Goods," is written to suggest a different approach to the cultural significance of consumer goods. It draws on the fields of anthropology, sociology, psychology, consumer behavior, American studies, and material culture to create a theoretical scheme of the cultural meaning that adheres in consumer goods. The scheme is designed to show how this meaning gets into and is got out of the goods. The emphasis here is not on what people "say" with the meaning in goods but what they "do" with it. This chapter attempts to show how we use the meaning in goods to construct concepts of the self and world.

The organizing theme of this chapter is "movement." The meaning of goods is constantly in transit, constantly moving from one location to another in the cultural world. The chapter shows how meaning begins in the culturally constituted world and the process by which it is then "unhooked" by product designers, advertisers, marketers, and journalists and transferred to the consumer good. It then shows how we as consumers fetch this meaning out of the goods for our own purposes in the construction of our own worlds. Four different rituals are considered here, each of them important to the process of getting meaning out of goods. In sum, this chapter looks at how we make consumption a source of cultural meaning and use it in the construction of individual and collective worlds.

The third and final section of the book seeks to look more particularly at some of the cultural objectives of consumption. Chapter 6 looks at how consumer goods and behavior are used to accommodate and create new notions of gender. Chapter 7 looks at their use in the preservation of certain of our ideals. Chapter 8 considers their dual role in the preservation of lifestyles or their reform. Chapter 9 looks at how we use the meaningful properties of consumer goods as an instrument of continuity and change.

Chapter 6, "Consumer Goods, Gender Construction, and a Rehabilitated Trickle-down Theory," applies new theories of symbolism to a very old and venerable diffusion theory. The "trickle-down" theory of diffusion was for a long time the most compelling model for describing how the clothing behavior of one group could influence the clothing behavior of another. In the last twenty years this model has been elbowed aside by brash new models. The purpose of this chapter is to rehabilitate the trickle-down theory by wedding it to new theories of symbolism.

The ethnographic case in point here is the clothing innovations among professional men and women and especially the "dress-for-success" look. Here we see a classic case in which consumer goods are used to create and respond to a fundamental shift in gender definition. What this chapter shows us is how women have used the meaning in certain goods to create new images of themselves.

The seventh chapter, "The Evocative Power of Goods," is designed to show how we use goods to keep alive some of our ideals and hopes. It begins with the suggestion that societies deliberately take their ideals and remove them from harm by "displacing" them to another time or place. Thus, the mountain village that has experienced a high rate of domestic discord (and might begin to wonder whether its present definitions of "family" and "gender" are misconceived) can protect its present ideal of family life by claiming that it existed with perfect clarity and ease "in the days of our grandfathers." Now the ideal is displaced, "proven" by its "existence" in another cultural space and time. But once something has been displaced, how does one recover it and make it live in the here and now? Consumer goods are one of the answers here. They serve as bridges to displaced meaning without compromising its displaced status. The theory explains why we so often wish for objects beyond our reach and why we suppose that we will obtain with these objects a new happiness. Consumer goods have long promised the realization of personal and collective ideals (only rarely delivering them). Chapter 7 attempts to show how this happens.

Chapter 8, "Diderot Unities and the Diderot Effect," begins with a glimpse of the great French philosophe Denis Diderot in his study mourning the passing of his old dressing gown. It is about the cultural consistencies that draw a collection of consumer goods into a characteristic grouping (e.g., the yuppie's BMW, Burberry, and burgundy) and how these product complements are preserved and sometimes transformed by the Diderot effect. This chapter considers the implications of Diderot unities and the Diderot effect for theories of lifestyle, advertising, and consumer demand.

The object of the final chapter of the book, "Consumption, Change, and Continuity," is to show how consumer goods serve us both as instruments of continuity and as instruments of change. The meaning in consumer goods is one of the ways in which we give our lives a consistency in the face of the overwhelming change to which it is subjected. Goods help in this capacity by creating a largely undetectable record of existing cultural categories and cultural principles. Surrounded by these goods, we are encouraged to imagine that these categories and principles are somehow inherent in the very nature of things. It is partly because sexist distinctions between men and women are invested in the physical objects of our daily existence that new definitions of gender in this society have been so hard to establish. The cultural meaning in goods also helps them to disarm cultural innovations. What Sahlins calls the "object-code" incorporates innovations such as "hippie" aesthetics and principles and make them a harmless part of the mainstream. But goods also have a genuinely innovative capacity, and they are certainly one of the most powerful engines of change in our society. The object-code of goods allows individuals to take existing cultural meanings and draw them into novel configurations. They are a kind of language of invention with which radical groups can think about, refine, and ultimately advertise their ideologies. Goods then are instruments of innovation and conservation and in both capacities they serve us in our modern quest for order in a disorderly world.

Culture and Consumption is a systematic inquiry into the cultural and symbolic properties of consumer goods. The first three chapters show how we came to be a consumer society. The second two chapters suggest how we might think about the cultural properties of consumer goods to best understand their symbolic properties. The final four chapters consider different uses to which we put the meaning of goods. The largest objective of these chapters is to help demonstrate the extraordinary contribution that the meaning in consumer processes makes to the structure and process of contemporary society.

Part I
HISTORY

An understanding of the modern relationship between culture and consumption demands an appreciation of the historical context in which this relationship was fashioned. The purpose of these opening chapters of the book is to offer three very different treatments of this context. In chapter 1, I attempt to integrate the large number of scholarly books and articles into a single overview of the history of consumption. I have added to this overview my own understanding of the changes in consumption that took place in Elizabethan England. In the second chapter, we narrow our attention to one particular moment in the history of consumption, the transformation of the "patina" system of consumption. In the third chapter, we descend still more steeply to the particulars of an individual life and the ethnographic treatment of the "curatorial" system of consumption. Together, these three chapters provide a historical foundation for the chapters on modern culture and consumption that make up the remainder of the book.

ONE

The Making of Modern Consumption

The historical community, following the lead of Braudel and the example of McKendrick, has recognized that the "great transformation" of the West included not just an "industrial revolution" but also a "consumer revolution." This community now argues that this consumer revolution represents not just a change in tastes, preferences, and buying habits, but a fundamental shift in the culture of the early modern and modern world. The consumer revolution is now seen to have changed Western concepts of time, space, society, the individual, the family, and the state. This first chapter seeks to establish a single overview of the available literature in order to consider how Western culture became increasingly dependent on and integrated with the new consumer goods and practices that appeared from the sixteenth century onwards. It seeks to show the historical circumstances in which culture and consumption began to fashion their present relationship of deeply complicated mutuality.

Modern consumption is, after all, a historical artifact.[1] Its present-day characteristics are the result of several centuries of profound social, economic, and cultural change in the West. Just what these changes are and precisely how they gave rise to the consumption of the present day are matters of some dispute. What cannot be doubted is that an inquiry into the origins and development of modern consumption is now well under way, and that this task now occupies a growing segment of the historical and social scientific community.

The first appearance of consumption in its modern form was dramatic. Elizabethans said they thought they detected something that "did smell of beyond the seas." Somewhat later observers referred to it as an "epidemic" or an "act of madness." Modern observers have used equally dramatic language. They have referred to it as an "orgy of spending" (McKendrick et al. 1982:10) and the creation of "dream world" (Williams 1982:66). Modern consumption was the cause and consequence of so many social changes that its emergence marked nothing less than the transformation of the Western world. As one historian has suggested, the appearance of the "consumer revolution" is rivaled only by the Neolithic revolution for the thoroughness with which it changed society (McKendrick et al. 1982:9).

The consumer revolution is a piece of a larger social transformation to which a large amount of social scientific and historical inquiry has been devoted. Durkheim, Weber, Marx, Simmel, Sombart, and Tonnies all addressed themselves to what Polanyi (1957) has called "the great transformation." Indeed it does not exaggerate to say that the study of this transformation is responsible in some part for the foundation and development of the social sciences. What is striking about this vein of scholarship, however, is that it has devoted very little of its attention to the development of consumption. As McKendrick notes, it is the study of the legal, economic, industrial, and other revolutions that has preoccupied the students of the great transformation. Only recently have scholars, with McKendrick as perhaps the most conspicuous and remarkable party, begun to look at the role of changes of consumption in the transformation of the West.

The work of this new group of scholars is diverse. There is no consensus on even the most fundamental terms of the consumer revolution. For instance, McKendrick (1982) claims to have discovered the birth of consumer revolution in eighteenth-century England, Williams (1982) has discovered it in nineteenth-century France, and Mukerji (1983) has discovered it in fifteenth- and sixteenth-century England. This diversity of outlook and approach is useful. It allows us to see the disparate aspects of the consumer revolution from several points of view. It is the purpose of this chapter to review these points of view and to show how they can be organized and interrelated in the creation of a general perspective on the origins and development of modern consumption.

The first part of the chapter will review the chief contributors to the study of the origins and development of modern consumption. The second part will examine three moments in the history of consumption, drawing together a diverse range of historical materials to create three "snapshots" of the Western world as it moved from the sixteenth century to the present day. This will include diverse topics, including new categories of goods; new times, places and patterns of purchase; new marketing techniques; new ideas about possessions and materialism; changed reference groups, lifestyles, class mobility, diffusion patterns, product symbolism, and patterns of decision making. Our concern throughout will be the transformation of culture that took place in the consumer revolution.

It must be emphasized that the chapter does not pretend to assemble these disparate aspects of the consumer revolution in any comprehensive way. Still less does it claim to provide a historical treatment that would satisfy the high standards of evidence and argument established by historians. If this chapter engages in speculation from which most historians fastidiously abstain, it does so because even speculation is preferable to the confusion that now surrounds this vital academic question.

THE STATE OF A NASCENT ART: THREE PIONEERS

The Birth of A Consumer Society: The Commercialization of Eighteenth-Century England is the most thorough, well-grounded and impressive of the works from which this essay draws.[2] Its most striking characteristic, perhaps, is its tone. There is nothing guarded or tentative about this piece of history. While some historians write to a Lilliputian scale and rarely stray beyond, say, the wills and probates of a single village in the third decade of the fifteenth century, McKendrick and his colleagues set out to take on a "big question" and present their arguments without faint-hearted qualification or reticence. This book also has a slightly "whiggish" quality insofar as it construes the past as a prelude to the present.[3] This is as much "history for the sake of the present" as it is "history for the sake of the past." Third, this book has the great advantage of being written in the effortless prose for which historians are deservedly famed. Its exposition of the complexities of the eighteenth century is elegantly clear. These three qualities, forthrightness, relevance, and clarity, make *The Birth of a Consumer Society* an unusually valuable and pertinent piece of historiography. It is easily the strongest contribution to the present field.

The larger terms of McKendrick's project are simple. He seeks to supply a neglected aspect of the social transformation that took place in eighteenth-century England. He insists that the traditional approach to this transformation gives us only half the picture. He argues that we have emphasized the industrial revolution to the exclusion of other, equally important developments. What has gone ignored is the "consumer revolution" that was the necessary companion of the industrial revolution. A change in productive means and ends, he says, cannot have occurred without a commensurate change in consumers' tastes and preferences. Nevertheless, historical scholarship has emphasized the "supply" side of the transformation and ignored the "demand" side. The purpose of *The Birth of A Consumer Society*, then, is to document the development of the demand side of the industrial revolution and illuminate how this transformation of tastes and preferences contributed to the great transformation.

One of the opening events of this revolution was the wild enthusiasm with which the English consumer greeted the cheap calico and muslins imported from India in the 1690s. The sudden demand for this fashion was an early indication of the new consumer tastes which would act as an engine driving domestic production and foreign importations to a new scale of activity. McKendrick, taking this as his cue, examines the "commercialization of fashion" as one of the chief areas in which consumer demand changed and was changed by eighteenth-century innovations. These innovations include a new, intensified tyranny of fashion, a more rapid obsolescence of style, the speedier diffusion of fashion knowledge, the appearance of marketing techniques such as the fashion doll and the fashion plate, the new and more active participation of previously excluded social groups, and finally, new ideas about consumption and its contribution to the public good. He turns, then, to the study of the commercialization of pottery and the entrepreneurial genius of Josiah Wedgwood, who both followed and led the consumer boom of the period. Especially interesting here is the account of the ease and skill with which Wedgwood manipulated the tastes of the "opinion leaders" of this period, the aristocracy. Finally, McKendrick examines the story of the commercialization of eighteenth-century fashion and the contribution of George Packwood, who did so much to develop newspaper advertising in the period.

McKendrick's contribution to this question is so important and remarkable that criticism has a churlish quality. We owe him a debt of gratitude, not carping disagreement. Still it must be observed that McKendrick's work is seriously flawed on two counts. First, on a point of historical fact, it appears that McKendrick has misread the empirical record. He claims that fashion did not govern the clothing of Elizabethan England with the rapidity it was to assume in the eighteenth century. There is, he says, no evidence of annual fashion in this half of the sixteenth century (1982:40). This is mistaken. Both primary and secondary sources make it clear that annual fashion was very much alive in Elizabethan England (cf. Fairholt 1885; Linthicom 1936; Norris 1938).[4]

This seems a small error, but it is in fact a major one. For McKendrick's study depends on two assumptions: that the consumer revolution was a sudden break, a genuine revolution, and, second, that this revolution took place in the eighteenth century. Furthermore, his evidence, as he willingly concedes (1982:12), comes chiefly from one product category, clothing. To advance his case he must successfully argue, then, that clothing became the sudden captive of a highly innovative fashion and that it did so in the eighteenth century. It appears that both of these contentions are not only groundless but a surprising departure from the well-established facts of the matter.

The second ground for complaint has to do with McKendrick's analytic approach. In order to investigate the "consumer boom" of the eighteenth century, he adopts two ideas from the social sciences: the notion of conspicuous consumption developed by Veblen (1912) and the "trickle-down" notion refined by Simmel (1904). Examined in the light of these ideas the consumer boom of the eighteenth century becomes a war of status competition in which goods serve chiefly in status-marking and status-claiming capacities. Certainly this is a fair characterization of one of the ways goods were used in the period and why they proved so popular. It is highly doubtful, however, whether this sociological explanation is an exhaustive account. But this is precisely what McKendrick attempts to make of these ideas. He entertains no additional or competing explanations. He subjects these concepts to no careful scrutiny. Simmel and Veblen are made to pull this argument through the unfamiliar soil of the eighteenth century unaided by the assistance of the author or fellow social scientists.

McKendrick's uncritical attachment to the ideas of Simmel and Veblen prevent him from taking up some of the questions his research raises. For instance, if a new fondness for novelty was at the base of the acceptance of fashion, whence did this fondness come? As McKendrick (following Braudel 1973) notes, fashion change is by no means universal (1982:36). When McKendrick's study of the new intensity of this fashion in the eighteenth century tells us that novelty had become an "irresistible drug" (1982:10), he leaves us to wonder just how this fundamental change in "mentalitie" had taken place. Similarly, when he tells us that much of the new spending was competitive and emulative (1982:11), he leaves it to the reader to work out whether consumers were slavishly imitating their betters or challenging them, and whether they were competing with their peers in a status war or merely putting social distance between themselves and their own imitative lessers.[5] These important differences are decisive to our understanding of the social context of the consumer revolution.

On balance, however, McKendrick's work makes an important contribution to our understanding of the historical origins and development of the consumption of the present day. His account of the commercialization of fashion, potteries, and shaving, and the additional work of Brewer and Plumb on the commercialization of politics and society respectively make a significant contribution to this question and, more important, raise the question to a new position of academic prominence and legitimacy.

Dream Worlds: Mass Consumption in Late Nineteenth-Century France by Rosalind H. Williams is another contribution to this growing field of historical study. This book is also striking for its tone which is, if anything, even more forthright than McKendrick's. Williams's work is also more whiggish insofar as it is unabashedly devoted to the discovery of the present in the past. Finally, it is clearly written and well crafted. What distinguishes these two books in matters of tone is the moral character of Williams's history. The "big question" to which this book is devoted is not only a clearer understanding of the nature of consumption in the modern day. It also thoroughly condemns the commercialization of modern society and the excesses and deception of the "dream world of consumption."

Those who sympathize with this now familiar point of view on the consumer society will admire the skill and intelligence with which it is developed here. But even those who sympathize with the moral vision that informs this book must agree that it commits Williams irretrievably to certain relatively grave difficulties in her treatment of nineteenth-century France. For instance, there is an unmistakable "presentism" here. We see nineteenth-century France only as an anticipation of the present day and never as a juncture of possibilities that might have turned out otherwise. Second, we see France and its nascent consumerism only in the most pessimistic, disapproving terms. However much one admires morally purposive scholarship, it must be acknowledged that genuine understanding of the origins and development of modern consumption is inhibited by such a perspective. History that is the recitation of modern articles of faith tells us much more about the present than the past (cf. McKendrick et al. 1982:30).

Williams's work is divided into two parts. The first means to show the origins and development of the "consumer revolution" and the second to outline the development of "critical thought" about this revolution. For Williams, the origins of the consumer revolution are late nineteenth-century France. The pioneering efforts of the French in retailing and advertising turned Paris into a kind of "pilot plant of mass consumption" (1982:11). Williams suggests the Paris expositions of 1889 and 1900 were the first planned environments of mass consumption and that they made decisive contributions to the development of the department store and the trade show (1982:12). In the second part of the book, Williams reviews the social critics and social scientists of France who sought to come to terms with the consumer revolution which was transforming their society. French intellectuals proved to be as innovative as their commercial brethren. While merchants and entrepreneurs

were creating the consumer revolution, French thinkers were struggling to create a
social theory capable of comprehending the massive social and economic changes
the revolution brought about. Williams devotes the second part of the book to a
study of the development of this thought and its creation of a "sociology of consumption."[6]

Williams begins her work with a study of the "closed world of courtly consumption," in which she examines the consumption of the seventeenth-century
French aristocracy. She calls this noble class "the first people in modern society
to experiment with discretionary consumption" (1982:57) and notes in particular
the relation of these people to Louis XIV, the "consumer king." She suggests that
Louis sought to tame his subordinates by turning them into "insatiable consumers"
(1982:30). Williams turns then to the consumption behavior of the bourgeoisie, the
group to whom discretionary consumption descended in the eighteenth century; to
the ideological war of words that was conducted between Voltaire, who argued that
consumption aided civilization, and Rousseau, who claimed the contrary; to the
effects of the French Revolution and, finally, to the works of Balzac as an indication
of the burgeoning consumer habits of the bourgeoisie. She moves then to the "dream
world of mass consumption" as this was constructed by the world expositions and
the department stores of late nineteenth-century Paris. Williams completes the first
part of her book with a study of four lifestyles that emerge from this dream world:
bourgeois, mass, elitist, and democratic.

One of the special virtues of Williams's work is that it sees the consumer
revolution broadly and uses a rich armory of social scientific concepts. She observes,
as McKendrick does, the implications of the consumer revolution for status competition (1982:54), but she also sees beyond this relatively pedestrian sociological
phenomenon to the more remarkable ways in which new consumer goods and habits
entered into the fabric of Western society as a decisive agent of change and sociality.
For instance, she notes that in the hands of Louis XIV, consumption became a
political instrument, a "method of rule" (1982:28). This point is vitally important
to the history of consumption and I will return to it below. Williams also uses
Elias's (1978) notion of the civilizing process to suggest the possibility that new
habits and a new scale of consumption were being driven by the massive social
change of which Elias has written. This too is an intriguing idea, but it must be
noted that it appears here as an assertion and not an argument or demonstration.
Third, Williams notes how the bourgeoisie imitated the aristocracy even as they
adopted new consumption strategies, such as private economy to permit public show
(1982:35). The emergence of new symbolic strategies is everywhere evident in the
consumer revolution and needs more attention of just this sort. Finally, Williams
observes the mutual influence of different lifestyles, a matter of some interest for
those interested in lifestyles, reference groups, and diffusion. These four points are
just the kind of inquiry that is so strikingly absent from McKendrick's study of
eighteenth-century England. They are potential opportunities for real insight into
the origins of the consumer revolution.

The weaknesses of Williams's work do something to diminish these accomplishments. It has already been noted that her use of Elias's argument is a piece of academic legerdemain. Williams simply asserts that as the "civilizing process" put new constraints on social behavior, new consumer goods appeared (1982:24). A relationship of this complexity needs more than simple assertion. Williams also makes a fundamental error in her historical particulars when she suggests that one of the first purchases of the nobleman was "leisure time" (1982:34). This argument demonstrates a misunderstanding of the significance of labor for the cultural definition of social actors in the early modern period and does nothing to advance the larger argument.[7] Finally, there is a "swiftness" to this analysis which results in its raising more questions than it can possibly answer. While intelligent and imaginative, Williams's position does not always have the foundation of full development and documentation. Williams's chief contribution to this debate, beyond the information she provides on nineteenth-century France, is her attention to the diverse and sometimes hidden factors which helped create the consumer revolution and which in turn were created by it.

From Graven Images: Patterns of Modern Materialism (1983) by Chandra Mukerji is a third attempt to discover the origins of the consumer revolution and to trace its development into the modern period. Mukerji locates the rise of a "consumerist culture" in fifteenth- and sixteenth-century Europe. She examines the emergence of early modern printing, eighteenth-century cotton, and the development of three aspects of materialism: consumerism, capital goods, and materialist thought. She finds here evidence of "hedonistic consumerism" in the early modern period. She discovers this non-utilitarian consumption even among Protestants whom Weber supposed had forsworn it.[8] Mukerji uses this discovery to argue that consumerism predates the rise of capitalism and, further, that consumerism helped to create the capitalism it is conventionally supposed to have followed. According to this new account of the genesis of modern Western society, consumerism was present in the very beginning.

Mukerji's general argument bears a certain resemblance to McKendrick's. Both argue that the story of the great transformation of the West has been consistently told from the point of view of the industrial revolution. What has been consistently neglected is the consumer revolution that was a necessary companion of industrial developments. In Mukerji's language, traditional scholarship has emphasized "industrial capitalism" at the expense of "commercial capitalism" (1983:8). The burden of Mukerji's analysis is to demonstrate just how it was that an early consumer revolution contributed to the rise of capitalism in the West and to the great transformation of this society. She undertakes this demonstration with the study of the "proliferation" of early consumer goods, particularly printed writing, pictorial prints, and maps as well as non-traditional fabrics such as calicoes.

Of all of the work reviewed here, Mukerji's is potentially the most rewarding. For when Mukerji seeks to explain how it was that consumption contributed to the great transformation, she attends to the "symbolic and communicative character of all objects" (1983:12). Drawing on the work of Douglas and Isherwood (1978) and Sahlins (1976), Mukerji is concerned with the cultural analysis of economic behavior and with the way in which consumer goods carry cultural meaning. It is in these terms that she wants to assess the impact of consumption on the growth of the modern world. In this scheme goods become a medium for the expression, transformation, and even the innovation of existing cultural ideas.

This theoretical approach takes the study of the history of consumption beyond the sociological transparencies of Simmel and Veblen and even beyond the more sophisticated ideas that Williams attempts to launch in *Dream Worlds*. Indeed this approach takes us to what ought to be the heart of any contribution to the history of consumption. It is precisely as expressions, creators, and innovators of a range of cultural meaning that goods have contributed to the rise of the modern West. It is precisely here that the study of our so-called "materialism" has a vital contribution to our understanding of the genesis of the modern world. The historical and social sciences will contribute to our understanding of this genesis only when they recognize the full range and complexity of the cultural meaning carried by goods and then begin to determine just how this meaning, in the medium of consumer goods, began to help transform the modern West. The first step must be to go beyond the simple reckoning of the "status meaning" that inheres in goods and that enters into status competition. This is only one, and perhaps the most obvious, of the kinds of meaning contained in goods.

Mukerji promises us a study that will inquire into cultural meaning but she fails, finally, to fulfill this promise. Mukerji uses the terms "culture" and "meaning" throughout her study but never does she succeed in using them in a manner that will satisfy anthropological definition and standards. The "symbolic properties" of goods are examined again and again but never does the study succeed in treating these properties in the terms proposed by Douglas and Isherwood and Sahlins. Throughout this study Mukerji mistakes social implications for cultural ones, institutional changes for meaningful ones, and economic factors for symbolic ones. In short, this study never succeeds in realizing the promise of its statement of theoretical intent (McCracken 1984b).

The history of consumption and an appreciation of its role in the larger history of the modern West is beginning to draw more and more scholarly attention. The three contributors reviewed here represent the best and most provocative of this recent work. Even this summary treatment suggests the diversity of approach that exists within this nascent field. This in turn suggests the enormous amount of scholarly labor that must be done both empirically and theoretically before this study hits "full stride." What is chiefly lacking is a full account of the cultural aspects of consumer goods and behavior. It is here that the contributions of consumption to the transformation of the West are most readily to be discovered.

THREE MOMENTS IN THE HISTORY OF CONSUMPTION

This section will treat three decisive episodes in the history of consumption. Each of these episodes consists in a consumer boom in which consumption took a decisive step forward, assuming a new scale and a changed character. Each of these episodes served as a reflection of new patterns of production, exchange, and demand, and each served as an incitement of new such patterns. Reviewed here as a group, the episodes give a picture of consumption in the West at three moments in its development.

THE CONSUMER BOOM IN SIXTEENTH-CENTURY ENGLAND

In the last quarter of the sixteenth century, a spectacular consumer boom occurred. The noblemen of Elizabethan England began to spend with a new enthusiasm, on a new scale. In the process they dramatically transformed their world of goods and the nature of Western consumption. They rebuilt their country seats according to a new and grander standard, and they began to assume the additional expense of a London residence. They changed their patterns of hospitality as well, vastly inflating its ceremonial character and costs. Elizabethan nobleman entertained one another, their subordinates, and, occasionally, their monarch at ruinous expense. A favorite device was the ante-supper. Guests sat down to this vast banquet only to have it removed, dispensed with, and replaced by a still more extravagant meal. Clothing was equally magnificent in character and expense. Fortunes were spent on wardrobe (Stone 1965). In this conspicuous expenditure nobles were surpassed by their monarch. With greater resources at her disposal and with greater ceremonial demands to satisfy, Elizabeth I engaged in a level of consumption unthought of by previous Tudors, including her liberal father, Henry VIII. Despite her otherwise parsimonious nature, Elizabeth's expenditures on housing, hospitality, and clothing were staggering (Strong 1977).

This outburst of spending can be attributed to two important developments in the period. First, Elizabeth I used expenditure as an instrument of government. This new use of consumption has been observed in Renaissance Italy by Braudel (1973), and it was no doubt from the Renaissance courts of Italy that Elizabeth drew inspiration. The object of this new pattern of expenditure was to make the court, in Braudel's words, "a sort of parade, a theatrical spectacle . . . [and, with luxury] a means of government" (1973: 307). Faced with extraordinary difficulties within and without her kingdom, Elizabeth exploited the expressive hegemonic power of things that has been used by English rulers ever since (cf. Thompson 1974, McCracken 1982b, 1984c). Objects, especially in the context of a highly ceremonial court, could be made to communicate the monarch's legitimacy of rule, aspirations for the kingdom, qualities of power and majesty, and, finally, godlike status as an individual seen increasingly in mythical, religious, and literary terms (McCracken 1985a; Montrose 1980; Strong 1973, 1977). The supercharged symbolism of the monarch's court, hospitality, and clothing became the opportunity for political instruction and persuasion.

But Elizabeth's use of goods as an instrument of rule goes beyond her exploitation of their expressive properties. With a characteristically intelligent piece of policy, Elizabeth also succeeded in persuading the nobility to foot a large part of the bill for this ceremony. She forced the nobility to spend conspicuously on her behalf and to squander vast resources in the process. As part of the larger Tudor project to centralize power and tame the "over-mighty subject," Elizabeth took new control of the resources in her domain. She insisted that she was to be not only the original source of royal bounty but also the immediate source of this bounty. What once moved through intermediaries from the court to the nobility was now to pass directly from her hand. This new arrangement forced noblemen to look directly to Elizabeth, rather than her representatives, for their share of royal bounty. It was now necessary to abandon country seats and come to court to bid for the Queen's attention. Newly discriminating, Elizabeth smiled only on those who showed their loyalty and deference through active participation in the ceremonial order of her court. The cost of such participation was ruinous. It increased the nobleman's need for resources and made him additionally dependent on his Queen. An important part of Elizabeth's genius as a ruler was the skill with which she exploited the expressive power of her world of goods. A further part of this genius was the skill with which she forced others to participate in this world to her advantage and their own detriment.

The second factor responsible for the consumer boom of the sixteenth century was the social competition that took place among the Elizabethan nobility. The position of sixteenth-century noblemen was a difficult one. As we have seen, they found themselves increasingly dependent on royal favor for their survival. The effect of this dependence was not only increased expenditure on the Queen's behalf. It also led indirectly to additional expenditure on their own behalf. When each no-bleman was drawn to court to bid for the Queen's attention, he was drawn away from the locality in which he was the undisputed apex of a steeply hierarchical society. Drawn to court and to London, this nobleman was suddenly one of a number of individuals with a claim to preeminence. His reaction to this new crowd of status-seekers was one of anxiety-stricken concern for his honor, his social standing, and his relationship to the monarch. It was almost inevitable that he should have been drawn into a riot of consumption. Williams suggests that the roughly equivalent spending of French noblemen made them the first "discretionary" consumers (1982:57). But the pressures of status competition make this consumption "discretionary" in only the most literal sense of the term. In point of fact, the Elizabethan nobleman had no choice but to risk his fortune and spend like a sailor home on leave.[9]

Developments in consumption have a way of creating circumstances which give rise to still further developments in consumption. Causes become effects which in turn become causes. As we shall see in the remainder of this section, the two developments discussed here created important social change in Elizabethan England which in turn created further change in the consumption of the period. When no-blemen began to establish new patterns of consumption as a result of Elizabeth's prompting and their own status anxieties, they began to change the fundamental nature of both the Elizabethan family and the Elizabethan locality. These changes had their own profound implications for the consumption of this and later periods in England's history.

The Elizabethan family as a unit of consumption was devoted chiefly to establishing and maintaining "the cult of family status" which had preoccupied English families from the medieval period onward (Thrupp 1948:123). Family status rose and fell as a result of the efforts of each generation to increase the standing and honor of the lineage (Stone 1965; James 1974). This was a reciprocal process insofar as the success of one generation was seen to reciprocate the efforts of past generations and to indebt future ones (Marston 1973:23; McCracken 1983a). Family consumption was a collective matter undertaken by a corporation that spanned the generations. One generation bought goods that would represent and augment the honor of previous generations even as these goods established the foundation for the honor-seeking efforts of the next. Purchases were made by the living but the consumption unit included the dead and the unborn. The Tudor family as a consuming corporation was concerned with a great many parties who were not immediately present to the transaction, and it sought goods that could carry and augment status claims over several generations.

The character of the durable consumer good in the Tudor period was profoundly shaped by this "cult of family status" and the responsibility of the present generation to past and future ones. In order to satisfy the cult of family status and the reciprocal bargain that each generation had with proximate generations, these goods were required to have special qualities. It was necessary that they possess the peculiar and, from a modern point of view, mysterious ability to grow more valuable as they grew more ancient and decrepit. According to the prevailing ideology of status, newness was the mark of commonness while the patina of use was a sign and guarantee of standing. This is a topic that will be explored in depth in the next chapter. It is developed only briefly here.

No purchase contributed to the cult of family status unless it brought into the family an object that was capable of assuming "patina" and of surviving several generations of family ownership. The "patina" system of consumption meant that only certain homes could qualify as a desirable consumer good. It meant also that only certain furnishings, those with antiquity, were goods of value to the noble family. Most conspicuous among the furnishings was the family portraiture, tangible proof of a noble lineage and an exact measure of the number of generations it had claimed high standing. But in a manner of speaking, all the remaining furnishings were family portraits. All were representations of long-established wealth and distinguished ancestors.

This image of Tudor consumption and its relationship to the family corporation is too general, but it will aid in suggesting some of the effects of the new consumption on the sixteenth century. The Elizabethan nobleman, now driven by his new status anxieties into exceptionally fierce social competition, began to spend more for himself and less for the corporation. This shift in his consumption had several consequences. First, it helped weaken the reciprocal contract that bound the family. Second, it changed the nature of decision making. Third, it changed the nature and the dynamic of the unit of consumption. Fourth, it changed the nature of consumer goods. Goods that were purchased for the immediate demands of a social war assumed very different qualities. They were no longer constructed with the same concern for longevity. They were no longer valuable only when ancient. Certain goods became valuable not for their patina but for their novelty. In the last quarter of the sixteenth century a change in the consumption of the nobility helped set very significant larger changes in train.

Another of the Elizabethan institutions to feel the impact of the nobleman's new pattern of consumption was the "locality." The locality was the community in which the nobleman, as the highest-ranking member of local society, had special political, social, and economic responsibilities. The local nobleman had traditionally been the "port" through which certain national and royal resources entered the locality. Members of the local community therefore looked to the nobleman and his largesse for important resources and obtained these resources at the gate, at the table, or in the fields of his manor. When the nobleman began to spend his time and his money away from the locality, some of this largesse was suspended. The nobleman began in effect to withdraw from the reciprocal bargain he and his ancestors had established with the locality. Contemporaries called this development the "death of hospitality," and they complained bitterly at the betrayal that local communities suffered when noblemen ate and drank and built and dressed their way through family fortunes in London (Heal 1984).

Here was another reciprocal agreement that had previously constrained and directed the nobleman's consumption. Reciprocal obligation had once put a kind of lien on the nobleman's consumer expenditure. What had descended to the nobleman as a subordinate was expected to descend (diminished and eventually) to his subordinates. The entire community was entitled to a share of certain of the resources of his household. With the nobleman's new socially competitive spending in London, however, the local community was cut out of its participation in this consumption. With the death of hospitality, the local community was excluded from "trickle-down" consumption.

But the consequences of the nobleman's new pattern of consumption for the local community were more serious and thoroughgoing than mere exclusion from modest resources. More important, perhaps, was the fact that the nobleman now consumed on a new scale, for new social purposes and according to new values, tastes, and preferences. The contemporary observer complained that noblemen now adopt products and services that "smell of beyond the seas" (Anon. 1579:39). Thus did local members of the community view the new standards of consumption adopted by their superordinates as these latter began to take direction from the court and a more general European elite.

Two developments resulted from the shift in superordinate tastes. The first is that superordinate and subordinate tastes were radically differentiated. Where once there had been differences of degree between the consumption of superordinates and subordinates, now there were differences of kind. Superordinates and subordinates now wanted different things. A kind of lifestyle differentiation was taking place. Differences in social location were becoming differences in style, aesthetic preference, and attitude. Superordinate and subordinate parties were beginning to build, and live in, different worlds of goods.

In addition to this growing attitudinal distance between the high and the low, the betrayal of the reciprocal bargain by the superordinate party meant that there was also a growing social distance between them as well. Subordinate parties saw less of their superordinates, they interacted with them less often in the ceremonies and events of the locality, and they received less from their households. The gap in attitude was matched by a gap in social relations.

Despite these differences, the influence of the superordinate parties as leaders of opinion and shapers of taste and attitude continued. In the profoundly hierarchical world of sixteenth-century England, the tastes of subordinate parties were always dictated by those of superordinate parties. The leader of men was also inevitably the leader of their consumer tastes and preferences. The sudden change of superordinate consumption patterns meant a radical change in the chief influence on the subordinate consumer. Willy-nilly, this subordinate was now subject to styles and fashions from a larger court society and an involuntary witness to the speed and whimsy with which court society changed its consumption behavior. In the language of sociology, the reference group of subordinates had changed profoundly.

It was now true that this reference group no longer had the kind of authority it once did. Envy and awe were sometimes replaced by confusion and contempt. The new consumer affectations of the aristocracy struck their lessers as foreign inventions of a suspect nature. Noble consumers were no longer an unchallenged, irreproachable source of influence for their subordinates. Nevertheless, in this hierarchical society, subordinates continued to watch their superordinates' consumption with constant and careful attention. Even when they disapproved of this behavior they took it in. Gradually, the idea, if not yet the reality, of new consumer patterns had begun to insinuate itself into the tastes and preferences of subordinate consumers. This gradual shift helped prepare the way for later consumer explosions and the eventual participation of social groups that were now excluded.

In summary, we see in Elizabethan England a consumer explosion of extravagant proportions. This boom is due chiefly to the new consumption of two groups. Elizabeth, for her own political reasons, had learned to use consumption as a means of creating a vast theater devoted to the aggrandizement of her power as a monarch. She had also learned to use it as a device for the impoverishment of her potentially over-mighty subjects. Noblemen, on the other hand, found themselves spending reactively. Elizabeth demanded that they do so. The unaccustomed presence of social competitors prompted them to do so as well. The escalation of this spending meant that they were very soon the slaves of competitive consumption.

These two parties and their radical new scale of consumption created important changes in the family and the locality. The demands of their new consumption made it very much more difficult for noblemen to fulfill their economic and symbolic responsibilities to these groups. Indeed these noblemen appear to have withdrawn from reciprocal bargains on which both of these social units were founded. With this withdrawal, the cult of family status and the practice of local hospitality were profoundly compromised. The compromise of these two institutions had still more consequences for the consumption of the period.

Betrayal of the cult of family status created a change in the consumption unit, shifting it from family to the individual. It created a change in the consumer decision process which now looked to the immediate needs of status competition at the expense of the long-term status needs of the family corporation. Finally, it helped begin a change in the symbolic properties of the consumer good and initiate a shift from "patina" to "fashion." Goods no longer needed to be able to assume the patina of long-term ownership to satisfy the symbolic needs of their owners.

Betrayal of hospitality of the locality had its own consequences. With this betrayal the close social relationship between superordinate and subordinate parties began to deteriorate. Uniformity of lifestyle began to diminish, and the specter of new and radical differentiation of lifestyle appeared. Finally the influence of the superordinate class, which served as the chief reference group for the subordinate class, began to change as well. Superordinate and subordinate parties became distant, estranged, and dissimilar, and the context of consumption changed dramatically. Noblemen now looked to a pan-European standard of consumption, while their subordinates looked on in astonishment at their new tastes and excesses. Sometimes disdainful of superordinate consumption, subordinates nevertheless followed this behavior with care. Thus were they primed for a round of consumer excess that would begin a century later.

In short, "ruinous" spending in London by noblemen did more than exhaust family coffers. It also changed the very nature of the Elizabethan family and locality, and from these changes were to flow a new round of developments in the history of consumption.

CONSUMPTION IN THE EIGHTEENTH CENTURY

The eighteenth century saw a consumer explosion of its own. The world of goods expanded dramatically to include new opportunities for the purchase of furniture, pottery, silver, mirrors, cutlery, gardens, pets, and fabric (McKendrick 1982:10). There were also new developments in the frequency with which goods were bought, the influences brought to bear on the consumer, the numbers of people engaged as active consumers, and the tastes, preferences, social projects, and cultural co-ordinates according to which consumption took place. McKendrick claims that the eighteenth century sees the "birth" of a consumer society (1982:3) and the beginnings of our own modern consumer culture. We will follow McKendrick's brilliant study in this brief survey of the eighteenth century, drawing on other studies where this is possible.

Following Simmel and Veblen, McKendrick suggests that social competition was the motive force of this revolution.

> These characteristics—the closely stratified nature of English society, the striving for
> vertical social mobility, the emulative spending bred by social emulation, the compulsive

power of fashion begotten by social competition—combined with the widespread ability to spend (offered by novel levels of prosperity) to produce an unprecedented propensity to consume. . . . (1982:11)

By this rendering the consumer revolution was driven by the viciously hierarchical nature of eighteenth-century England. Goods had suddenly become tokens in the status game and they were being consumed with alacrity. As the history of consumption continues, many more causes will be identified. But McKendrick's argument will continue to serve as a guide to one of the most compelling forces that helped transform the West into a consumer society.

McKendrick also helps us see clearly the new characteristics of consumption itself and how important and thoroughgoing these changes were.

What men and women had once hoped to inherit from their parents, they now expected to buy for themselves. What were once bought at the dictate of need, were now bought at the dictate of fashion. What were once bought for life, might now be bought several times over. What were once available only on high days and holidays through the agency of markets, fairs and itinerant pedlars were increasingly made available every day but Sunday through the additional agency of an ever-advancing network of shops and shopkeepers. As a result "luxuries" came to be seen as mere "decencies", and "decencies" came to be seen as "necessities". Even "necessities" underwent a dramatic metamorphosis in style, variety and availability. (1982:1)

Some of these factors we have seen before. The purchase for self instead of for family that began in the sixteenth century is now well established. So, too, is the growth of obsolescence through fashion change. Some of the factors are new. The explosive growth of markets in time and space is a special eighteenth-century innovation. So is the explosion of consumer choices. So, especially, is the participation rate. Subordinate classes, which in the sixteenth century could only watch in horrified fascination as the nobility cultivated a new scale and new tastes in their consumption, could now become participants in this consumption. The new prosperity of the period brought all of these factors, old and new, to a pitch of intensity that suggested to some contemporary observers that an "epidemical madness" had taken hold of England.

In general terms the implications of this "madness" are unmistakable. Consumption was beginning to take place more often, in more places, under new influences, by new groups, in pursuit of new goods, for new social and cultural needs. It was growing from a small corner of domestic life to a major activity. The West was engaged in a grand experiment in which culture and consumption were becoming inextricably linked. To see the full significance of this conjunction of culture and consumption, it is necessary to take a closer look at some of the developments that McKendrick brings to our attention.

In his discussion of the career of Josiah Wedgwood, for instance, McKendrick observes a major development in the field of marketing, and what must be the first success in the conscious control of marketing forces.[10] Wedgwood took careful reckoning of the trickle-down effect and began systematically to exploit it for his own purposes.

A hierarchical Europe had always seen fashions in clothing begin with the court, move through the nobility, the gentry, the middle class, and the lower classes, driven inexorably by the dual engines of subordinate imitation and superordinate differentiation. The point of entry for a fashion was the upper classes and, until Wedgwood, their choice of a new fashion was a relatively discretionary matter made according to their own pleasure and the court's direction. After Wedgwood, the upper classes became a target of marketing influence. Wedgwood sought to insinuate his goods into the lifestyle of this group in the hope that these goods would then trickle downward to the lower classes.

Once Wedgwood had mastered the trickle-down effect, he was able to exploit the competitive spending of the period to his own advantage. This "domestication" of a natural market force must rank as one of the important developments in the market's growing sophistication in the manipulation of demand. The industrial revolution of this period was driven in large part by the successful exploitation of previously unharnessed forces of nature. The parallel consumer revolution was also driven by a new understanding and mastery of the world, in this case the perceived regularities not of nature but of society and its marketplace.

McKendrick does not treat this theme but it is essential to the full assessment of individuals such as Wedgwood. When Wedgwood glimpsed and exploited the trickle-down effect he began a process that has contributed mightily to the consumer revolution. He began the process by which the manufacturer (and later the marketer) made themselves the students of social phenomena that were not otherwise studied. These "market ethnographers" watched for patterns and regularities in the highly dynamic circumstances of the eighteenth century, turning what they learned into the instruments of marketing. The application of this knowledge then fed back into the dynamism of the situation and created even more dramatic changes. It can be argued that this "participant observation" anticipated the scholarly and interventionist undertakings of the social sciences in some cases by hundreds of years. This new attention to and manipulation of the regularities of society helped to propel the West forward and create new and more intimate connections between consumption and culture.

McKendrick's study of the eighteenth century gives ample evidence of the new use and sophistication of other marketing devices, especially fashion magazines, fashion plates, and the English fashion doll. Considered with the advertising columns of the press, the trade cards of retail merchants and the roving Manchester Men, Scotch drapers, and Scotch Hawkers who carried commercial goods into the provinces, it becomes clear that the eighteenth century consumer had access to a new volume of influence and information.[11] This consumer was the object of more and more sophisticated attempts to awaken wants and to direct preferences. This consumer was beginning to live in an artificially stimulated climate that removed his/her tastes and preferences from the hold of convention and local tradition, and put them increasingly in the hands of the emerging forces of the marketplace. It is difficult to know how much of the "epidemic" of spending of the eighteenth century was indeed a response to these new forces, and how much must be attributed to other factors external to the marketplace. It is likely that new tastes and the new means to manipulate them existed in a dialectical relationship, one encouraging the other while the two worked together to create the consumer revolution of the eighteenth century.

While McKendrick is perhaps wrong to argue that fashion did not begin in earnest until the eighteenth century, it is true that by this time it had begun to affect more social groups and more products and to proceed with new rapidity. Fashion so consistently transforms the tastes and preferences of the modern day that it is difficult to imagine an economy in which it did not enjoy full sway. It is equally difficult to appreciate how great a change it introduced into the lives and expectations of the Western consumer. With the growth of fashion grew an entirely new habit of mind and pattern of behavior. Increasingly, aesthetic and stylistic considerations took precedence over utilitarian ones. That an object had not exhausted its usefulness was no longer sufficient grounds for its preservation. Whether it could satisfy the more important condition of fashionableness was now the deciding factor.

This development represents a triumph of style over utility, of aesthetics over function. More important, it represents a radical redefinition of the idea of status and the use of goods to express status. If goods had once carried the status message through their "patina," now they carried the status message through their novelty. This had been true of certain goods such as clothing since the Elizabethan period, but now it came to encompass new product categories such as potteries and furniture. A new relationship between novelty and status was being established. This is a topic that will be more fully explored in the next chapter.

It appears then that in the eighteenth century goods began to carry a new kind of status meaning. This gave them very different implications for the status system and the organization of society. It is also likely that goods were becoming the carriers of other kinds of meaning as well. It is possible that the kind of role information carried by goods in the present day (Solomon 1983) began to emerge in this period. Belk (1984a) has suggested that growing role differentiation and anonymity in Western society has encouraged the use of goods as an expression of and guide to social identity. Both role differentiation and anonymity were well under way in this period and it is likely that goods began to assume this additional semiotic burden. The cultural meaning of goods was increasingly a way an anonymous society could maintain its center. As Sahlins puts it, goods allow Western societies to turn "the basic contradiction of its construction into a miracle of existence, a cohesive society of perfect strangers" (1976: 203).

Before the topic of fashion is abandoned here, it is worth observing the several implications of the obsolescence it created. First and most simply, fashion had the effect of requiring that objects be replaced over and over again. This simple consequence of fashion helped to make consumption a new, more frequent, and taxing activity. The consumer had to devote more time to the activity of purchase. More important, however, the consumer had to devote more time to consumer learning.

The consumer now needed a whole range of additional information to distinguish the fashionable from the unfashionable good and to know what message he or she would send with its purchase.

Consumers now occupied a world filled with goods that carried messages. Increasingly they were surrounded by meaning-laden objects that could only be read by those who possessed a knowledge of the object-code. Of necessity they were becoming semioticians in a new medium, the masters of a new code. In sum, more and more social behavior was becoming consumption, and more and more of the individual was subsumed in the role of the consumer.

What does it mean to be defined as a consumer? One of the themes that McKendrick's status-based explanation does not touch on is how the consumer revolution was both cause and consequence of new cultural definitions of the person. As Mauss (1985) and subsequent anthropologists (e.g., Carrithers, Collins and Lukes 1985) have pointed out, the concept of the person varies from culture to culture and the prevailing notion of the person in Western cultures is a highly peculiar one. The consumer revolution has played an intimate role in shaping the Western concept of the person, but the historical scholarship on this question is scant. One fascinating treatment appears in Campbell (1983) who argues that new patterns of consumption were both cause and consequence of Romantic definitions of the self. The Romantic insistence on the uniqueness and autonomy of the self, and its insistence on the realization of the self through experience and creativity, both drew from, and drove, the consumer revolution. Increasingly, individuals were prepared to suppose that "the self is built through consumption [and that] consumption expresses the self" (1983:288). This connection between consumption and individualism, largely wrought in the eighteenth century but begun, as we have seen, in the sixteenth century, is one of the great cultural fusions of the modern world. Each of these ideologies could now use the other as a powerful engine for its own advancement. Their connection and their mutuality continues to the present day and can be glimpsed in any commercial that invites the observer to "be all that you can be."

Another ideational or cultural development that McKendrick does not capture because of his status-based explanation is the development of new attitudes. As O'Neill (1978) and Leach (1984) have pointed out, the consumer revolution required a fundamental reform of certain attitudes and outlooks. One of the chief of these is the inculcation of a willingness to consume. O'Neill observes that "the consumer is not born, but produced by processes that teach him or her to want to want . . ." (1978:224). This process of instruction happens necessarily for each new generation of consumers, but it had to be undertaken for the first generation of consumers, and it is reasonable to suppose that this generation lived sometime in the eighteenth century.

As McKendrick notes, fundamental changes were taking place in the cultural definition of space and time. In the eighteenth century it became possible to pursue consumption activities throughout the week and throughout an urban area. Space and time were being reconfigured to accommodate consumption and to make it a centerpiece of social activity and personal interest. Thompson has examined the reconfiguration of time for the purposes of a new industrial order (1967). A similar study is needed to observe the reconfiguration of time for the purposes of the new consumer order.

The reconfiguration of space is somewhat better studied. Braudel (1973) argues that privacy was an eighteenth-century innovation and he has observed the way in which this idea is played out in new building form and home furnishings (cf. Tuan 1982:52–85). Here too there is reason to think that the eighteenth century merely carries forward an innovation of the sixteenth century. Hoskins (1953) notes the substantial rebuilding of England to accommodate new ideas of privacy. But clearly this vital cultural notion of space was transforming, and being transformed by, the consumer goods of the period.[12]

The eighteenth century is an important period in the history of consumption also because of the numbers of people who were able to participate. The consumption of the Elizabethan period was restricted largely to a noble class while other social groups looked on in wonder and disdain. The eighteenth century was the opportunity for this social group to take a fuller part in the consumer revolution. Their participation makes this the first period of "mass consumption" in the Western tradition.[13]

It is difficult working from secondary sources to follow Elizabethan developments in the history of consumption into the eighteenth century. It is clear however that purchase-for-self rather than purchase-for-family continued and indeed Mc-Kendrick explicitly suggests that this transition was completed in the eighteenth century for a great many product categories and most social groups. The consumer good also continued in its transformation from an object with "patina" to an object that was fashionable. Fashion had become unambiguously the uppermost design consideration for most of the consumer goods of the eighteenth century. With this shift in the symbolic properties of consumer goods, these goods came to assume a very different gatekeeping significance for the socially mobile. As we shall see in the next chapter, these goods now helped to conceal the status origins of their owners and to this extent encouraged mobility. In sum, the consumer decision-making process was increasingly informed by the new status and fashion considerations that emerged in the sixteenth century.

What appears to be novel to the eighteenth century is the explosive growth of consumption in space and time. Another novelty of the period is the explosion of choices. So, too, is the participation of subordinate groups. It is also possible to observe new kinds and amounts of advertising, a new intensity to the control of fashion over consumer goods, an increase in obsolescence, and an overall increase in the sophistication of marketing techniques as well as changing definitions of the person and of desire.

The implications and consequences of these developments are striking. Producers had learned how to exploit a social dynamic such as the trickle-down effect and to harness the power of social competition. This was the beginning of an effort to understand and manipulate the marketplace that continues to the present day.

The necessity of purchase for one's self and frequent re-purchase in the course of one's lifetime, both the result of obsolescence, had profound effects for the individual members of society. Increasing amounts of time and attention had to be devoted to the process of consumption, more information was required for its successful execution, and more of the individual's world was occupied by message-carrying objects. New concepts of the person were driving, and driven by, new consumer patterns.

In short, the eighteenth century saw a transformation of consumption and the world in which it took place. Consumption was beginning to take place more often, in more places, under new influences, by new groups, in pursuit of new goods, for new social and cultural purposes. The "world of goods" was steadily making itself co-extensive with the world of social life.

CONSUMPTION IN THE NINETEENTH CENTURY

There was no "consumer boom" in the nineteenth century. By this time the consumer revolution had installed itself as a structural feature of social life. What had started as a modest dynamic confined to one corner of society had made itself the magnetic center of society. The transformation that had begun in the sixteenth century and expanded in the eighteenth century was, by the nineteenth century a permanent social fact. Profound changes in consumption had created profound changes in society and these in turn had created further changes in consumption. By the nineteenth century, consumption and society were inextricably linked in a continual process of change. There was, then, no "consumer boom" in the nineteenth century because there was now a permanent and continual dynamic relationship between social and consumer changes which together drove a perpetual transformation of the West.

Some of the changes of this period are essential to our understanding of the modern character of consumption. These changes include the emergence of the department store, which contributed fundamentally to the nature and context of purchase activity as well as the nature of information and influence to which the consumer was subjected. The nineteenth century also saw the emergence of new "consumer lifestyles" and their novel patterns of interaction between persons and things. New marketing techniques such as the employment of new aesthetic, cultural, and sexual motifs were devised to add value to products. More and more social meanings were being loaded into goods through new and more sophisticated devices for meaning transfer. Social changes created new and more pressing communicational needs than the language of goods could claim to answer. The nineteenth century saw the introduction of features that still characterize the consumption of the present day.

Williams's *Dream Worlds: Mass Consumption in Nineteenth Century France* is our chief guide to consumption in this period, and it moves our attention from England across the channel to France. Surprisingly, the patterns of consumption established by the aristocracy survived the destruction of the French court in the eighteenth century. The important change from a consumption point of view was that the production of certain goods moved out of the private realm of noble house-holds into the public marketplace. In the 1790s, chefs moved from aristocratic hotels to public restaurants while dressmakers and tailors who had once served noble patrons now opened public shops. Increasingly it was public consumption rather than private consumption that directed the work of the producers of luxury goods (Williams 1982:48).

The French Revolution that changed so much of eighteenth-century France left the tastes of the mass of French consumers relatively unchanged. Even the Jacobin hostility to these tastes and aristocratic consumption that had been inspired by Rousseau had no apparent effect on the consumer patterns of the next century. The bourgeoisie of nineteenth-century France continued to aspire to what Williams calls the "courtly model" of consumption. Indeed they seized upon the consumer patterns of the aristocracy as weapons in their continued battle for higher social status (Williams 1982:53).

This French affection for the aristocratic model of consumption did not continue for the whole of the nineteenth century. In the course of the century the aristocratic model was supplemented by three additional and eventually more important styles of consumption. Williams elucidates each of these styles with great skill and elo-quence. The first of these was the lifestyle of mass consumption which adopted new and fantastic ideas of luxury even as it preserved those of the aristocracy. This model of consumption was especially encouraged by the astonishing developments in the department store to which later reference will be made. The second was the elite lifestyle which insisted that a special mode of consumption could create a new aristocracy, setting those with superior aesthetic and artistic vision above the mass of men. This is the model of consumption inspired by Beau Brummel and the dandies who followed his example in both England and France. Dandies ridiculed the excesses of bourgeois and aristocratic consumption and declared themselves the new elite, an aristocracy by taste instead of breeding. The third was a democratic mode of consumption that emerged out of the decorative arts movement. This movement was also opposed to the aristocratic pretensions of the bourgeoisie. It sought no new aristocracy but a mode of consumption that was accessible, modest, and dignified. Williams suggests that what is distinctive about the consumption of the nineteenth century is the emergence of this "distinctive grouping of interde-pendent lifestyles" (1982:110) and the end of the preeminence of the courtly model of consumption.

Williams treats each of these emergent lifestyles as an attempt to come to terms with the development of a consumer society. The style of mass consumption, for instance, is seen as an artifact of new marketing techniques. The style of elitist consumption is seen as an attempt to contend with the excesses and banality of a bourgeois society preoccupied with goods and indifferent to ideas or standards. The style of democratic consumption is seen as an attempt to draw the mass consumer away from his/her preoccupation with goods by creating a manner of consumption that encouraged a simplicity of lifestyle and the dignity of the common man. These are illuminating explanations but they also reflect the limitations of Williams's point of view. Each of them draws too much on this book's guiding assumption that consumer goods are silly distractions that individuals buy out of only the basest and most superficial of motives. Too rarely does Williams entertain the possibility that consumer goods were fascinating for consumers of the nineteenth century because they were increasingly the residence of cultural meaning and new opportunities for defining self and the world.

It is possible to see each of these lifestyles treated by Williams as a new experiment in the expressive powers of goods. The aristocratic model of courtly consumption was the earliest of these experiments. As we shall see in the next chapter, the "patina" sought for goods by this model had a very particular meaningful character that was crafted to a very particular social end. It allowed the aristocracy to encode their status claims in a manner that discouraged counterfeit claims. This model survived into the seventeenth, eighteenth and nineteenth centuries as one of the schemes by which goods can be made to carry cultural meaning. Williams's study allows us to see some of the competing models of consumption that appeared in the nineteenth century to challenge the patina model. Each of these styles represents a new way to exploit the cultural character of consumer goods in the accomplishment of new cultural objectives.

The style of mass consumption is a particularly interesting opportunity to determine what additional meanings could be loaded into goods. Some of these meanings were new notions of status. Still others were concerned not with status but a whole range of new cultural meanings. Both the expositions and the department stores of late nineteenth-century France cultivated a style of interior design that Williams calls "chaotic-exotic" (1982:71). Extravagant interiors crowded with contradictory allusions to different ethnic, geographical, and even mythical themes were common. In Williams's dark view this represents the increasing use of art in the service of commerce. The "ornamental delirium" of these public places represents in her view "the submission of truth, of coherence, of taste, of all other considerations to the ends of business" (1982:64). It may indeed have been this, but it was also, and perhaps more important, an experiment in the new expressive abilities of consumer goods.[14]

Williams suggests that the symbolic purpose of this new aesthetic was a crude one. It was simply to "bring together anything that expresses distance from the ordinary" (1982:71). But it is also possible to say that we see in this period the use of goods to communicate much more coherent and purposeful messages. A more careful analysis of these experiments, one that is less quick to suppose aesthetic anarchy and moral compromise, is needed before the style of mass consumption is fully understood. Williams's larger project leads her to assume that aesthetic experimentation of the period is devoted to the creation of a dream world. Someone must now examine the evidence from a different point of view. It is necessary to determine whether the "ornamental delirium" of the nineteenth century had more coherence and meaning than Williams allows.

The elitist style of consumption is a more obvious gesture in the use of goods to shape and carry cultural meaning. The cultivation of this elite style is nothing less than the effort to use the emerging language of goods to create a single omnibus cultural concept that specified a new definition of the person, a new definition of this person's relationship to his/her larger society, and a set of orienting concepts and values for social action. The language of goods was being used here very deliberately and skillfully to undertake a piece of social invention: the creation of a new order of social life. Innovation of this order was previously impossible not only because a traditional society would brook no such experimentation but also because there was no system of discourse that would allow for the necessary re-thinking and invention out of which a new concept of social life could emerge. We may see the dandy who epitomizes this new elitist style of consumption as a figure who very self-consciously took advantage of a disordered society to make a place for himself that had not existed for anyone before. In the person of Beau Brummel we see nothing less than the abrogation of powers of influence that had previously been possessed only by the monarch. In both cases the necessary condition of this social innovation was the possession of a means of communication that only a growing inventory of products charged with new meaning and a new potential for meaning could allow.[15]

In the case of the decorative arts reform movement and the emergence of democratic consumption we see the expressive potential of goods explored in a different way. The meaning carried by goods is intended in this case to resocialize "the people," changing their concepts of themselves, their concepts of society and, most of all, their social aspirations by changing their concept of consumption and consumer goods. This experiment in the language of goods puts it to a proselytizing purpose. It uses goods to carry a new concept of goods into an unsuspecting com-munity. If the dandies had used goods to create and announce a new style of life for themselves, the advocates of democratic consumption used them for instructional purposes in their attempt to reform a social group different from their own.

Each of the lifestyles identified by Williams gives us a glimpse of larger, more complicated process by which Western society sought to explore and tap the cultural significance and communicative value of a new and vital means of communication that had come so suddenly into its possession. Indeed it is not too much to say that the consumer revolution provided some of the cultural resources that were needed to contend with the social dislocation wrought by the industrial revolution. Some significant part of the history of consumption must consist in the study of this development.

One of the great developments of the nineteenth century was the emergence of the department store. Williams notes the similarity of the department store to the world exposition of this period. She demonstrates that both used the unprece-dented design of their interiors to create a new environment for shopping, purchase, and consumption. Their extravagant, enveloping scale and the exotic-chaotic style allowed them to create a "new and decisive conjunction between imaginative desires and material ones, between dreams and commerce . . ." (1982:65). Williams also observes that the commercial possibilities of the new medium of motion picture film were immediately glimpsed and exploited.[16] Expositions, department stores, and film were all-important contributors to the dream world of mass consumption.

Perhaps even more important than the contribution of the exposition, department store, and film to the aesthetics of consumption was their contribution to the purchase process. First of all, all three represented the effort to expose the consumer to a range of persuasive and informational stimuli without any expectation that this stimuli would result in immediate purchase. Consumers were encouraged to wander through the department store at will absorbing its fantastic representation of exotic worlds and consumer goods, and they were allowed to participate in this extraordinary environment without obligation. The rhetorical object of the marketplace had changed. It was now devoted to the "arousal of free-floating desire" instead of merely the "immediate purchase of particular items" (1982:67).

Second, when purchase was undertaken in the department store institutions it had very different characteristics. The prices of consumer goods on display were not subject to the barter process. Prices were fixed and the consumer consented to them in the act of purchase or simply did not buy. Williams suggests that this new pattern of interaction between marketplace and consumer encouraged a new passivity on the consumer's part.

Third, the department store encouraged the introduction of credit. Borrowing was made possible by the creation of a "large-scale, impersonal, rationalized system of installment purchase" (1982:93). Suddenly the unobtainable was within one's grasp. This innovation especially helped to give modern consumption an especially dreamlike quality, as Williams notes.

Michael B. Miller broadens our understanding of the department store significantly in *The Bon Marché: Bourgeois Culture and the Department Store 1869–1920* (1981). Miller's treatment resembles Williams's insofar as it insists that the department store must be seen not only as a reflection of changing consumer patterns but also as a decisive agent which actively contributed to the culture in which this consumption took place. Like Williams, Miller examines the contribution of the department store to changing tastes and preferences, changing purchase behavior, a changing relationship between buyer and seller, and changing marketing techniques.

Where Miller is most interesting is precisely in his treatment of the influence of the department store on the culture of nineteenth-century France. He begins with an assertion of the department store's determinative cultural role. "Far more than a mirror of bourgeois culture in France, the Bon Marché gave shape and definition to the very meaning of the concept of a bourgeois way of life" (1981:182). He then systematically examines how the department store worked to shape and transfer cultural meaning. His first observation is that the goods of the department store gave material expression to the values of the bourgeoisie. Goods made these values concrete and gave them a "reality all their own" (1981:180). Miller suggests that fundamentally important values such as "respectability" and "certitude" were anchored in the clothing and furnishings of this group. Furthermore, the distinctions that segment the bourgeois ceremonial categories of space and time are also expressed in clothing and furnishings. In this brief discussion goods are seen to make a fundamental contribution to the hold these values had on the bourgeoisie. This study brings Miller as close as any of the historians considered here to taking up the cultural properties of consumer goods discussed by Sahlins (1976) and Douglas and Isherwood (1978).[17]

Miller's second observation is more ambitious. He claims that as the Bon Marché poured the values, attitudes, and aspirations of the bourgeoisie into goods, it succeeded in shaping and transforming them. When this department store infused goods with cultural meaning both the meaning and the culture underwent revision. The brevity of Miller's treatment of it is therefore especially problematical. Still the point is an intriguing one and deserves more careful study. We see here the use of goods as a kind of historical and cultural "operator" (Boon 1973). Operators are material symbols which help to reorganize the cultural meaning of the "global structure" so that new historical contingencies can be incorporated into the existing cultural order (McCracken 1983b, 1985a; Sahlins 1977, 1981).

Miller's third observation is that goods possessed of cultural and historical meaning were the agency by which one social group socialized another. He suggests that the Bon Marché and its catalogues became a kind of "cultural primer" which showed a certain class "how they should dress, how they should furnish their home, and how they should spend their leisure time" (1981:183). As a study in diffusion, this is a most interesting opportunity for future study. But it is still more promising as an opportunity for the study of the hegemonic powers of things. Elizabeth I had learned to rule through objects and their consumption, and this instrument of government continued to be exploited three centuries later. In general terms, Miller demonstrates with unusual sophistication how the department store served as an important site for the conjunction of culture and consumption in the nineteenth century.[18]

The nineteenth century saw the creation of a permanent interaction between consumption and social change. Consumption now bred constant social change. This social change bred constant reforms in consumption. The dialectical relationship between these two forces created an engine that helped drive the "great transformation" into the nineteenth and twentieth centuries. This engine now consistently violated one of the fundamental laws of thermodynamics. It needed no source of energy external to itself. It had created its own dynamic, one that might break down but would never wear out.

From Williams we get a study of consumption in the nineteenth century that traces the eclipse of the "courtly model of consumption" and the rise of four competing lifestyles each of which expresses another response to the characteristic problems and difficulties of life in a consumer society. I have suggested that these lifestyles might also be regarded as experiments in the exploitation of the expressive, cultural power of goods.

From both Williams and Miller we get a study of the fundamental importance of the department store to the developments of this period. Williams notes the role of the store in changing the aesthetics and stimuli of the shopping environment, in creating a new pattern of interaction between buyer and seller, and in developing innovations such as credit. Miller observes the department stores' manipulation of the meaningful properties of goods. These stores not only made certain values manifest and somehow more immanent in consumers' lives, they even assisted in the transformation of these values. Finally, the goods of the department store became instruments of instruction and politics. In general terms, it might be said that the powerful dynamic created out of the dialectical relationship between consumption and social change had found in the department store a physical locus and an institutional home. As a permanent structural feature of modern society, it now had a place to stay.

CONCLUSION

This chapter has reviewed recent literature on the making of modern consumption. It has examined three crucial moments in the history of consumption. This undertaking does not represent a perfect inventory of the issues that must be addressed by future historians of consumption. It is suggested instead as a map of the present terrain according to which certain landmarks can be made plain, certain hazards warned against, certain opportunities made conspicuous, and a far-flung and various terrain made more comprehensible.

It is a curiosity for the sociology of knowledge that the role of the consumer revolution in the "great transformation" was so long and systematically ignored. It is a further curiosity that this period of neglect should end so suddenly with the appearance of not one but several substantial works devoted to the topic. If the causes of this long neglect are not apparent, its consequences are. The history of consumption has no history, no community of scholars, no tradition of scholarship. It is, in the words of T. S. Kuhn, "preparadigmatic." Or, perhaps more accurately, it is "neo-natal."

The absence of a scholarly tradition gives this field a necessary diversity of quality and approach. Each of the scholars reviewed here has had to assume not only the responsibilities of a scholar but also those of a pioneer. Each has had to find his or her own way through uncharted territory. Each has suffered what Veblen called "the penalty of taking the lead." If the three works reviewed here fail to illuminate fully the dialectical engine that made consumption and social life mutually transforming in the modern West, it is because they could not fully see the terrain they have helped to survey.

This seven-league-boots tour of the history of consumption brings certain details, events, and actors plainly into view. We have observed how the consumer revolution served as cause and consequence of the transformation of Elizabethan England. Caught up in Elizabeth's strategic use of consumption as an instrument of government, Elizabethan noblemen were forced in patterns of conspicuous consumption that had profound consequences for their relationships with their families and localities. Spending more and more for their own immediate purposes, these noblemen withdrew from their reciprocal contracts with the family and the locality. For the family, this withdrawal had the effect of helping to narrow its scope and corporateness. For the locality, it had the effect of diminishing the influence of the superordinate.

When we pick up the story of the consumer revolution in the eighteenth century, consumption has moved a little closer to the center of the historical stage. Institutionally it is a more active and a more formal presence. Merchants were now marketers and the masters of diffusion effects and new media of communication. The number of goods was rising steadily and they could be bought in more places on more opportunities than before. The transforming power of fashion now touched more product categories and the rate of fashion change had increased. This required more frequent purchase and a wider scope of social knowledge. Fashion also destroyed the "patina" system that had served so well as a status gatekeeper. Most striking of all, certainly, was the fact that consumption was now a mass activity. The epidemic metaphor used by contemporaries was apt. The virus that had restricted itself to a minor aristocratic community had now infected everyone.

By the nineteenth century the consumer revolution had installed itself as a permanent social fact. The vigorous dialectic that bound consumer change and social change was now a structural reality. Indeed this revolution had even found an institution locus, a place of its own, the department store. This new institution helped change the nature of aesthetics by which goods were marketed, introducing powerfully persuasive techniques in film and decor that are still being refined. The department store also changed the very nature of the place in which people consumed, what they consumed, the information they needed to consume, and the styles of life to which this new consumption was devoted. It helped create the meaning that goods carried and even "rewrote" this meaning when social change demanded it. Finally, department stores were agents of diffusion, serving as vast schoolrooms in which the citizens of the nineteenth century could learn the arts and skills of their vital new role as consumers. The consumer revolution could not have been better housed.

New experiments in the manipulation of the cultural and symbolic properties of goods are the great and neglected secrets of the history of consumption. Elizabeth and her aristocracy were perhaps the first consumers to have the opportunity to experiment with this new medium. By the nineteenth century the medium had grown vastly more complicated and powerful both as a means of cultural invention and as a means of symbolic expression. Now all social groups engaged in this creative enterprise in an effort to both build and accommodate to a perilous and liquid world. With the growth of social disorganization and indeterminacy, due in some part to the consumer revolution itself, it was now necessary for everyone to resort to use of the expressive and culturally constitutive powers of this new medium. The use of this cultural inventory and instrument was no longer a discretionary opportunity but an increasingly urgent necessity.

The consumer revolution is a strange chapter in the ethnographic history of the species. For what may have been the first time in its history, a human community willingly harbored an nonreligious agent of social change, and permitted it to transform on a continual and systematic basis virtually every feature of social life. The scholarly community has not been slow to recognize the extent of the "great transformation." Nor has it been slow to declare the great transformation a vital topic of academic study. But it has been extraordinarily and inexplicably slow to examine the contribution of the consumer revolution here. The works reviewed in this chapter suggest that this reticence is now at an end. There is now both a precedent and a foundation for the study of the consumer revolution.

TWO

"Ever Dearer in Our Thoughts"

Patina and the Representation of Status
before and after the Eighteenth Century

In the first chapter we considered the broad sweep of the history of consumption. In this chapter we will look at one particular aspect of this history, the "patina" system of consumption. Patina, as both a physical and a symbolic property of consumer goods, was one of the most important ways that high-standing individuals distinguished themselves from low-standing ones, and social mobility was policed and constrained. As a system of consumption, it served as a mainstay of social organization until its eclipse in the eighteenth century. Supplanted by the "fashion" system of consumption, patina dwindled to its present status: a status strategy used by the very rich alone. This chapter attempts to establish a theoretical sense of patina, drawing inspiration from both Veblen and Peirce, and to show the career of the patina system before and after the eighteenth century.

MATERIAL CULTURE AND
THE STATUS MESSAGE

The field of material culture has established a detailed understanding of the symbolic properties that adhere to objects of human manufacture. It has surveyed the range, the depth, and the many communicative uses of these properties, and we are now in possession of a thorough record of how material culture makes culture material. One of the special interests of this literature is the ability of material culture to carry status messages. Scholars across the social sciences have sought to demonstrate how individuals and communities use inanimate objects to claim, to legitimate, and to compete for status meaning. It does not exaggerate to say that status has been a kind of "fixed idea" for certain communities of scholars. For all this careful study, however, the study of status symbolism is incomplete. We do not possess a systematic idea of what may be the most important of the symbolic properties that have to do with status. We have not yet cultivated an idea of what this chapter will call "patina."

This chapter examines the idea of patina in four parts. The first defines and discusses the concept "patina." The second considers existing theories of status representation through material culture and offers a formal theory of patina as a means of status representation. The third gives a brief history of patina in the modern West, noting particularly how patina status symbolism was affected (and largely displaced) by the advent of the fashion system in the eighteenth century. The final part offers a treatment of patina in the modern world and discusses its present role in the current representation of status.

PATINA: PHYSICAL AND SYMBOLIC PROPERTY OF MATERIAL CULTURE

Patina is, first of all, a physical property of material culture. It consists in the small signs of age that accumulate on the surface of objects. Furniture, plate, cutlery, buildings, portraiture, jewelry, clothing, and other objects of human manufacture undergo a gradual movement away from their original pristine condition. As they come into contact with the elements and the other objects of the world, their original surface takes on a surface of its own. As these objects are minutely dented, chipped, oxidized, and worn away, they begin to take on "patina."

In Western societies, this physical property is treated as a symbolic property. In these societies, the surface that accumulates on objects has been given a symbolic significance and exploited to social purpose. It has been seized upon to encode a vital and unusual status message. What makes this message unusual is that it is not, strictly speaking, concerned with claiming status. This relatively simple, even banal, message is left to other, more mundane, aspects of status symbolism. Patina has a much more important symbolic burden, that of suggesting that existing status claims are legitimate. Its function is not to claim status but to authenticate it. Patina serves as a kind of visual proof of status.

A sixteenth-century example will serve to illustrate what is intended here. An Elizabethan family used silver plate to make a status claim (Jones 1917). They used it to represent their high standing, wealth, and taste. Taken by itself, this status claim had no need of patina. Perfectly new plate, utterly without patina, could make a compelling visual claim to high standing. But patina added something vital to this symbolism. It demonstrated that the plate's status symbolism had foundation. It said that the plate's owners were no pretenders to their symbolism. It served as a kind of proof of the family's longevity and the duration of their gentle status. In this sense, the plate's status claim was quite naked without the finely worked cover of patina with which time, accident, and, most important, long-standing ownership had endowed the silver's surface. The presence of this patina reassured an observer that the plate had been a possession of the family for several generations and that the family was, therefore, no newcomer to its present social standing.

It is hard to overestimate the value of this kind of symbolic property. One of the very great liabilities of status claims made by way of material culture is the ease with which they are counterfeited. Any newcomer with the necessary taste and money could buy the objective correlatives of gentle standing. Indeed every generation in the medieval and early modern West saw merchants systematically acquire the trappings of high standing with the purchase of a country seat and lifestyle (Hexter 1961; Thrupp 1948). It is Macfarlane's argument that this is a defining feature of the West: that it encouraged a constant and relatively unconstrained mobility in social standing (Macfarlane 1978). In such a social context, the presence of a symbolic property that could affirm (or betray) the duration of status and provide to this extent visual evidence of the authenticity of status claims was a very valuable piece of symbolism indeed. Elizabeth's principal secretary, the great Lord Burghley, put the matter concisely: "Gentility is nothing else but ancient riches" (Burghley 1930).

PREVIOUS STATUS STUDIES AND A THEORY OF PATINA

Goffman, in an early piece entitled "Symbols of Class Status," observed that "a symbol of status is not always a very good test of status" (Goffman 1951). The difficulty, he observed, is that these symbols may be used in a "fraudulent" way. Some members of every community have engaged in acts of status misrepresentation. In the sixteenth century, Sir Thomas Elyot expressed his irritation with the "taylour or barbour [who] in the excess of apparayle [would] counterfaite and be lyke a gentilman" (Elyot 1907).

This difficulty has increased as people have moved from face-to-face societies in which the status of each individual is a matter of common knowledge to relatively anonymous societies in which status must often be inferred from an individual's physical possessions. Form and Stone observed this social phenomenon and they, too, note the opportunity it creates for status forgery. They speak of status being "temporarily appropriated by the "correct" display and manipulation of symbols" (Form and Stone 1957).

Any society that depends on status representation exposes itself to the possibility of this kind of deception. With their intense mobility and their growing anonymity, Western societies have been especially plagued by this problem. Inevitably these societies have created a set of symbolic correctives that would protect them from pretenders.

There are many of these correctives. One of the earliest is sumptuary legislation.[1] By the simple expedient of an act of Parliament, England declared status forgery illegal and created the disincentive of trial and punishment (Baldwin 1926; McCracken 1982a; Hooper 1915). This punishment was severe and sometimes humiliating. One Thomas Bradshaw, an Elizabethan merchant tailor, was seized by an official of the Crown who fulfilled the law by tearing and slashing at Bradshaw's "excessive" clothing. His clothes now in tatters, Bradshaw was paraded through the city streets, and when he reached his home the process was renewed, this time in full view of his neighbors (Hooper 1915:441). For all this fierceness of punishment, however, sumptuary legislation was less and less regarded as an effective means of dealing with status misrepresentation, and England did not draft laws of this kind after the sixteenth century. Ostensibly the most effective means at the disposal of the state, legislative action has proved an unsuccessful and little-used option.

It can only be speculation but there would seem to be a logical reason for the ultimate failure of sumptuary legislation to control status misrepresentation. The problem with this legislation was not that it failed in the detection and punishment of crimes against exclusivity. The problem was that detection and punishment were placed in the wrong hands and came too late. It was necessary for a body of law-makers to deliberate on what was and what was not appropriate clothing for each social group, then for someone to be made responsible for the execution of this law, and then for offenders to be detected and punished. This process was cumbersome and, as with any legal remedy, effective only in the long term and for the collectivity. It did nothing to protect the individual who might fall prey to an act of status forgery. It did not give that individual early warning of the forgery. The detection and punishment of status misrepresentation proved, with other social matters, to be something better left in the hands of the individual.

Another of the strategies with which societies have sought to come to terms with status forgery might be called the "invisible ink" strategy. Here certain social groups cultivate certain kinds of knowledge (of songs, poems, plays, dances, wines, decorum, clothing, and so on) and they make these the crucial and most telling signs of belonging (Bourdieu 1984; Davis 1958; Douglas and Isherwood 1978). The most cunning thing about this strategy is that it is often invisible to those it is used against. The pretender may, for instance, identify the wrong composer as a personal favorite. Immediately he has announced his "outgroup" status as plainly as if he had placed a sign around his neck reading "not one of us." But he will likely remain entirely oblivious to his error and its consequences. This strategy has long been a successful one and it remains an active means of discovering pretenders. The disadvantage of the strategy is that it requires an extremely well-organized, close-knit social world, with a stable group of participants, the sort of world that appears, for instance, in the fiction of Henry James. Any world that is more porous, more rapidly changing, or more anonymous cannot hope to establish and maintain the very fine distinctions that allow for this kind of social discrimination.

A third strategy is to make status contingent on the possession of certain closely guarded objects. This strategy has a long and distinguished history. The seals and insignia of high office have been associated with Western forms of government from their origins to the present day. Western militaries have also made extensive use of them. The difficulty of this technique is that it demands a duly constituted authority to supervise the attribution and use of these objects (e.g., a court dispensing honors, a herald dispensing coats of arms). This authority usually finds it easy enough to confer honors but virtually impossible to recover them. These signs of status, once given, cannot be retrieved. As a result these honors are not very fluid. They do not reflect in a perfectly current way the present and proper state of status allocation.

Now let us consider the strategy implicit in the symbolic property here called "patina." This means of dealing with the pretender has certain advantages. First, the patina strategy very neatly separates ingroups from outgroups. The observer can tell at a glance from the physical possessions of the status-claimer whether there is foundation for these claims. The patina of these possessions says plainly that they have been in the family of the status-claimer for several generations. The lack of patina says just as plainly, "this wealth is new wealth." To this extent, patina works as well as any of the status-detection devices that have been acknowledged by the social sciences. Still more significantly, it succeeds in incorporating many of the advantages of these devices while transcending many of their disadvantages.

First of all, patina gives the opportunity of immediate detection and punishment which rests not with some agent of the state, as in sumptuary legislation, but with every social actor. It creates a category of status symbolism that is immediately detectable by all. On first sighting, before entering into social interaction, the observer is able to use patina for the purposes of a status assessment and make his or her own determination of legitimacy or fraudulence.

Second, patina has the virtue of the "invisible ink" strategy. Patina's status symbolism is often better known and understood by those with long-standing claims to status than those without. Sombart pointed out the tendency of the newly rich to betray their origins through certain styles of consumption (1967). Patina works as a hidden code immediately intelligible to those of genuine standing and well concealed from all but the most sophisticated pretenders. But best of all, this strategy has a universality that the "invisible ink" strategy does not. Even in porous, rapidly changing, and anonymous worlds of status, the patina strategy continues to serve its discriminating purpose.

Finally, patina does have a certain fluidity and therefore can reflect with passing accuracy the present state of status allocation. Patina accrues only on objects of financial value. When a family undergoes a loss of financial resources it is forced eventually to sell some of its patina objects for their cash value. The real tragedy of this action (and the real difficulty of the decision) stems from the fact that it is not just the objects that are lost but their very considerable status value as well. The once high-standing family is in this way systematically dispossessed of the objects that help legitimate its status claims.

In sum, patina status symbolism has several manifest advantages in the detection of status misrepresentation. Furthermore, it is a technique that has been used consistently and extensively in Western status communities. It has served as an invaluable gatekeeper, controlling the status mobility that has been endured and encouraged in the rapidly changing West. But for all this, it has not been given formal treatment in the social science scholarship devoted to the study of status symbolism. It is not too much to say that patina has been utterly neglected in the academic world. Let us see now whether a theory of patina can be fashioned that will enable the social sciences to recognize and contend with it.

A THEORY OF PATINA

The patina of an object allows it to serve as the medium for a vitally important status message. The purpose of this message is not to claim status. It is to verify status claims. Patina allows this verification by permitting the observer to engage in a process of inference about an individual who is making status claims. This process consists roughly in the following assumptions:

1) An object possesses patina in direct proportion to its age.

2) The age of an object stands in direct proportion to the duration of its ownership by a family (with the assumption that the family had bought the object new).

3) The duration of ownership of an object by a family represents the length of time that this family had enjoyed a certain level of discretionary income.

4) The duration of the possession of income level represents the length of time that this family has enjoyed a certain social status.

More simply, patina permits the inference: The greater the patina on certain objects, the longer the owner has enjoyed certain status. It allows the observer to read the duration of a family's status from the amount of the patina on its possessions.

The first thing to be observed about this account is that it makes patina a peculiar species of symbolism. With the advent of structural linguistics and the influence of de Saussure, it has been fashionable to insist on a restricted definition of meaning and to argue, more particularly, that the relationship between the signifier and the signified is an arbitrary one. This perspective says that at least for the preeminent process of communication, language, there is no "natural" connection between the signifier and signified. The contention is that linguistic meaning comes not from the connection between the two, but from a "structure" of the relationship between sets of signifiers and signifieds. These contentions stand at the very heart of the structuralism that now looms so large in certain parts of anthropology in particular and the social sciences in general (Culler 1975; Lévi-Strauss 1963; Sahlins 1976; de Saussure 1966).

The theory of patina proposed here departs from this approach. The present argument is precisely that patina, as a "signifier," stands for status, as a "signified," because of the "natural" connection between them. It is precisely because patina is a kind of non-arbitrary sign that it allows the observer to infer certain kinds of economic and status information about object owners. Patina is, first of all, a physical property and only then a symbolic property of things. This gives it a "real" connection to the thing it signifies. In order to account for patina as an instance of status symbolism we must move beyond what is currently fashionable in certain analytic circles.

There is nothing very radical or adventuresome about this departure. For the approach proposed here has appeared before in the study of the status symbolism of material culture. Indeed it appeared in the work of a scholar who may be the parent of the modern study of status symbolism, Thorstein Veblen.

In *The Theory of the Leisure Class*, Veblen took the position that clothing and other categories of material culture make their status claims by serving as "good prima facie evidence" of income (Veblen 1912). His contention was simply that observers read from the cost of an article of clothing to the purchasing power of the individual wearing it. This is a pre-symbolic formulation. It does not posit the elaborate theoretical apparatus required by twentieth-century structuralists. It does not require "codes," "messages," "syntagmatic chains," "paradigmatic classes," "encoders," and "decoders." Indeed it dispenses with the very notion of "inter-pretation." Veblen's theory simply posits an intelligent observer capable of drawing inferences from the cost of the goods that figure in acts of conspicuous consumption. In Veblen's scheme, the observer is not "decoding" symbolic messages, he or she is "inferring" symbolic implications.

A very similar proposal is being made here for patina. Like the consumer goods discussed by Veblen, patina represents status claims by providing visual evidence from which the observer draws certain social inferences. No "code" underlies this communicative act. No "encoding" or "decoding" is necessary for it to accomplish its symbolic task. Patina works on another principle, one outside the explanatory reach of the structuralist paradigm.

The best way in which to characterize this principle is with the theory of Charles Sanders Peirce and his definition of the "icon" (Peirce 1932). According to Peirce, an icon is a sign that reproduces some of the qualities of the thing it signifies. An example of an icon in language is onomatopoeia where the sign vehicle (e.g., "buzz") imitates the thing it signifies (i.e., the noise of a bee). Other examples of icons include diagrams which are structurally isomorphic with the object they stand for and replicas where the physical properties of signal and object signaled are indistinguishable (Silverstein 1976).

In this instance, patina serves as an icon to the extent that the patina of the object reproduces the duration of the family's claim to status (inferential steps 1 and 4 above). It shows the duration of the family's claim to status by demonstrating the age of the object it adorns. In this case, the relationship between signifier and signified is largely natural and motivated.[2] Patina serves a communicative purpose precisely because of its physical qualities and the kinds of information that can be inferred from these qualities. The status symbolism of patina may be outside pre-vailing structuralist conventions but it is nevertheless readily comprehensible in the theoretical terms proposed by Peirce. From this perspective, the most useful account of patina's expressive power is that it is "iconic."

A HISTORY OF PATINA

The patina strategy of status representation is still widely used in the present day, as we shall see in the final section of this chapter. But its modern manifestation is a pale version of its former self. For the patina strategy was once a mainstay of the processes by which communities protected themselves from status misrepre-sentation. It was, for instance, preeminent in the medieval and early modern periods of European history. With the advent of the consumer revolution and the fashion system in the eighteenth century, the patina strategy was substantially eclipsed. Let us examine it before and after this development.

PATINA IN THE ASCENDENCE

Medieval and early modern English families may be seen as corporations devoted to creating, augmenting, and validating honor (James 1974, 1978). Honor was the most precious of the family's possessions, the foundation of its social standing, and the "gold standard," as it were, on which the family depended in order to negotiate its social transactions. The most striking thing about honor was its dynamic character (Marston 1973). Families could destroy honor and they could increase it. Positive action was needed even to maintain it. Honor was constantly changing in its quantity and quality.

Honor was fluid and mutable in large part because the social order of this period was itself highly dynamic. The mobility of this period was ceaseless. Families rose and fell in the hierarchy with only a few of the ascendent ones able to achieve and then maintain greatness for more than a few generations (Stone and Stone 1984).[3] The currency of this movement was honor. The family that increased its honor rose in the hierarchy. The family that damaged its honor fell. Honor was the fuel of mobility.

One of the most important pieces of status mobility in this period was the transition from ungentle to gentle standing. This was, for instance, the transition that was required of a merchant before his family could be regarded as a member of noble society. But it was also the transition for yeomen, professionals, and noncommercial ranks that sought to claim gentle standing. This transmutation of social substance was an exceedingly difficult one. After all, it required that an individual and a family cross what was unquestionably the best defined and most strongly guarded social distinction in a society preoccupied with distinctions (Stone 1965:49). This transition was perhaps the single most demanding event for which honor was accumulated.

Elizabethan commentators referred to the "five generation" rule (Cooper 1970:16; Ferne 1586:87).[4] This was the number of generations that was required for a family to accumulate sufficient honor and standing to be regarded as fully gentle. Only a period as long as this could wash away the taint of commonness. Only a social apprenticeship of this duration could earn a family rights of full participation in the privileges of gentle standing.

These five generations of apprenticeship were a period in which a family was expected to conduct itself as the gentle family it aspired to be. The logic was, apparently, that five generations of gentle appearance could create gentle reality. The family was expected to devote its wealth to the acquisition of the style of home, clothing, furnishings, and hospitality that characterized those of high standing. Very substantial investments of money in exactly the right bundle of consumer goods were therefore an essential part of the ennobling process on which the family had embarked. As Stone put it, "Money was the means of acquiring and retaining social status, but it was not the essence of it: the acid test was the mode of life . . . " (Stone 1965:50).

It is not hard to see why patina was so useful to a society with these social characteristics. Patina provided individuals a visual manner of determining where families stood in the process of gentrification and mobility. When the consumer goods of a family had patina, it was clear that the process of transformation had fully taken place. Patina said that the family had lived in a gentle manner for generations and therefore legitimately lived in that manner now. This simple physical and symbolic property allowed the members of this fiercely hierarchical society a way of protecting against status misrepresentation.

But we can look at patina not just from the point of view of individual families but also from that of the entire society. From this point of view, patina appears as an essential part of a larger process by which this society turned money into status, commoners into gentlefolk, and in the process kept wealth and standing consonant. That society was a rigid hierarchy was one of the realities of English life in this period. That it was also a place of intense and constant mobility was another. To accommodate these two potentially hostile realities it was necessary to have some way of absorbing new wealth without disrupting the social order.[5] It was necessary to allow new wealth to enter the hierarchy but not in a manner that disrupted the existing status hierarchy or encouraged pretenders. The five-generation rule satisfied this requirement. It allowed entry but only over time and only after a process of qualification. The virtue of patina was that it allowed this society to make publicly demonstrable where individuals stood. Patina made certain that those who merely enjoyed wealth but who had not yet qualified for standing could be identified as such. It marked those who had completed their apprenticeship. In short, patina acted as a kind of gatekeeper, baring pretenders, admitting those who belonged.

PATINA IN ECLIPSE

Patina suffered an eclipse in the eighteenth century. It did so because of the dramatic appearance of a "consumer society" in this period. As we have seen in the previous chapter, England was, suddenly, caught up in what one contemporary observer called an "epidemical madness." Driven by new tastes and preferences and exposed to a brilliant range of new consumer choices, the English had given themselves over to what a modern observer calls "a convulsion of getting and spending" (McKendrick et al. 1982). The English had discovered conspicuous consumption on a modern scale (Braudel 1973).

The consequences of this consumer revolution are extraordinarily numerous and diverse, as we have noted in the preceding chapter. What concerns us here is the development of a new kind and tempo of fashion change. Eighteenth-century England saw the rate of fashion change increase dramatically. What had once taken a decade to move through the fashion cycle now did so in a year. What had once taken a year now took a season. Still more remarkable, categories of objects previously untouched by fashion were now drawn into the process of ceaseless change (Braudel 1973:315–25). Marketers now understood the dynamics of fashion and worked to increase its pitch. New techniques to create new styles and discredit old ones were constantly being developed (McKendrick et al. 1982:34–99). This was the birthplace of the fashion system that dominates consumption in the present day.

The consequences of this development for the patina strategy of status representation were cataclysmic. Suddenly, high-standing individuals could find more status in things that were new than in things that were old. Worse than this, the new concern for fashion in houses, furniture, cutlery, silver, and pottery meant that high-standing individuals were throwing over objects that had patina for those that did not. Again in the words of McKendrick, "novelty became an irresistible drug" (1982:10). With novelty in the ascendent, patina fell into eclipse.

The end of patina as the preeminent means of controlling status misrepresentation set in train a series of unhappy events for the status system. The first of these was simply that there was now no longer any way of discerning through material culture the difference between those of high standing and the wealthy of low standing. When the latest fashion was the rage, anyone with the necessary taste and resources could take possession of the latest innovation and use it for status purposes. This meant that first-generation wealth was now indistinguishable from five-generation gentry.

The second event followed irresistibly from the first. There was now an explosion of imitative behavior on the part of low-standing consumers. Fashion had erased one of the most important ways of differentiating the belongings of the high from those of the low. The low standing could now counterfeit high standing without fear of detection. McKendrick documents the fierce and overwhelming enthusiasm with which they did so. He does not see that the end of the patina strategy helped to make this orgy of status emulation possible.[6]

The third event was the systemic implications of subordinate imitation. When low-standing individuals began to borrow high-standing status markers, high-standing individuals were forced to move on to new status markers. This "trickle-down effect," first identified by Simmel, had operated throughout the early modern period (Simmel 1904). But now, without patina to protect certain status markers, this diffusion pattern assumed new proportions and a new rapidity. Now virtually every status marker could be imitated by wealthy subordinate social groups. As a result, superordinate groups were forced to adopt new innovations in all product categories. There was no rest. No sooner had the high-standing group moved to a new innovation than this, too, was appropriated by subordinate groups, and movement was required again. Aristocratic classes had become the captives of a "chase and flight" cycle.[7] The fashion innovations they had adopted out of fancy, they now had to adopt out of necessity. With no patina strategy to protect them from fraudulent status claims, the only way of doing so was to continually invent new ones.[8]

The advent of a fashion system opened up the possibility of imitation, and with imitation, the loss of symbols, and with this loss, the drive to still more innovation. The advent of this system spelled the end of patina as a means of controlling status misrepresentation. The end of this system deprived the high-standing groups of their first line of defense against status misrepresentation. High-standing parties were now forced continually to adopt new fashions to recreate the distinction patina had previously supplied them. They were now, in a more than figurative sense of the phrase, the prisoners of fashion.

Traumatic as this episode was for high-standing parties and the history of their status strategies, there were benign effects from a more general point of view. The advent of the fashion system of status allocation did mean that a new consistency between wealth and standing was possible. Now an individual could turn income into status immediately and with no need of a long, expensive, and perilous wait over five generations. This allowed the status system to incorporate the upwardly mobile immediately. It allowed it to reward those who by dint of initiative and talent had proven themselves worthy of advancement. This new system of status allocation favored initiative and accomplishment rather than mere standing. It encouraged new mobility and the recognition of ability. The patina strategy had served the cause of relative rigidity, fixity, and immobility. The fashion system served the cause of mobility. We must wonder what contribution the end of patina made in this particular way to the transformation of the West.

PATINA IN THE MODERN WORLD

Patina lives on in the modern world. It has been displaced by fashion, but not entirely supplanted. It remains a useful means of discriminating between old and new status. While it is no longer the terrible gatekeeper, the unforgiving test of who could, and could not, claim gentle standing, it continues to make itself useful. Patina may no longer control status representation, but it remains a skillful and devoted servant in its cause.

Warner and Lunt in their now classic study of status in America, *Yankee City*, glimpsed patina on several occasions. In their discussion of "antiques, heirlooms, and other properties that have been handed down from the past" they noted the importance of these objects to the relations between generations:

> The inheritance of ritual objects from the past and their use by living lineal descendants provide the members of the upper-class group with a symbolic apparatus which ties the sentiments of the living with those of the dead. The house, its furnishings, and the gardens thus become symbolic expressions of the relations not only between household members but also between the living and the dead. (Warner and Lunt 1941:107)

Warner and Lunt saw patina more directly when they commented on the homes of upper-upper-class families. "A home with a distinguished lineage is concrete evidence of upper-class status." They also noted how these objects could help a family to gather status. " . . . after a few generations, the 'new people' who live in these homes and who have adopted upper-class behavior will become members of old families and enter the upper-upper class" (1941:107, 108). But nothing more dramatically acknowledges the presence of the patina strategy in the new world than the clipper ship episode.

One of the families of highest standing in Yankee City, the Altons, were forced by financial exigency to sell one of their most prized status objects. This was a model of a clipper ship which represented the activity from which the Altons had gained their wealth, and more important, it implied the duration of the Altons' claim to high standing. The Altons appreciated the status value of their clipper ship and took it to Boston where a dealer was instructed to sell it "on the quiet." This strategy did not prevent the Starr family, a family of new wealth and great social ambition, from buying the clipper ship and displaying it in their Yankee City home (Warner and Lunt 1941:131).

The clipper ship episode shows us an America in which patina remained active. It shows us a family trying to appropriate an object with patina in order to use it to turn wealth into standing and legitimate status claims. On the one hand, this reassures us that patina was still a status strategy in eastern America in the 1930s. On the other hand, it tells us just how much this strategy had been diminished and distorted in the new world. The subterfuge undertaken by the Starrs was unknown to the Elizabethan world. No such undertaking would have been taken seriously in that period; no family could have hoped to appropriate status in that manner.[9]

The patina strategy has been noted by other more recent studies in the social sciences. Pratt in her exemplary study, "The House as an Expression of Social Worlds," has caught glimpses of its existence among high-standing families in Vancouver, British Columbia (Pratt 1981). Pratt identifies two groups in this study, the "Shaughnessy" group, characterized by a traditional point of view, old money, private school educations, and classical tastes in its interior design, and the "West Vancouver" group, characterized by a more modern point of view, new wealth, public school education, and much more fashion-conscious tastes. Pratt suggests that the first group, the "Shaughnessy" women, were preoccupied with "classical" interior design and especially attached to family heirlooms because they were conventionally minded and indifferent to media influences. What she fails to see is that this attachment reflects the fact that these heirlooms have patina and serve to acknowledge the duration of a family's claim to status.[10]

Pratt's failure to see the operation of a patina strategy on the part of the Shaughnessy women also prevents her from understanding that the West Vancouver women adopt a high-fashion strategy for essentially reactive reasons. The "West Vancouver" women are given to a style of furnishing and clothing that is extremely sensitive to fashion. Pratt attributes this sensitivity to the fact that these women are individualistic ("low grid, low group") in a way that the Shaughnessy women are not. What she fails to see is that the West Vancouver women recognize that the recency of their high standing prevents them from using the patina strategy. They have no patina objects with which to make this claim. Their response is to make the best of a difficult situation by using the status-conferring potential of fashion currency in an aggressive, thoroughgoing manner. Unable to use patina, they use its terrible rival, fashion, to make their status claims.[11] Without a formal idea of patina, Pratt is unable to analyze the aesthetic and social principles that motivate the Shaughnessy group or the reactive strategies of their "new money" rivals.

By this evidence the patina strategy lives on in contemporary society. It would appear to be the case, however, that it has retreated from general use and is now the special preoccupation of only the most high-standing groups. For the rest of society it is of little value. Virtually no one buys furniture with the expectation that it will be of utilitarian and symbolic value to the next generation. No one in the mass of society buys a home with the idea that it might become a "family seat." Some middle- and upper-middle-class families will purchase silver with the expectation that this will be passed down as a "family heirloom" and indeed many middle-class families use such collections for their patina significance. However, these collections, especially those that show any trace of fashion sensitivity, begin very quickly to show their age more convincingly than their status. By the second generation they are not developing a more and more distinguished patina but threaten instead to become an embarrassment. Indeed the very notion of a family heirloom, while still active in the way in which families think about their possessions and distribute them from generation to generation, bears so little resemblance to the Elizabethan operation of patina as to obscure our vision of this once distinguished status device. For the mass of society, the notion of patina is itself hopelessly antique, a charming notion that has passed from fashion. Patina, if it lives on, does so in tiny social enclaves where it keeps the gate with all of its former perspicuity but precious little of its former glory.

THREE

Lois Roget

Curatorial Consumer in a Modern World

This chapter continues our descent from general matters to more particular ones. We narrow our focus to the minute examination of a single modern consumer, Lois Roget. What is remarkable about Mrs. Roget is that she engages in a pattern of consumption that has almost completely disappeared from modern North America and that has not prevailed anywhere in the West since the early modern period. Indeed the present author felt a little like a nineteenth-century naturalist who had stumbled upon a species long thought extinct. Here living in quite ordinary domestic circumstances and the twentieth century was a woman with a strongly "curatorial" pattern of consumption. An examination of this life allows us to peer into the "lived reality" of consumption before the creation of the modern marketplace. It gives us a modest sense of consumption as it existed in what Laslett has called the "world we have lost."

Lois Roget's style of consumption does not appear in any of the literature reviewed in the first or the second chapters. It has not been captured, and probably cannot be captured, in any of the historical scholarship that is now being written. Facts of this delicate ethnographic nature almost never survive. Plainly, the reconstruction of this pattern of consumption from the example of a living individual is a perilous undertaking fraught with the possibility of error and misrepresentation. It is undertaken here with the hope that the advantages outweigh the dangers.

The final section of the chapter considers the implications of curatorial consumption for the individual. Mrs. Roget's pattern of consumption gives her important comforts, continuities, and securities that are generally now absent from the modern world. But it also works to constrain and coerce her existence in ways that most of us would find intolerable.[1]

LOIS ROGET: CURATORIAL CONSUMER

Lois Roget is the keeper of her family's possessions.[2] Her house is literally crowded with objects that have descended from her family and from the family of her husband. Her attitude toward them is charged with a sense of responsibility. She is bound by familial duty to store, display, and conserve these objects. This curatorial pattern of consumption touches many aspects of her life. Her sense of purpose, her concept of family, her attachment to place, and her relationship to her children, all of these are strongly implicated in her relationship to her possessions.

Lois comes from a family that has occupied the same local farmhouse for seven generations. Not surprisingly, the family has an extraordinarily strong sense of its own continuity, and Lois a very strong sense of being a descendant. Both of these were well illustrated recently when Lois was asked to take a position in a church restoration society because her mother had previously served there. ("My mother was a director on that board and so guess who is on that?") The Gresham region has a place for the living representative of this long-lived family, and when Lois fills it she does so almost as a family representative. Lois's husband's family ("John's people," as she likes to call them) is also able to claim an unbroken chain of several generations and he, too, appears to have a strong sense of himself as a descendant.

These two farm families have built up a large and impressive stock of household furnishings, and they have used these furnishings as a kind of archive. This family has written its history into its possessions. Relatively few North American families exhibit this special enthusiasm for the use of material culture to signify their continuity, and I wondered how the Rogets had developed it. Perhaps this is a rural farm tradition, but it is also possible that they learned this lesson from the things themselves. After all, they have owned at least two objects with quite remarkable powers of instruction. The farmhouse in which the family has lived for seven generations is one of these. Here, in circumstances more modest than the ones normally intended by the phrase, was a "family seat," a center for the family, a proof of its longevity, a container for its memories. As each generation bequeathed it to the next, this farmhouse must have given the family a vivid lesson in the mnemonic power of things.

Equally important as a source of instruction, perhaps, was the deed to the farm. This is, as Lois describes it, "parchment paper with a red seal which shows [the farm] was paid for in pounds and pence." Many objects serve as title to certain social claims, but here is a title that is also a title. The family has treasured it for its historical and social value and in doing so perhaps learned something about the symbolic value of things. Both the farmhouse and the deed vividly demonstrated to the family that objects can serve as an archive, and it is to them possibly that the family owes its enthusiasm for collecting and conserving. For this family, things of meaning were perhaps an early source of instruction in the meaning of things.

Lois's heirlooms consist in a wide range of furnishings which have descended from an astonishing number of relatives. The special historical and memorial significance of these furnishings constantly impresses itself upon their curator. Lois often looks up from a book to gaze at a table or a chair and recalls the ancestor who owned it. This individual returns as an image and a memory that can be glimpsed and let slip, or explored in exhaustive detail. Lois pursues one or the other option, depending on her mood. The constant presence of this visual archive make the family history ever present and ubiquitous. Lois can return to it as she will return to her book, picking up the narrative at her leisure.

The relatives are so well represented I felt that she was reading me the family tree instead of showing me her living room. Each of the objects has its provenance. This includes the kinship term appropriate to the previous owner(s). An English aunt is recalled by some "pretty little plates," Lois's great-grandmother by a chair in the hall. Often the provenance will include something about the character, home, life of the owner, and perhaps a story that concerns the piece and its connection to Lois. But the diversity and range of the family information recorded in these objects must not be allowed to imply that Lois is discursive or muddled when she discusses the mnemonics of a piece. On the contrary, she is precise and almost scholarly when she recites the history that exists in her family's goods. She is, after all, speaking not for herself but the family.

Sometimes the archival meaning of these goods concerns the important ceremonies in the family's past. The wedding of Lois's mother, for instance, is recalled by "that little green cookie jar." But this collection of things also includes objects of memorial value created by Lois's own household. Objects commemorate her wedding, her children's graduation, her husband's retirement, her wedding anniversaries, and a range of other family events. Some of these objects have been given her by junior generations to whom they will someday return charged with historical family meaning. This family is not only a site for historical meaning but also a place for its manufacture.

The second set of meanings contained in this family's possessions is related to the first and has to do with place. Lois and her husband's families have a strong sense of attachment to this local area. Indeed it does not exaggerate to say that the family is attached to the locality with some of the intensity that the generations of the family are attached to one another. Tie to family and tie to place are mixed together. The furnishings of Lois's home also express this tie to place. They recall farmhouses throughout the local area. They are made of wood that comes from local forests. They were made by local craftsmen. They have been admired and coveted by hundreds of local residents. These things are as much a part of the locality as the Rogets.

Lois, then, is in possession of objects that are charged with a profound significance. She appreciates that she is, as a result, charged with a very profound responsibility. The family's longevity, the strength of its corporate connection, and its tie to this locality are expressed in her possessions. Her duty is to see that these most important pieces are kept from harm, properly displayed, and passed to the next generation.

The fact and the strength of Lois's sense of her curatorial responsibilities was everywhere evident in the interview. When asked to describe her possessions, she made a strong and consistent distinction between the pieces that were family pieces and those that were not. She tended to dwell on the family pieces and to recite the family members and stories associated with them. The other non-family pieces, on the other hand, were often dismissed as being "of no significance" and "just a chair."

Lois's attitude toward antiques was especially illustrative of the depth and nature of her curatorial feeling for her things. Lois likes to look at antiques that are being offered for sale but she would never consider buying one. She has no interest in possessing objects for their age, beauty, stylistic characteristics, or historical associations. She has no interest in antiques qua antiques. All of the things in her possession are valued and conserved for their family connection.

It is interesting to see the way in which Lois plays out her curatorial role. Any good curator feels the responsibility to preserve objects in such a way that their care will persist even when the curator does not. When it comes to the care of objects, succession is a key issue. Lois has systematically groomed her daughter to take over her curatorial responsibilities. She has versed this child (now forty) in a reverence for these objects and in the family history attached to them. She has even given her daughter a chance to practice by putting in her home several pieces from the collection.

This responsibility for seeing to the continued care of the collection has certain anxieties attached to it, however. First of all, Lois wonders whether her daughter will indeed have the space and the inclination fully to protect the collection. Certainly, the daughter expresses an enthusiasm and certainly she has been well trained but what if . . . Appalling prospects rush in upon the curator and she wonders if she has done enough. Maternal and curatorial anxiety here combine to trouble Lois and make her fear for the future of the family collection.

Second, it is plain that Lois's son has absolutely no curatorial feeling. He has expressed an interest in one piece of the collection and one piece only: a tea service that has the family name on it. His concern for this piece demonstrates, ironically, just how little curatorial sensitivity he really has. For what has caught his eye from the entire collection is the one piece that is branded with the family name. All of the other pieces, many of them to Lois's way of thinking much more charged with family significance, are ignored. Otherwise a good and devoted son, this child has no feeling for the project that so preoccupies his mother.

But the very greatest source of anxiety for Lois is the fact that her children refuse to talk about the collection and its eventual disposition. Lois would like to attach to the back of all of her pieces a piece of tape that identifies the child to whom it is to go. However, her children simply refuse to listen to her when she raises this topic. "I try to pin them down, you see, because they must have liked some bits [of the collection]. They just laugh at me, they think we [Lois and her husband] are going to live forever." This conflict is an interesting one. On the one hand, Lois is attempting to satisfy her curatorial responsibility by seeing that her children assume it on her death. She is concerned to see that her own memory and that of her family will be preserved in death. Her children, on the other hand, want no part of a discussion that looks forward to a time when their mother joins the lineage. They wish to have the mother's memory and that of the family preserved in life. Each party is structurally disposed to contradict the other's wishes.

It is therefore especially interesting that Lois has made no attempt to recruit the next generation. The grandchildren, as we shall see, have been raised to value and appreciate the collection. But it appears they have not been fully instructed in its historical significance. They do not know all the stories that inhere in these things. This is an important opportunity missed. Another of the respondents interviewed has contrived to move her collection into her grandchildren's lives by stages so that they are not only well aware of its significance but already trained in the responsibilities of the curator.

AN INTERACTIVE EXHIBIT

But this most recent generation of a long-lived family has been given a chance to participate in the memorial significance of their grandmother's collection. Indeed, one of the most effective ways Lois plays out her curatorial role is through a policy of "interactive exhibits." In her living room she has a little oil lamp of which she is very fond. In her words: "When I was a little girl and we didn't have hydro [i.e., electric power], I used to take a lamp like that to bed every night and so it means a lot to me." This lamp is put at the center of the table at Christmas time as a centerpiece. It is also put at the center of the table when the grandchildren come to visit. On these occasions the lights are turned off and the children have a special meal around the lamp.

This is a skillful use of the collection. It uses an object charged with historical family significance in the creation of an event charged with contemporary family significance. But better than that, it creates a memorable childhood event for one generation by using an object from the childhood of another. The object will pass into their possession and there evoke not only their childhood but the childhood of a grandmother. Their past will contain an object that contains the past of the family. Lois has created a living exhibit that puts the otherwise passive observer into participatory contact with the museum piece, and an otherwise distant generation in touch with its lineage.

Lois's family ritual may be seen as a technique for loading events of a corporate, family significance into the individual's past. This technique has the effect of making the individual's past (and to this extent, the individual) a part of the family. We may take this to be a kind of "securing" activity on the lineage's part. Thus does the lineage integrate each generation into the lineage. Thus does it see to its own continuity and preservation. In analytic terms, we are witnessing here the use of person-object relations to create person-person relations.

The fact that Lois choose a lamp for this ritual is interesting. Can it be only accidental that when the grandchildren gather in the light of this lamp, they are brought together in the small circle of the family? Is it accidental that the flame that creates this pool of light also necessarily creates a surrounding darkness from which it gives protection? Is it accidental that lamps are often used for memorial purposes and as a symbol of sustained faith and devotion? When Lois chose one of her possessions to create a little family ritual of continuity, she enjoyed very great luck or quite remarkable skill.

Being a curator has not always been easy. Lois has recently had problems with her physical plant. For twenty-three years she lived in a house that was almost perfect for storage and display, a red brick house of large and beautiful proportions. The exterior strongly resembled local farmhouses in material and shape and therefore had a certain appropriateness. The interior was very large and possessed a living room, a dining room and a hall that together provided graceful display space. Three years ago, however, Lois and her husband moved into their "retirement" home. Blessed with one or two superb features and much more manageable from the standpoint of cleaning, this house was a disaster from a curatorial point of view. First, it was modern and therefore quite inappropriate as a place to display the collection. Second, it was small, which meant that some things had to be removed from display and the remaining pieces shown to dramatically different effect.

A change of site has substantially diminished Lois's ability to mount the exhibit properly but she has persevered. She sighs a little at the difficulties imposed by her present house, but she understands they are as nothing compared to the difficulties that are to follow. She understands that the next move, to an apartment or a retirement home, will take her into very much smaller circumstances in which she will have virtually to abandon her attempts to display and store the collection. So much of her sense of self is presently caught up in and realized through her role as family curator that it is impossible for Lois to imagine (or for us to speculate) what the consequences of this move will be.

For the time being, Lois continues with her responsibilities. As any curator knows, collections must be continually cultivated and tended to. One of Lois's current projects is to find a chair that will enable her to complete a set of chairs that have descended from an aunt. This is the only situation in which Lois will consider buying an old object. She justifies this purchase with the contention that it will make the collection more complete. Curators and especially restoration experts know how often a little artifice helps to bring out the essential truth of an object or collection. She also takes very great pleasure in restoring a decayed family piece to its former glory. In both cases, she is working the collection to increase its memorial value.

Extensive as the collection is, it does not furnish the house entirely, and it has been necessary to buy several major and minor pieces. This is made more difficult by Lois's prohibition against the purchase of antiques, noted above. Lois must somehow buy pieces that conform to the collection without actually being ancient themselves. Lois has solved this display problem by choosing pieces that are both old and quite bland in appearance. Together, these properties prevent the pieces from drawing attention to themselves and allow them to serve as "bit players," which create a backdrop for the important pieces without threatening their place of preeminence.

Plainly, then, person-object relations in this household consist, in part, in a powerful and consistent pattern. We have called this pattern "curatorial consumption" and defined it as a pattern of consumption in which an individual treats his or her possessions as having strong mnemonic value, and entertains a sense of responsibility to these possessions that enjoins their conservation, display, and safe transmission. The difficulty with this approach is that it threatens to conceal the person. The metaphor that casts Lois as a curator threatens to make these quite extraordinary aspects of her consumption appear to be mere extensions of itself. It makes them appear simple operations of the metaphor rather than the unusual and very real characteristics of a life.

Before we go further then it is necessary to insist that this is no idle metaphor. Lois does attach an historical, powerfully mnemonic significance to these objects. She does regard this collection as organized according to a specific principle, and she protects it from the intrusion of pieces that are merely old. She has made herself the keeper of each piece and its provenance. She has cultivated a successor. It is not Lois who is shaped to the metaphor but the metaphor that conforms to her.

CURATORIAL AND MODERN CONSUMPTION: A CONTRAST

Plainly the curatorial aspect of Lois's consumption is rare and almost eccentric. Most modern-day consumers do not take a curatorial interest in their possessions. Indeed few of us own objects that would admit of this treatment. There is virtually no product category, with the possible and unpredictable exception of cutlery, plate, and certain items of art and furniture, that are passed from one generation to another. These few exceptions having moved from one generation to another are highly unlikely to make the transition to a third generation. Multi-generational transfer has become rare. This is, of course, a modern development, the origins of which have been located in the eighteenth century by the historian Neil McKendrick (1982) who notes that from this period onward an individual family becomes less and less likely to inherit their possessions and more and more likely to buy them.

So there is no question but that Lois is a very rare bird. Indeed her curatorial pattern of consumption makes her a valuable limiting case. She is a kind of exception that helps us see the rules that govern more mainstream patterns of consumption. Let us look more closely at the nature of her curatorial consumption. What are its origins, what are its implications for Lois and her family, what is its significance from a person-object point of view? How does this family differ from more conventionally minded ones?

In the conventional pattern in contemporary society each family chooses its consumer goods for itself. Increasingly the social sciences see this act of choice as something that involves the family in an act of identity construction. The family is buying not merely the economist's bundle of utility, but also a set of signs that will serve to represent and to constitute the family's character (McCracken 1986b). The conventional family then is called upon to select from a range of possible consumer goods and the range of quite different cultural meanings these goods carry.

From one point of view we can say that this process of choice is forced. The fact that no goods descend to the modern family compels them to make their own choices. From another point of view, however, we can say that the process of choice is free. The absence of inherited goods leaves a family with a clean slate. It allows them to constitute physical and symbolic surroundings for the family without literal or figurative baggage. In sum, the act of choice that confronts the modern family is both a necessity and an opportunity. Each family must and may make its own set of consumer choices and avail itself of the meanings that are contained in consumer goods.

Moreover, the consumption necessity and opportunity of the modern family has a perpetual quality. Families are often free and forced to make a continual series of purchases and, with each of these changes, to undertake a transformation in the family's concept of itself. In a sense, modern families are not allowed to inherit from themselves. Things do not necessarily descend to them from their previous manifestations. In short, conventional families have free and forced access to a large and changeable body of meaning through their consumer choices.

Lois, on the other hand, has a pattern of consumption with very different implications. She has had her choices strictly constrained. A great many of her purchase choices were preempted by inheritance, and the remainder were made with a careful eye to protecting the preeminence and character of the collection. Furthermore, these inherited possessions come charged with very particular meaning: the places, the people, and the events of previous generations. For Lois, then, there is little discretionary opportunity, either in her possessions or in the meanings thereof.

This lack of elective opportunity is of course a condition some people dream of. It represents for them one of the most valuable aspects of a pre-industrial, pre-consumer society. The individual finds his or her life ordered by tradition and continuity. Each generation is heir to and the beneficiary of the values and meanings of the previous ones. Neither individuals nor generations need to reinvent themselves but may rely instead on the work of the ancestors.

On the other hand, this pattern of consumption has potentially irksome characteristics. The inheritance of objects preempts opportunities for choice, and the inheritance of heirlooms delimits the range of meaning to which one has access. It does not exaggerate to say that there is very little room for Lois in these possessions. They are already packed with meaning, the work of seven generations eager for memorial. Indeed, these objects are so fully "prerecorded," that to take possession of these objects is to risk being swamped by their meaning. Their simple presence represents a daily, voluble insistence that the family is a lineage and Lois a descendant. This tyranny is compounded by the fact that once one has accepted these things, one must then become their steward.

In the difference between Lois's curatorial pattern of consumption and more modern ones, we are confronted with a classical confrontation between the corporation and the individual. For Lois, the individual, is submerged within the corporation. She has the comfort, continuity, security, and embeddedness of this relationship. As part of a corporation, Lois has been gifted with a way to define herself and her world and blessed with a powerful sense of belonging. She has been gifted even with a kind of immortality. In these things she will live on and be remembered. But as part of the corporation she also suffers the loss of individuality and a diminished freedom of development and expression. For modern families, on the other hand, the family is limited in its connection to previous and future generations. There is no clarity and depth of definition to be drawn from the ancestors. Nor is there any sense of continuity, precedent, or tradition from which to take definition. Each family (and increasingly each individual) must make its own way, cobbling together a sense of itself out of its own resources and the consumer goods at its disposal. In the place of this legacy, however, there is great elective range. The family is largely a blank slate, on which it alone is permitted to write.

Lois is a curiosity, almost a throwback. Her pattern of consumption was once the prevalent one. As McKendrick tells us, until the eighteenth century, most individuals inherited more than they purchased and were heir in this way not only to their ancestors' possessions but also to their meanings. This pattern of consumption was one of the ways in which the individual remained submerged within the corporation. Clearly, however, the individual in the West has been escaping the controlling grasp of corporations, domestic and otherwise. Stone (1977) documents this process as it takes place in the period 1500–1800. By the eighteenth century, a new pattern of corporation and consumption was fast emerging, one in which the individual was now forced and free to make both his/her own choices in consumption and self-definition.

Objects play a key part in the old and the new patterns. For the old system of family and inheritance, the movement of goods from one generation to the next was an important method of preserving the corporation, insuring its continuity, relaying its values, and of bringing each successive generation into the lineage. Lois gives us a glimpse of how this old system worked as a way of communicating meaning from one generation to the next.

For the new system, goods are equally important. They are one of the sources to which families and their individuals turn for the meaning that no longer descends to them from the lineage. These goods are useful in this manner only because they are the products of a meaning-producing system and perpetually revised for new social circumstances. The currency of their meaning makes them quite useless to successive generations. As a result, they now rarely move from one generation to another; and rarely are they useful in memorializing past generations as a corporation in any substantial way. The use of objects as a record of the family and as a means of its continuity is very difficult to achieve in the new pattern of consumption.

So what does Lois have that we don't have? This is another way of asking what is the nature of what Laslett (1971) has called the "world we have lost"? When you ask Lois to give an account of the value of her antiques this is what she says:

> LR: "Yes, well they are precious, not for the value so much, as [that] I can look at them all and know exactly the home they came from."
> GM: "Do you find yourself doing that from time to time?"
> LR: "Oh yes. When I see that buffet I know the aunts had it in their dining room."

The past lives on in the present. Lois lives in a world that is rich in attachment.

Her physical surroundings constantly speak to her of her family and their lives. A family's possessions have been called its archive. But they are much more than that. The material culture of a home like Lois's gives the past a certain presence. As a result, Lois lives in a "home" the likes of which the rest of us can only dimly imagine. Her home is a place of astonishing "placeness." It is richly worked and deeply rooted. What does she think of the "places" in which the rest of us live? I showed her a picture of a modern living room and she responded in a way that takes issue squarely with the mainstream.

> LR: "Well, of course that is not my idea of home at all. That's modern."
> GM: "How do you feel about a place that looks like that?"
> LR: "I haven't any feeling for it, none at all."

The "place" Lois lives in reverberates with meaning and the entire family sounds when memory sets this reverberation off. Other places, the places in which the rest of us live, do not reverberate. She cannot hear anything in them and they cannot elicit any feeling in her. She has no "feeling" for these places because there is, from her perspective and within her sense of person-object relations, no feeling there. We live in places that have no history. For some of us this is exhilarating. We may write upon these places as an act of self-expression and self-definition. But for Lois these places are empty and intensely vacant.

CONCLUSION

Lois and her collection are, in a sense, merely different versions of the family. Both are the issue of a family enterprise that stretches over seven generations. Both are historical artifacts of a sort. These objects are so densely vested with the memory of human beings, and the human beings so densely vested with the meaning of these grand old pieces of furniture, that the two appear as different moments in a historical process that endlessly converts ancestors into objects and objects into descendants. Lois is a participant in a process that has almost entirely vanished. She is, to this extent, not only the curator of her family's past but also of a much broader Western one.

Part II

THEORY

This second part of the book is devoted to theoretical matters. It is here that we shall attempt to take account of the meaningful properties of consumer goods and the interpenetration of culture and consumption from a theoretical point of view. The social sciences have been exceedingly slow to develop theoretical resources in this area. It has also suffered some important false starts. The "product as language" argument is one of these. In chapter 4 we shall examine this argument as it has been used in the study of the symbolism of clothing. We shall demonstrate here that the language-clothing comparison is unsound. In chapter 5, an attempt is made to transcend the "language-product" approach and create a more satisfactory theoretical account of the cultural characteristics and symbolic properties of consumer goods.

FOUR

Clothing as Language

An Object Lesson in the Study of the
Expressive Properties of Material Culture

Some years ago a new and influential metaphor captured the attention of the social sciences. This metaphor suggested an essential similarity between language and inanimate objects. Suddenly it became fashionable to talk about the "language" of clothing, the "language" of food, the "language" of houses. This metaphor has helped to point out the symbolic properties of material culture and consumer goods. But it has also created some thoroughgoing misconceptions about what these symbolic properties are and how they operate. This chapter suggests that clothing, one of the most expressive of the product categories, is *not* usefully compared to language. It argues that clothing is a very different system of communication, the cultural significance of which cannot be fully assessed until the "language" metaphor is abandoned or revised.

THE EXPRESSIVE PROPERTIES
OF MATERIAL CULTURE

The study of clothing as an instance of material culture has several dimensions.[1] This chapter will focus on only one: clothing as an expressive medium. The first section of the chapter will review thematically the anthropological literature which treats clothing from this point of view. It will consider how the study of clothing has been used to examine cultural categories, principles, and processes as well as social distance and social change. The second section of the chapter will critically and empirically examine the widespread contention that clothing may be regarded as a kind of language. I will seek to demonstrate that the metaphor that treats clothing as a language is in one respect problematical. I will argue that the metaphor conceals from us much that is important to our understanding of clothing as a means of communication. The third section of the chapter will take up the implications of this argument for the more general study of material culture. I will argue that if the metaphor that links material culture and language is to continue to serve us, it must do so not as a study in comparison but as a study in contrast. We must concern ourselves much more with the differences between language and material culture and much less with the similarities between them. I shall note four research opportunities that follow from this perspective. It is hoped that this three-part undertaking will serve a larger purpose: to advance and clarify one aspect of our growing interest in the expressive character of material culture.

It is plain that theoretical developments in recent years, particularly those accomplished in the areas of symbolic, structural, and semiotic anthropology, have encouraged a long-standing interest in the expressive aspects of material culture. Pitt-Rivers in 1875 expressed his interest in material culture as the "outward signs and symbols of particular ideas in the mind" (1906:23). But it was not until relatively recently that we have been prepared theoretically and methodologically to show how material culture achieves the outward expression of inward ideas. The work of Lévi-Strauss in particular has given us a way to investigate material culture as ethnographic data in which culture is made material. In the hands of Lévi-Strauss and others, structural analysis has demonstrated how the categories, principles, and processes that constitute culture may be discerned in the concrete, tangible objects of material culture.

This and other kindred theoretical developments have advanced the study of material culture to a new place of importance. They have played a signal role in the rehabilitation of the field and its recovery from the neglect and disdain suffered since the eclipse of the evolutionary paradigm. For the anthropologist concerned to examine culture, the study of material culture is a newly vital opportunity.

Material culture's rehabilitated standing is widely acknowledged and needs no special emphasis here. What is not so widely acknowledged, however, is that the revitalization of material culture has brought forth new opportunities for controversy, imprecision, and imperfect anthropology. As material culture plays host to more, and more vigorous, ethnographic activity, it is called upon to redouble the vigilance with which it reflects upon itself. Our rehabilitation has brought new responsibilities. This chapter is an attempt to meet this responsibility by clarifying one of the theoretical issues implicit in our efforts to treat material culture as an expressive medium.

ANTHROPOLOGY AND THE STUDY OF CLOTHING: A THEMATIC REVIEW

Existing studies of clothing as an expressive medium reveal the several ways in which clothing may be seen as a concrete manifestation of "particular ideas in the mind." In this section, I will review these studies with an eye to demonstrating what the student of material culture can hope to discover of culture in the consideration of clothing.

CLOTHING AND THE STUDY OF CULTURAL CATEGORIES

Bogatyrev in his early study of Moravian folk costume (1971) demonstrated the number and range of cultural categories that may be discerned and investigated through the study of clothing.[2] His project, though couched in the language of the

Prague Linguistic Circle, is compatible with the terms of analysis introduced by de Saussure (1966) and later used to nonlinguistic purpose by Lévi-Strauss (1966).[3] Moravian folk costume is treated as a collection of material "systems of difference" which encode a collection of parallel conceptual "systems of difference." Thus, for example, the age-grade discriminations of the Moravians (a system of difference which discriminates categories of person by age) finds correspondence and representation in the costumes worn by Moravians of different ages (costumes which are themselves a system of difference that discriminates categories of person by the differential distribution of clothing color, shape, fabric, etc.). Other categories of person, as defined by rank, sex, marital status, occupation, etc., are also evident in Moravian clothing which serves thus to give them material representation in the social world. Categories of time, place, and activity are also represented in clothing. In Bogatyrev's work we have a relatively comprehensive demonstration of how clothing makes manifest conceptual systems of difference that would otherwise have no nonlinguistic "objective correlative."

Clothing is to this extent an opportunity to establish the basic co-ordinates into which a world has been divided by culture. Clearly, not all of the distinctions that organize the Moravian folk world were evident to Bogatyrev in Moravian costume, but it is fair to say that all of the fundamental axes according to which this world was ordered were made accessible to him there. It is characteristic of clothing to provide this record of and guide to cultural categories. As Sahlins puts it in his study of contemporary American clothing: " . . . the system of American clothing amounts to a very complex scheme of cultural categories and the relations between them, a veritable map—it does not exaggerate to say—of the cultural universe" (1976:179).

CLOTHING AND THE STUDY OF CULTURAL PRINCIPLES

If cultural categories are evident in clothing, so too are cultural principles.[4] Clothing reveals both the themes and the formal relationships which serve a culture as orienting ideas and the real or imagined basis according to which cultural categories are organized. We may use any one of a number of studies as our ethnographic case in point. Adams's (1973) study of Sumbanese textiles, Drewal's study of Yoruba art (1983), Schwarz's (1979) study of South American clothing, and my own efforts (1982a) to account for the sumptuary legislation and ornament of Elizabethan dress, all reveal how readily organizing cultural principles may be drawn from clothing. In Adams's case, textile design is shown to display three basic formal patterns which are also observed in the organization of Sumbanese spatial distinctions, marriage practices, formal negotiations, ceremonial language, social organization, and distinctions of ritual time and occasion. The principles that organize these diverse aspects of social life are thus found represented in the abstract design of the textile. In my study of Elizabethan clothing, I have sought to show how the contradiction between hierarchical and egalitarian ideas that informed the organization of the social world were variously represented and mediated by the design of the ornamentation of Elizabethan doublets and breeches. In both studies, the principles of a world are found woven into the fabric of its clothing.

It is worth emphasizing that clothing is a particularly valuable source of evidence for the study of cultural principles. Cultural categories are first of all linguistic categories and can therefore be elicited from the informant with relative ease through verbal testimony. Cultural principles, on the other hand, are often less explicitly and consciously entertained by the informant and therefore more difficult to obtain through conventional interview techniques. What is not apparent to the informant in a conscious manner may nevertheless be given voice by the characteristic design and distribution of the informant's clothing.

CLOTHING AND THE STUDY OF CULTURAL PROCESS

Clothing is, then, a means by which cultural categories and principles are encoded and made manifest. Because it serves in these capacities, it is also a valuable means of communication for ritual in general, and rites of passage in particular. Charged with semiotic effect and potential, clothing is one of the chief opportunities for exercising the metaphoric (Fernandez 1977) and performative (Tambiah 1977) powers of ritual. Clothing can also be used to mark and even to effect the transition from one cultural category to another that occurs in the rite of passage. Each of the three stages described by Van Gennep (1960) and elaborated by V. Turner (1967) can be represented in ritual and actualized for the participant and observer through the strategic use of the communicative aspect of clothing (cf. Leach 1961).

Studies that examine this use of clothing are too few. One rare effort, T. Turner's study of Tchikrin body ornament (1969), demonstrates how much of the logic of this Brazilian group's age-grade transition is to be found inscribed in the self-decoration that attends the rite of passage. Kuper (1973b) has considered the Ncwala ritual of Southeast Africa and Wolf (1970) the color symbolism of a Chinese mourning ritual. Winick (1961) makes passing reference to the use of shoes as a marker of transition in contemporary North America but detailed studies of this phenomenon are almost nonexistent. Here, too, the study of clothing serves as a productive "way in" to the study of a meaningful universe.

CLOTHING AND THE STUDY OF SOCIAL DISTANCE

The study of clothing presents other opportunities for the study of culture. For example, the treatment of social distance has been undertaken by Murphy (1964) through the examination of the Tuareg veil and by Messing (1960) through the examination of the Ethiopian toga. The veil is used by the Tuareg to acknowledge status differences, shifts in the tone of a relationship, and, most of all, to remove the individual from situations in which conflicting roles create conflicting expectations. For Ethiopians, the toga is used to create social distance according to mood and to reflect differences in status, role, and function.

In these two instances we find clothing used as a more active, individual, and variable means of communication. The use of clothing to represent cultural categories, principles, and processes is a largely collective enterprise in which the individual as a communicator plays a relatively passive role. In the examples provided by Murphy and Messing, clothing allows the individual to communicate particular information on a more active, individual, and changeable basis. In short, this manifestation of the expressive character of clothing is, to use the standard semiotic distinction, more a matter of *parole* than *langue*. The study of this aspect of clothing opens up the possibility of examining culture as it is enacted by individuals in their negotiation of daily life. It allows us the observation of material culture as an active, daily means of communication.

CLOTHING AND THE STUDY OF CHANGE AND HISTORY

It is also possible to undertake the study of change and history through clothing. Kuper (1973a) has examined the role of clothing in colonial southeast Africa. She has demonstrated, among other things, the use of clothing as an instrument of both the hegemonic influence of the West and the indigenous attempts to resist this influence. For my own part (1985a), I have sought to show how clothing can be used as a historical operator which serves not only to reflect changing historical circumstances but also as a device which creates and constitutes this change in cultural terms. Taking the color of the clothing of two groups at the court of Elizabeth I, I have tried to show how clothing served as an agent of history by giving cultural form and order to a highly innovative, dynamic historical moment.

Clothing plays its diachronic role variously. One of its chief manifestations as a reflection and agent of change is the phenomenon of fashion (Barthes 1983; Gibbins and Gwyn 1975; Kidwell and Christman 1974; Richardson and Kroeber 1940; Roberts 1977; Sapir 1931; Schwartz 1963; Simmel 1904; and Wills and Midgley 1973). In this and other forms, clothing is sometimes a confirmation of change and sometimes an initiation of change. It is sometimes a means of constituting the nature and terms of political conflict and sometimes a means of creating consensus. It is sometimes an instrument of attempted domination and sometimes an armory of resistance and protest.

These various aspects of the relationship between clothing and history have not been widely studied. But this too is material culture in an active dynamic mode. In this diachronic role, clothing serves as a communicative device through which social change is contemplated, proposed, initiated, enforced, and denied. Its study allows us to observe the expressive aspect of material culture in one of its most radically creative forms.[5]

In sum, previous studies of clothing reveal how much of culture can be examined in the material culture of clothing. Cultural categories, principles, processes, social distance, daily communication, and history are all accessible to the student of material culture through the study of clothing. It is indeed not too much to argue that all of this ethnographic material, and the "primary ideas" they represent, are not only accessible but particularly comprehensible when viewed from this perspective. Clothing makes culture material in diverse and illuminating ways.

CLOTHING AS LANGUAGE:
REQUIEM FOR A METAPHOR

It is characteristic of these and other studies of clothing to resort to a particular metaphor when talking about the expressive aspect of clothing. Again and again the critical literature suggests that clothing is a kind of language. Thus, Bogatyrev notes the resemblance between Moravian folk costume and language (1971:84), Turner call Tchikrin body language a kind of "symbolic language" (1969:96), Wolf speaks of the "vocabulary" of the symbolic system of Chinese mourning costume (1970:189), Messing calls the Ethiopian toga a "nonverbal language" (1960:558), and Nash refers to one aspect of contemporary clothing as a "silent language" (1977:173). In Sahlins the comparison is a detailed one and includes references to the "syntax," "semantics," and "grammar" of clothing (1976:179). Neich is still more exacting in his comparison and advocates the use of an "explicitly linguistic model" for the study of New Guinea self-decoration (1982:214). This tendency to compare clothing to language is not limited to anthropological studies; it exists in the work of other social scientists (Gibbins 1971; Gibbins and Schneider 1980; Holman 1980b, 1980c, 1981; Roach and Eicher 1979; Rosenfeld and Plax 1977) as well as those of popular writers (e.g., Lurie 1981).[6]

Plainly, this comparison of language and clothing is not always intended with the same degree of seriousness or conviction. Sometimes it serves only as a rhetorical ornament. Furthermore, even when the metaphor is used more purposefully, it is hard to fault the reflex from which it springs. For it *is* a helpful figure of speech, and it succeeds in illuminating certain properties shared by clothing and language. It is also apparent that the comparison follows the same worthy instinct that has informed so much work and progress in recent anthropology. It continues in the tradition of applying linguistic models to the study of nonlinguistic phenomena (e.g., Lévi-Strauss, 1963).

Still, it must be observed that the metaphor has been used so liberally that it has started to cool and take on the fixity of conventional wisdom. What was once a lively and illuminating suggestion of similarity is more and more a statement of apparent fact. This latter-day development in the history of the metaphor radically changes its value as a rhetorical device and academic instrument. As a "dead metaphor" it now threatens to conceal as much as it once revealed. It now dulls our critical senses as it once stimulated our imaginative faculties.

The time has therefore come to bury this metaphor or rehabilitate it. It is necessary to examine the relationship between clothing and language and determine where the similarities hold and where the differences exist. This new scrutiny of the metaphor promises a clearer idea of the expressive properties of clothing and the other instances of material culture which appear to give voice to culture.

RESEARCH REPORT AND CRITICAL COMMENT

In order to investigate some of the similarities and differences which exist between language and clothing, a study was undertaken in the fall and winter of

1982–83.[7] The purpose of this study was to design a research project which would examine how clothing is "decoded" or interpreted by the observer. A larger study will help to substantiate the findings of this initial project but the pilot gives sufficient data to address the issue raised in this chapter.[8]

It was while examining the twenty-five hours of interview testimony generated by the pilot study that I began to have grave doubts about the wisdom of a thoroughgoing language-clothing comparison. In order to demonstrate this skepticism, it is necessary to resort briefly to the terms and concepts of structural linguistics.

Speech, Jakobson and Halle argue (1956:58–62), implies the operation of two linguistic principles (cf. de Saussure 1966; Barthes 1967). One of the principles, that of selection, occurs when the speaker selects a linguistic unit from each paradigmatic class to fill each of the corresponding "slots" that make up the sentence. Each class consists of all of the units that can potentially fill the same slot in a sentence. These units are capable of substitution one for the other and therefore enjoy a relationship of equivalence. But they are also defined by their difference to one another and therefore enjoy a relationship of contrast. The units of each paradigmatic class may be viewed as a vertical plane not altogether dissimilar to the rolling wheel of the slot machine. Any particular unit in a sentence is invisibly attended by all the other units of its class. These units stand ready to take its place and so change the meaning of the sentence. When the speaker employs the principle of selection he evokes one unit from each paradigmatic class and thus exploits the system of contrast that each of these classes represents.

The second linguistic principle, that of combination, occurs when the speaker combines the units selected from the paradigmatic classes into a syntagmatic chain. This chain consists in the various slots for which paradigmatic alternatives exist. Rules of combination specify how units are to be combined into a syntagmatic chain. This is the horizontal plane of language that gives language its linear, discursive aspect. Any syntagmatic chain creates a sequential context which acts on the meaning of each unit as it is entered into speech. The unit, already defined by its paradigmatic relations, undergoes a further process of definition when it is conjoined with other items in a syntagmatic chain.

The code of any particular language consists in a specification of the units of the paradigmatic classes and the rules for their syntagmatic combination. The code establishes how the principles of selection and combination are to be used in any particular linguistic exercise.

Each speaker of a language is both constrained and empowered by the code that informs his language use. He or she has no choice but to accept the way in which distinctive features have been defined and combined to form phonemes. He or she has no choice but to accept the way in which phonemes have been defined and combined to form morphemes. The creation of sentences out of morphemes is also constrained but here the speaker enjoys a limited discretionary power and combinatorial freedom. This discretionary power increases when the speaker combines sentences into utterances. By this stage the action of compulsory rules of combination has ceased altogether. The speaker is no longer constrained but free in his combinatorial activity. Jakobson and Halle refer to this characteristic of language as "an ascending scale of freedom" (1956:60). At the bottom of the scale the speaker is fully constrained, at the top he or she is completely free. It is this dual character of language that allows it to stand both as a collective and systematic means of communication and as an instrument of endlessly various expressive potential.

This model of language is for present purposes well illustrated by Neich (1982) in his study of self-decoration in Mount Hagen, New Guinea. Neich suggests that we may treat this self-decoration as a code which specifies paradigmatic choices appropriate for syntagmatic combination. The Hagener chooses a decorative unit from each paradigmatic class and combines these in a syntagmatic chain, his clothing outfit. Does the Hagener thus create a message about status and role on formal and informal social occasions? Whether the Hagener is a donor, donor's helper, warrior, etc., can be read by the observer from the decoration of his/her body. For Neich, this decoration demonstrates both principles of language. He argues that the self-decoration of Hageners, examined in the light of a structural linguistic model, reveals a languagelike character, and that we may call it a "semiotic or system of signs" (1982:217) (cf. Barthes 1967:111).

My research suggests that the application of the structural linguistic model to clothing is problematical. While clothing does bear a resemblance to language in some respects, it departs from it in a fundamental way. Ironically, when clothing most fully conforms to language and its principles of selection and combination, it fails completely as a semiotic device. Or, to put this another way, when clothing as a code is most like language, it is least successful as a means of communication. There is to this extent a fundamental difference between language and clothing. This difference must be taken into account if we are to make a successful examination of the communicative aspect of clothing.

In examining my research data, I sought to determine how informants interpreted examples of clothing. The external assessment of an internal activity of this sort is of course extremely difficult. The best I could hope to do was to establish a characteristic pattern of interpretation, and hope that this pattern was a reliable guide to the inner activity itself. While this latter assumption is itself problematical, it does seem to me that there is a characteristic pattern, and that this pattern does serve, at least in a negative way, to cast doubt on one of the supposed similarities between language and clothing.[9]

Informants were asked to respond to a series of slides which pictured a variety of instances of contemporary North American clothing. There were three categories of response to these slides. These categories represent levels of relative ease of interpretation.

In the first category of interpretation, informants were swift and sure in their reading of the clothing portrayed. Typically, they delivered their response to the slide almost instantaneously. Selecting a term from our vocabulary of social types, the informant would identify the person pictured as a "housewife," "hippie," "businessman," etc. Sometimes this term would be accompanied by a demographic adjective (e.g., "middle-class," "uneducated," "wealthy").

It is difficult to judge from these external signs just what internal process had occurred. But it did appear unlikely that the informant had performed a "reading" of the clothing portrayed in anything like the terms we associate with language proper.

First, there was no evidence of a linear reading of the clothing outfit. Informants did not appear to begin their interpretive activity with one body slot and work their way through to others. They did not sort through the syntagmatic chain in order to determine how each paradigmatic selection modified the meaning of other selections and the chain itself. They appeared instead to read the clothing outfit before them as an ensemble. It was clear that the outfit was examined to discover the differential effect of its various parts, but the successive combination of these parts did not seem to play an important part in the informant's account of their meaning. The parts of the outfit did not present themselves in a linear way to the informant (for they exist not in sequence but as co-present elements), and the informant did not read them this way. Instead, clothing presents the parts of its "syntagmatic combination" simultaneously, and it is simultaneously that they are read.

Second, the meaning of the outfits was always rendered in terms of a limited vocabulary of adjectives and nouns. By their own account, informants sought to determine the "look" of the outfit before them. These "looks" did not constitute a set of infinite possibilities but a delimited universe. The informant showed no expectation that the message of a particular clothing outfit would constitute a novel piece of discourse. And more important, he or she showed no evidence of possessing the interpretive resources necessary to deal with such a message. He or she had at his disposal the use of only a limited set of adjectives and nouns that did not allow for novelty.

In the second category, informants experienced hesitation and difficulty in making their interpretation. Unable to make an immediate identification of an outfit, they began a more careful examination of the "body sentence" and its component parts. Often they would deliver comments of the following kind: "Let's see, they're wearing 'x' so they might be 'a', but they're also wearing 'y' so perhaps they're 'b'." Typically, the informant would then complain that the parts of the outfit did "not really go together," and that it was therefore difficult to read the individual pictured. This period of hesitation and uncertainty would be resolved by one of two strategies. The informant would either take the most salient item of clothing and offer its meaning as an interpretation of the clothing message, or, he/she would attempt to reconcile contradictory messages with an explanatory vignette (e.g., "Well, he wears that jacket because he used to be a businessman, but it doesn't fit with the pants and shoes because he's lost his job and is on the skids").

This second, more difficult, category of interpretation shows a characteristic similar to the first. Here again, no evidence of a linear reading of the body-sentence presents itself. Despite the fact that the informant was now attending with greater attention to the body-sentence, he was apparently not reading each item of clothing in its syntagmatic relation to other items of clothing. Indeed it appeared that the informant employed his careful reading not to decode a sentence, but to solve a puzzle. He engaged in a hunt for clues that would allow him to disambiguate a potentially opaque message.

This category of interpretation also allows us to see what becomes of this code when it is confronted with a modestly novel message. The informant did not treat a novel combination of clothing parts as a sentence that could be rendered intelligible by an application of the code. He treated it as a puzzle that could be resolved only by ignoring one of its contradictory elements or by inventing a story that explained the contradiction away. Again, and perhaps here more strongly, we see the informant possessed of limited interpretive resources. A clothing outfit either conformed to one of the terms contained in his limited exegetical set or it remained ambiguous. The exercise of even a small degree of combinatorial freedom by the wearer created not discourse, but confusion.

The third, most difficult, category of interpretation also conforms to the pattern noted here. When confronted with still more anomalous outfits, informants would hesitate, begin their answers by fits and starts, and then give up the interpretive effort altogether, often with an explanation such as: "Oh, he [the person pictured in the slide] could be anyone, I can't read this guy at all." The individual pictured in the slide departed so completely from a prescribed "look" that he was impossible to read even in speculative terms. Thus, when the individual pictured had exercised the combinatorial freedom characteristic of language and begun to group clothing elements in novel combination, the interpreter was least able to make sense of the resulting message. When clothing was most like language, it was least successful as a means of communication.

DISCUSSION

The most apt explanation of this decoding behavior is, perhaps, that we have in clothing a peculiar kind of code. It appears that clothing as a means of communication has no genuine syntagmatic aspect. The code does not provide rules of combination for the manipulation of paradigmatic selections to semiotic effect. The combination of clothing elements is, therefore, not a crucial part of the creation of clothing messages. In short, the code has no generative capacity. Its users enjoy no combinatorial freedom.

The clothing code, to use the terms of Jakobson's point discussed above, is almost fully constrained. It does not have a complete ascending scale of freedom. The code specified not only the components of the message, but also the messages themselves. These messages come, as it were, pre-fabricated. Because the wearer does not have this combinatorial freedom, the interpreter of clothing examines an outfit not for a new message but for an old one fixed by convention. Combinatorial freedom can be exercised by the wearer only with the effect of baffling the interpreter. Combinatorial freedom cannot be exercised in clothing without depriving this clothing of its combinatorial potential and effect.

This aspect of the clothing code was anticipated by Jakobson. In an article entitled "Language and its Relation to Other Communication Systems" (1971), Jakobson argued that for certain nonlinguistic means of communication, the code is a collection of messages rather than a means for their creation. Unlike language, which establishes signs and the rules for their combination into messages, a system such as clothing gives no generative opportunity, and must therefore specify in advance of any act of communication the messages of which the code is capable (cf. Culler 1975:3–54).

It is because of the absence of the principle of combination (and the generative freedom it allows) that informants decode clothing ensembles as they do. The decoding process consists in accurately identifying a clear message (already specified by the code) through the accurate identification of the highly redundant, mutually presupposing elements in which the message consists. Or it consists in struggling with an interpretation made difficult by a heterogeneous set of elements for which the code has made no provision. For the clothing code, novelty of the sort possessed by language is not an opportunity for communication but a barrier to it.

It should be noted that Neich attributes a syntagmatic aspect to clothing only with considerable misgiving. He acknowledges, first, that clothing does not appear to have the same combinatorial freedom that is evident in language; second, that clothing does not have the same linear, discursive quality as language; and, third, that there are among the Hageners fixed clothing syntagms—messages "that the individual no longer has to combine for himself" (1982:221). But these are only cautions. Neich insists finally that self-decoration has sufficient linearity and combinatorial freedom to be grouped with language and treated according to the terms of a structural linguistic model. It is my contention that the model does not apply. The interpretive efforts of my informants suggest that clothing does not exhibit combinatorial freedom, and is therefore encoded and decoded in a way quite incompatible with the structural linguistic model. Indeed, I would go further and say, as I have done above, that when a clothing message exhibits the combinatorial aspect of language it renders itself imprecise. The model therefore does not only fail to bring to light aspects of clothing, it positively misleads us in our attempt to understand its expressive properties.

THE EXPRESSIVE PROPERTIES
OF MATERIAL CULTURE RECONSIDERED

Students of material culture have resorted more than once to a model of language to aid them in their attempts to understand the expressive properties of their data. It is the burden of this chapter to suggest that this critical reflex is, perhaps, ill advised. Those of us who seek to take account of the expressive aspect of material culture in these terms are condemned to work in the failing light of an ill-chosen metaphor. There is no question that the metaphor once encouraged insight and research of a valuable kind. But as long as we continue to insist on the similarities between material culture and language, we will remain imperfectly aware of important differences.

This is not to suggest that the metaphor should be abandoned. It is to suggest that the terms of our analysis should perhaps be shifted to examine not the similarities but the differences between language and material culture. The metaphor will serve us just as well as a study in contrast as it once did as a study in comparison.

Let me propose four topics that come to light when one considers the differences between material culture and language as expressive media. For instance, we might consider whether the nonlinguistic codes of material culture communicate things that language proper cannot or, characteristically, does not. Do cultures charge material culture with the responsibility of carrying certain messages that they cannot or do not entrust to language? Forge, for one, argues (1970:288) that this is indeed the case, and it is likely that a critical eye to the ethnographic literature will reveal other instances in which material culture undertakes expressive tasks that language does not or cannot perform.

When we contemplate the possibility that language and material culture differ in their communicative ends, it becomes particularly important to understand how they differ as communicative means. Take, for example, the apparent difference identified in this chapter between the codes of clothing and language. It has been suggested that clothing does not possess a combinatorial freedom and that it is therefore incapable of creating new messages. This account of clothing suggests that it is, in a sense, a "closed" code. It suggests a passing resemblance between clothing and the mythic thought and the activity of the bricoleur described by Lévi-Strauss (1966:17). Like this thought and activity, clothing provides society with a fixed set of messages. It encourages the use of the code for the purpose of semiotic repetition rather than innovation. It allows for the representation of cultural categories, principles, and processes without at the same time encouraging their innovative manipulation. Language, on the other hand, is a much more "open" code and more closely resembles scientific thought and the activity of the engineer, which, as Lévi-Strauss notes (1966:19–20), are constantly creating new messages and allowing events to have an innovative effect on structure. Clothing is constant in its semiotic responsibilities, language is changeable.

In short, clothing is a conservative code. Culture can therefore trust to this instance of material culture messages that language might abuse. It can encode in clothing and material culture information it wishes to make public but does not wish to see transformed. As Miles Richardson puts it, "material culture continues to have an existence, as it were, apart from the drift and flow of opinions, attitudes, and ideas" (1974:4).

Second, we may ask whether material culture as a means of communication works in more understated, inapparent ways than language. Are its messages less overt and their interpretation less conscious than those of language? It is likely that future research will decide this question in the affirmative. The semiotic information of material culture appears typically to seep into consciousness around the edges of a central focus and more pressing concerns.

The inconspicuousness of material culture gives it several advantages as a means of communication. First of all, it makes material culture an unusually cunning and oblique device for the representation of fundamental cultural truths. It allows culture to insinuate its beliefs and assumptions into the very fabric of daily life, there to be appreciated but not observed. It has to this extent great propagandistic value in the creation of a world of meaning.

Furthermore, the inconspicuousness of the messages of material culture also permit them to carry meaning that could not be put more explicitly without the danger of controversy, protest, or refusal. Particularly when the message is a political one and encodes status difference, material culture can speak sotto voce. Political statement can therefore be undertaken with diminished risk of counter-statement (cf. Givens 1977; McCracken 1982b:82).

Third, it is possible that material culture and language differ in the relative universality of their codes. My research suggests that within a single speech community that shares a relatively uniform code for language, there can exist quite marked differences in the code for clothing. Different age-groups and classes will encode and decode clothing messages in a strikingly disparate manner and with a low degree of mutual intelligibility. The study of clothing and other instances of material culture may serve thus as an opportunity to study social and ideational diversity. Bernstein's pioneering work (1971) on the diversity of language codes in contemporary England may serve as a model for this study, but here again we must attend as much to the ways the codes of material culture differ from this model of language as we do to the ways they do conform to it.

Finally, it must be observed that material culture as a means of communication is severely limited in the number and range of the things it can communicate. And it cannot exercise the rhetorical powers which language possesses. No nonlinguistic code allows us to communicate the medical condition of an aunt in Winnipeg, our opinion of the Thatcher government, or our judgment of the latest South American novelist. Material culture allows the representation of only a very limited number of things in only a very limited number of ways. And it cannot be used to express irony, metaphor, skepticism, ambivalence, surprise, reverence, or heartfelt hope. Material culture allows very little expressive scope.

The study of the expressive properties of material culture must reckon with a paradox. Material culture is, as I have tried to demonstrate in this chapter, extremely limited in its expressive range. Deprived of combinatorial freedom and generative potential, it is a relatively impoverished means of communication. It stands as a kind of mystery, then, why culture should utilize it for any communicative purpose, when it has a code as subtle and sophisticated as language as an alternative. The answer to this paradox must be that material culture, for all its apparent limitations, has certain virtues not shared by language. It is apparently possessed of semiotic advantages that make it more appropriate than language for certain communicative purposes. I have sought to note three of these advantages above, and it seems to me that the study of material culture will be advanced by the discovery of others. The research strategy that seeks out the differences between material culture and language promises, I think, a more thoroughgoing understanding of the expressive nature of material culture. It promises to show us how and why it serves as a useful medium of communication.

In the remainder of this book, we will have the opportunity to address the paradox noted here. We will have the chance to glimpse why it is that culture should use so artless and so cumbersome a means of communication as material culture. The general answer to this mystery appears to be that material culture has a powerful and various instrumental function. It can be used to perform certain kinds of social and cultural work. This instrumental ability, this capacity to serve in the construction of the self and world, makes material culture indispensable to culture. If material culture is in some ways an imperfect means of communication, it has quite re-markable pragmatic powers. In the chapters to follow, we shall have occasion to document the several ways in which the meaning of material culture is put to work in the construction of the social and cultural world.

FIVE

Meaning Manufacture and Movement in the World of Goods

This chapter is in some respects the linchpin of the book. It looks back to the previous chapter by developing the theoretical terms suggested there in a much more comprehensive way. We need to move beyond the limitations and the banalities that now inhere in the "goods as language" approach, and this chapter proposes one of the theoretical schemes we might use to do so. But the chapter also looks back to the opening chapters of the book. In these opening chapters, I noted the historical process by which culture and consumption became increasingly interdependent. In this chapter, I seek to demonstrate the present state of this relationship and to show how culture and consumption operate as a system in the present day.

CULTURE AND CONSUMPTION

Consumer goods have a significance that goes beyond their utilitarian character and commercial value. This significance consists largely in their ability to carry and communicate cultural meaning (Douglas and Isherwood 1978; Sahlins 1976). In the last decade a diverse body of scholars has made the cultural significance of consumer goods the focus of renewed academic study (Arnould and Wilk 1984; Baudrillard 1968, 1970; Belk 1982, 1985; Bronner 1983; Felson 1976; Furby 1978; Graumann 1974–75; Hirschman 1981; Holman 1980a; Krampen 1979; Leiss 1983; Levy 1978; Prown 1982; Quimby 1978; Rodman and Philibert 1985; Schlereth 1982; Sellerberg 1976; Solomon 1983). Their work has established a kind of subfield across the social sciences which now devotes itself with increasing clarity and thoroughness to the study of person-object relations. This chapter seeks to contribute a novel theoretical perspective to this emerging field, to show that the meaning carried by goods has a mobile quality for which prevailing theories make no allowance.

One of the great limitations of present approaches to the study of the cultural meaning of consumer goods is the failure to observe that this meaning is constantly in transit. Meaning is constantly flowing to and from its several locations in the social world, aided by the collective and individual efforts of designers, producers, advertisers, and consumers. There is a traditional trajectory to the movement of this meaning. Usually it is drawn from a culturally constituted world and transferred

FIGURE

MOVEMENT OF MEANING

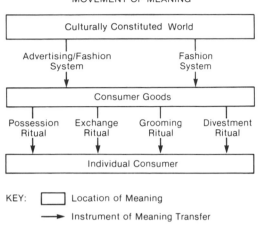

KEY: ☐   Location of Meaning
        ➤   Instrument of Meaning Transfer

to the consumer good. It is then drawn from the object and transferred to the individual consumer. There are, in other words, three locations of meaning: the culturally constituted world, the consumer good, and the individual consumer, as well as two moments of transfer: world-to-good and good-to-individual. It is the purpose of this chapter to analyze this trajectory and to show where meaning is located and how it is transferred. It will do so in five sections, considering each of the five moments of the trajectory in its turn.

The appreciation of the mobile quality of cultural meaning in a consumer society should help to illuminate certain aspects of goods, consumption, and modern society. This perspective asks us to see consumers and consumer goods as the way-stations of meaning. To this extent, it encourages us to attend to structural and dynamic properties of consumption that are not always fully emphasized. It also asks us to see such activities as advertising, the fashion world, and consumption rituals as instruments of meaning movement. Here, it encourages us to attend to the presence of a large and powerful system at the heart of modern society that gives this society some of its coherence and flexibility even as it serves as a constant source of incoherence and discontinuity. In sum, a fuller understanding of the mobile quality of cultural and consumer meaning can help to demonstrate some of the full complexity of present consumption and to reveal in a more detailed way just what it is to be a "consumer society."

LOCATIONS OF CULTURAL MEANING: THE CULTURALLY CONSTITUTED WORLD

The original location of the meaning that resides in goods is the "culturally constituted world." This is the world of everyday experience in which the phenomenal world presents itself to the senses of the individual, fully shaped and constituted by the beliefs and assumptions of his or her culture. This world has been constituted by culture in two ways. Culture is the "lens" through which all phenomena are seen. It determines how these phenomena will be apprehended and assimilated. Second, culture is the "blueprint" of human activity. It determines the co-ordinates of social action and productive activity, specifying the behaviors and objects that issue from both. As a lens, culture determines how the world is seen. As a blueprint, it determines how the world will be fashioned by human effort. In short, culture constitutes the world by supplying it with meaning. This meaning can be characterized in terms of two concepts: cultural categories and cultural principles.

MEANING STRUCTURE: CULTURAL CATEGORIES

Cultural categories are the fundamental co-ordinates of meaning.[1] They represent the basic distinctions with which a culture divides up the phenomenal world. For instance, each culture specifies cultural categories of time. In our culture these categories include an elaborate system that can discriminate units as fine as a "second" and as vast as a "millennium." Less precise but no less significant are the distinctions imposed between leisure and work time, sacred and profane time, and so on. Each culture also specifies cultural categories of space. In our culture these include categories of measurement and those of "occasion." The flora, fauna, and landscape of nature and supernatural worlds are also segmented by culture into a set of categories. Perhaps the most important of the cultural categories are those that segment the human community into distinctions of class, status, gender, age, and occupation.

Cultural categories of time, space, nature, and person create the vast body of categories. Together they create a system of distinctions that organizes the phenomenal world. It is thus that each culture establishes its own special vision of the world and thus that it renders the understandings and rules appropriate to one cultural context preposterously inappropriate in the next. Culture makes itself a privileged set of terms within which virtually nothing appears alien or unintelligible to the individual and outside of which there is no order, no system, no safe assumption, no ready comprehension. In sum, culture "constitutes" the world by investing it with its own particular meanings. It is from this world so constituted that the meaning destined for consumer goods is drawn.

CULTURAL CATEGORIES IN NORTH AMERICA

It is worth noting that cultural categories in North America appear to have their own special characteristics. First, they possess an indeterminacy that is not normally evident in other ethnographic circumstances. Cultural categories of person, for instance, are marked by a persistent and striking lack of clarity. Cultural categories of age, for instance, are not clear-cut.

A second characteristic of cultural categories in modern North America is their apparent "elective" quality. Devoted as it is to the freedom of the individual, this society permits its members to declare at their discretion the cultural categories they presently occupy. Exercising this freedom, teenagers declare themselves adults, members of a working class declare themselves members of a middle class, the old declare themselves young and so on. Category membership, which in most cultures is more strictly specified and policed, is in our own much more a matter of individual choice. In this culture, individuals are to a great extent what they claim to be, even when these claims are, by some sober sociological reckoning, implausible.

A third characteristic of cultural categories in North America that must be noted is the fact that they are subject to constant and rapid change. The dynamic quality of cultural categories plainly adds to their indeterminacy. More important, however, this quality also makes cultural categories subject to the manipulative efforts of the individual. Social groups can seek to change their place in the categorical scheme while marketers can seek to establish or encourage a new culture category of person (e.g., the ''teenager,'' the ''yuppie'') in order to create a new market segment. Cultural categories in North America are subject to rethinking and rearrangement by several parties.

THE SUBSTANTIATION OF CULTURAL CATEGORIES

Cultural categories are the conceptual grid of a culturally constituted world. They determine how this world will be segmented into discrete, intelligible parcels and how these parcels will be organized into a larger coherent system. For all their importance, however, these categories have no substantial presence in the world they organize. They are the scaffolding on which the world is hung, but they stand invisible to all those who live in this world.

But cultural categories are constantly substantiated by human practice. Acting in conformity with the blueprint of culture, the members of a community are constantly realizing categories in the world. They are constantly playing out these distinctions so that the world they create is made consistent with the world they imagine. In a sense, the members of a culture are constantly engaged in the construction, the constitution, of the world in which they live.

One of the most important ways in which cultural categories are substantiated is through the material objects of a culture. As we shall see in a moment, these objects are created according to the blueprint of culture and to this extent they make the categories of this blueprint material. They render them substantial. Objects contribute thus to the construction of the culturally constituted world precisely because they are a vital, visible record of cultural meaning that is otherwise intangible. Indeed it is not too much to say that they have a ''performative'' function (Austin 1963; Tambiah 1977) insofar as they give cultural meaning a concreteness for the individual that it would not otherwise have. The material realization of cultural categories plays a vital part in the cultural constitution of the world. The meaning that has organized the world is, through goods, made a visible, demonstrable part of it.

The process by which a culture makes its cultural categories manifest has been studied within anthropology in some detail. Structural anthropology has supplied a theoretical scheme for this study and several subspecialties, such as the anthropologies of art, clothing, housing, and material culture, have supplied areas of particular investigation. As a result of this work, there is now a clear theoretical understanding of the way in which linguistic and especially nonlinguistic media express cultural categories (Barthes 1967; Lévi-Strauss 1963, 1966: 116; Sahlins 1976; de Saussure 1966) as well as a wide range of empirical investigations in the areas of spatial organization (Doxtater 1984; Kuper 1972), house form (Bourdieu 1973; Carlisle 1982; Cunningham 1973; Lawrence 1981, 1982, 1984; McCracken 1984a, 1986b), art (Fernandez 1966; Greenberg 1975), clothing (Adams 1973; Joseph 1986; McCracken and Roth 1986; Schwarz 1979), ornament (G. Clark 1986; Drewal 1983), technology (Lechtman and Merrill 1977), and food (Appadurai 1981; Carroll 1982; Douglas 1971; Ortner 1978). The study of this material culture has helped determine in what way, and in what form, cultural categories are substantiated in the culturally constituted world. It has helped to show how the world is furnished with material objects that reflect and contribute to its cultural constitution.

THE SUBSTANTIATION OF CULTURAL CATEGORIES IN GOODS

Goods are an instance of material culture. They are an opportunity for the expression of the categorical scheme established by culture. Goods are an opportunity to make culture material. Like any other species of material culture, they permit the public, visual discrimination of culturally specified categories by encoding these categories in the form of a set of distinctions of their own. Categories of person divided into parcels of age, sex, class, and occupation can be represented in a set of material distinctions through goods. Categories of space, time, and occasion can also be reflected in this medium of communication. Goods help substantiate the order of culture.

Several studies have examined the way in which goods serve in this substantiation. Sahlins's study (1976) of the symbolism of North American consumer goods examines food and clothing "systems" and shows their correspondence to cultural categories of person. Levy's (1981) study of the correspondence between food types and cultural categories of sex and age in American society is another excellent illustration of the way in which one can approach the demographic information carried in goods from a structuralist point of view. Both of these studies demonstrate that the order of goods is modeled on the order of culture. Both demonstrate that much of the meaning of goods can be traced back to the cultural categories into which culture segments the world. The substantiation of categories of class in consumer goods has been considered by Belk, Mayer, and Bahn (1981), Coleman (1983), Davis (1956), Form and Stone (1957), Goffman (1951), Sommers (1963), Vershure, Magel, and Sadalla (1977) and Warner and Lunt (1941). The substantiation of categories of gender is less well examined but appears to be drawing more scholarly attention (Allison et al. 1980; Belk 1982; Levy 1959; Hirschman 1984). The substantiation categories of age also appears to be receiving more attention (Disman 1984; Olson 1985; Sherman and Newman 1977–78; Unruh 1983). Goods, with the other instances of material culture, serve in the substantiation of culture.

MEANING STRUCTURE: CULTURAL PRINCIPLES

Cultural meaning also consists in "cultural principles." In this case, meaning consists not in the categories of person, activity, space, or time but in the ideas or values according to which these and other cultural phenomena are organized, evaluated, and construed. If cultural categories are the result of culture's segmentation of the world into discrete parcels, cultural principles are the ideas with which this segmentation is performed. They are the charter assumptions or organizing ideas which allow all cultural phenomena to be distinguished, ranked, and interrelated. As the orienting ideas of thought and action, they find expression in every aspect of social life and, not least of all, they find expression in goods.

These principles, like categories, are substantiated by material culture in general and consumer goods in particular. It is worth observing that cultural categories and cultural principles are mutually presupposing and their expression in goods is necessarily simultaneous. Goods are therefore incapable of signifying one without signifying the other. When goods show a distinction between two cultural categories, they do so by encoding something of the principle according to which these categories are distinguished. Thus the clothing that shows a discrimination between men and women or between high classes and low also shows something of the nature of difference that is supposed to exist between these categories.[2] It communicates the supposed "delicacy" of women and the supposed "strength" of men, the supposed "refinement" of a high class and the supposed "vulgarity" of a lower one. Clothing communicates the properties that are supposed to inhere in each of these categories and that serve as the basis for their discrimination. Apparently the categories of class and sex are never communicated without this indication of how and why they are to be distinguished. The world of goods, unlike that of language, never engages in a simple signaling of difference. It is, in fact, always more forthcoming and more revealing. Its signs are always, in a sense, more motivated and less arbitrary than those of language.

Cultural principles in modern North America have the same indeterminate, changeable, elective quality that cultural categories do. Principles such as "naturalism" can fall into disrepute in one decade, only to be rehabilitated and advanced to a new place of importance in another, as occurred in the 1960s.[3] The principle of "disharmony" that the punk aesthetic finds so useful was once not a principle but merely the term for phenomena that had somehow escaped the successful application of another principle.

The ethnographic literature on the meaning of objects as principle may be found in Adams (1973), Fernandez (1966), McCracken (1982a), and Drewal (1983). Substantive literature which shows the presence and nature of meaning as principle in the objects of contemporary North American society is not abundant. Levy's article makes passing reference to it (1981) as does Sahlins (1976), and the idea is implicitly treated in the work of Lohof (1969) on the meaning carried by the Marlboro cigarette. It also surfaces in the attempt of sociologists to make objects an index of status and class. For example, Laumann and House (1970) sought to establish the meaning of household furniture and resorted to the principles of "modern" and "traditional." Felson in his study of "material life styles" (1976) posited something called a "bric-a-brac factor," while Davis (1958) sought the terms "Bauhaus Japanesey" to characterize a certain principle of interior design. The principle of "science" (or, more exactly, the concern for technical mastery of nature and the confidence that human affairs can be benignly transformed through technological innovation) was a favorite motif of the kitchen appliances and automobiles in 1950s and 1960s North America (Csikszentmihalyi and Rochberg-Halton 1981:52). Scholars in the material-culture arm of American studies and art history have made the most notable contribution here (Quimby 1978; Schlereth 1982). Prown (1980) and Cohen (1982), for instance, have examined the principles evident in American furniture.[4]

It is plain in any case that, like categories, the principles of culture are substantiated by consumer goods and that these goods so charged help make up the culturally constituted world. Both categories and principles organize the phenomenal world and the efforts of a community to manipulate this world. Goods substantiate them and therefore enter into the culturally constituted world as both the object and objectification of this world. In short, goods are both the creations and the creators of the culturally constituted world.

INSTRUMENTS OF MEANING TRANSFER: WORLD-TO-GOOD

Meaning then is first of all resident in the culturally constituted world. To become resident in consumer goods it must be disengaged from the world and transferred to the good. The purpose of this section is to observe two of the institutions that are now used as instruments of this transfer. It will examine the institutions of advertising and the fashion system.

ADVERTISING

Advertising works as a potential method of meaning transfer by bringing the consumer good and a representation of the culturally constituted world together within the frame of a particular advertisement. The creative director of an agency seeks to conjoin these two elements in such a way that the viewer/reader glimpses an essential similarity between them. When this symbolic equivalence is successfully established, the viewer/reader attributes certain properties he or she knows to exist in the culturally constituted world to the consumer good. The known properties of the world thus come to be resident in the unknown properties of the consumer good. The transfer of meaning from world to good is accomplished.

The mechanics of so complicated a process deserve more detailed exposition. The creative director is concerned with effecting the successful conjunction of two elements. One of these elements is specified by the client. In most cases, the director is given a consumer good, the physical properties and packaging of which are fixed and not subject to manipulation. The other element, the representation of the cultural constituted world, is constrained and free in almost equal proportions. The client, sometimes drawing on marketing research and advice, will specify the properties that are sought for the consumer good. So directed, the director then enjoys a wide range of discretionary control. Subject only to the negative constraints of budgetary limitations and the positive constraints of a continuous "brand image," the director is free to "deliver" the desired symbolic properties in any one of a nearly infinite number of ways.

This process of delivery consists in a lengthy and elaborate series of choices (Dyer 1982; McCracken 1980; Sherry 1985; Singer 1986; Williamson 1978). The first choice is a difficult one. The director must identify with sufficient clarity for his or her own purposes the properties that are sought for the good in question. This will sometimes result in a period of complicated discourse between client and director in which these parties alternately lead and follow one another into a sharpened appreciation of the properties sought for the good. In any case, the advertising firm will enter into its own consultative process to establish clarity sufficient for its own purposes. The second choice is equally difficult but perhaps less consultative. The director must decide where the desired properties are resident in the culturally constituted world. The director has at his or her disposal a vast array of possibilities from which to choose. "Place" must be selected, and the first choice here is whether the ad will have a fantasy setting or a naturalistic one. If the latter is chosen, it must then be decided whether this setting will be an interior or an exterior, an urban landscape or a rural one, a cultivated environment or a untamed one. Time of day and time of year must also be chosen. If people are to appear in the advertisement, their sex, age, class, status, and occupation must be selected. The clothing and body postures and affective states of these people must also be specified (Goffman 1979). These are the pieces of the culturally constituted world that can be evoked in the ad.

It must be noted that the process of selection can be made more or less well according to the skill and training of the director. There is no simple route from the properties that are desired for the consumer good to the pieces of the culturally constituted world that can supply them in the advertisement. This is, as members of the advertising profession point out, a "creative" process in which the most appropriate selections of the advertisement are not so much calculated as glimpsed. Imprecision and error in this creative process are not only possible but legion. It must also be noted that the process of selection, because it is creative, proceeds at unconscious as well as conscious levels. Directors are not always fully cognizant of how and why a selection is made, even when this selection presents itself as compelling and necessary (e.g., Arlen 1980:99, 119).

In sum, the director must choose from the alternatives that have been established by the network of cultural categories and principles in terms of which culture has constituted the world. These choices will be established by the director's determination of which of these categories and principles most closely approximates the meaning that the client seeks for the product. Once this process is complete, a third set of choices must be completed. The director must decide just how the culturally constituted world is to be portrayed in the advertisement. This process will consist in reviewing all of the objects in which the selected meaning has been substantiated and then deciding which of these will be used to evoke this meaning in the advertisement. It must then be decided how the product is going to be presented in this highly contrived context. Photographic and visual conventions will be exploited here so that the viewer/reader can be given the opportunity to glimpse an essential equivalence between world and object. The director must bring these two elements into a conjunction that encourages a metaphoric identification of "sameness" by the would-be consumer. World and good must be seen to enjoy a special harmony. They must be seen to "go together." When this sameness is glimpsed, through one or many exposures to the stimuli, the process of transfer has taken place. Meaning has shifted from the culturally constituted world to the consumer good. This good now "stands for" cultural meaning of which it was previously innocent.

Visual images and verbal material appear to assume a very particular relationship in this process of transfer. It is chiefly the visual aspect of the advertisement that conjoins the world and object between which a transfer of meaning is sought. Verbal material serves chiefly as a kind of prompt which instructs the viewer/reader in the salient properties that are supposed to be expressed by the visual part of the advertisement. Text, and especially headlines, make explicit what is already implicit in the image. They provide instructions on how the visual part of the advertisement is supposed to be read. The verbal component allows the director to direct the viewer/reader's attention to exactly the meaningful properties that are intended for transfer (cf. Barthes 1983:33–39; Dyer 1982:139–182; Garfinkle 1978; Moeran 1985).

All of this must now be successfully decoded by the viewer/reader. It is worth emphasizing that the viewer/reader is the final author in the process of transfer. The director can only bring the world and consumer good into conjunction and suggest their essential similarity. It is left to the viewer/reader to see this similarity and effect the transfer of meaningful properties. The viewer/reader is to this extent an essential participant in the process of meaning transfer, as Williamson (1978: 40–70) endeavors to note. The viewer/reader must complete the work of the director.

Advertising is a kind of conduit through which meaning is constantly being poured in its movement from the culturally constituted world to consumer goods. Through advertising, old and new goods are constantly giving up old meanings and taking on new ones. As active participants in this process, we are kept informed of the present state and stock of cultural meaning that exists in consumer goods. To this extent, advertising serves us as a lexicon of current cultural meanings. In large part, it is advertising that maintains a consistency between what Sahlins calls the "order of culture" and the "order of goods" (1976:178).

THE FASHION SYSTEM

Less frequently observed, studied, and understood as an instrument of meaning movement is the fashion system. Yet this system, too, serves as a means by which goods are systematically invested and divested of their meaningful properties. The fashion system is a somewhat more complicated instrument for meaning movement than advertising. In the case of advertising, movement is accomplished by the advertising agency and its effort to unhook meaning from a culturally constituted world and transfer it to a consumer good through the means of an advertisement. In the case of the fashion system, the process has more sources of meaning, agents of transfer, and media of communication. Some of this additional complexity can be captured by noting that the fashion world works in three distinct ways to transfer meaning to goods.

In one capacity, the fashion system performs a transfer of meaning from the culturally constituted world to consumer goods that is remarkably similar in character and effect to the transfer performed by advertising. In the medium of a magazine or newspaper, the same effort to conjoin aspects of the world and good is evident, and the same process of glimpsed similarity is sought. In this capacity, the fashion system takes new styles of clothing or home furnishings and associates them with established cultural categories and principles. Thus does meaning move from the culturally constituted world to the good. This is the simplest aspect of the meaning-delivery capacity of the fashion system and the one, ironically, that Barthes (1983) found so perplexing and difficult to render plain.

In a second capacity, the fashion system actually invents new cultural meanings in a modest way. This invention is undertaken by "opinion leaders" who help shape and refine existing cultural meaning, encouraging the reform of cultural categories and principles. These are "distant" opinion leaders: individuals who by virtue of birth, beauty, celebrity, or accomplishment, are held in high esteem. These groups and individuals are sources of meaning for those of lesser standing. It is suggested in fact that their innovation of meaning is prompted by the imitative appropriations of those of low standing (Simmel 1904).[5] Classically, these high-standing groups are a conventional social elite: upper-upper and upper-lower classes. These are, for instance, the origins of the "preppie look" that has recently "trickled down" so widely and deeply. More recently, these groups are the unashamedly nouveau riche who now predominate on evening soap operas such as "Dallas" and "Dynasty" and who appear to have influenced the consumer and lifestyle habits of many North Americans. Motion picture and popular music stars, revered for their status, their beauty, and sometimes their talent, are also the occupants of this relatively new group of opinion leaders. These groups all invent and deliver a species of meaning that is largely fashioned by the prevailing cultural co-ordinates established by cultural categories and cultural principles. These groups are also permeable to cultural innovations, changes in style, value, and attitude which they then pass along to the subordinate parties who imitate them.

In a third capacity, the fashion system engages not just in the invention of cultural meanings but also in its radical reform. Some part of the cultural meaning of Western industrial societies is subject to constant and thoroughgoing change. The radical instability of this meaning is due to the fact that Western societies are, in the language of Claude Lévi-Strauss (1966:233–234), "hot societies." They willingly accept, indeed encourage, the radical changes that follow from deliberate human effort and the effect of anonymous social forces (Braudel 1973:323; Fox and Lears 1983; McKendrick et al. 1982).[6] As a result the cultural meaning of a "hot," Western, industrial, complex society is constantly undergoing systematic change. In contradistinction to virtually all ethnographic precedent, they live a world that is not only culturally constituted but also historically constituted. Indeed it does not exaggerate to say that hot societies demand this change and depend on it to drive certain economic, social, and cultural sectors of the Western world (cf. Barber and Loebel 1953; Fallers 1961). The fashion system serves as one of the conduits for capture and movement of this category of highly innovative meaning.

The groups responsible for this radical reform of meaning are usually those that exist at the margin of society: hippies, punks, or gays (Blumberg 1974; Field 1970; Meyersohn and Katz 1957). These groups invent a much more radical, innovative kind of meaning than their high-standing partners in diffusion leadership. Indeed all of them represent a departure from the culturally constituted conventions of modern North American society and all of them illustrate the peculiarly Western tendency to tolerate dramatic violations of cultural norms. Each of these groups generated new cultural meaning, if only through the negative process of violating cultural categories of age and status (hippies and punks) or gender (gays). Their redefinitions of these cultural categories and a number of attendant cultural principles then entered the cultural mainstream. Innovative groups of this sort become "meaning suppliers" even when they are devoted to overturning the established order (as were hippies) and even when they are determined not to allow their cultural inventions to be absorbed by the mainstream (as were punks, cf. Hebdige 1979; Martin 1981).

If the sources of meaning are more dynamic and numerous, so are the agents who gather this meaning up and accomplish its transfer to consumer goods. In the case of the fashion system, these agents exist in two main categories. The designers of products are one. These are sometimes the very conspicuous individuals who establish themselves in Paris or Milan as arbiters of clothing design and surround themselves when possible with a cult of personality. Architects and interior designers sometimes assume a roughly comparable stature and exert an equally international influence (Kron 1983). More often, these designers are less well known and indeed most are anonymous to all of those outside of their industry (Clark 1976; Meikle 1979; Pulos 1983). The designers of Detroit automobiles are a case in point here, as are the product developers of the furniture and appliance industries. (Figures such as Raymond Loewy are exceptions that prove the rule.) The second category consists of fashion journalists and social observers. Fashion journalists may belong to print or film media and may have a high profile or a low one. Social observers are sometimes journalists who study and document new social developments (e.g., Lisa Birnbach 1980; Kennedy Fraser 1981; Tom Wolfe 1970; Peter York 1980), and sometimes they are academics who undertake a roughly similar inquiry from a somewhat different point of view (e.g., Roland Barthes 1972; Christopher Lasch 1979). Market researchers are beginning to serve in this capacity as well (e.g., John Naisbitt 1982; Arnold Mitchell 1983; and, possibly, John Molloy 1977).

Both of these groups are responsible for meaning transfer. Normally, they establish a relatively equal division of labor. Journalists perform the first part of a two part enterprise. They serve as gatekeepers of a sort, reviewing aesthetic, social, and cultural innovations as these first appear, judging some as important and others as trivial. They resemble in this respect the gate-keepers in the world of art (Becker 1982) and music (Hirsch 1972). It is their responsibility to observe, as best they can, the whirling mass of innovation and decide what is fad and what is fashion, what is ephemeral and what will endure. After they have completed their difficult and often mistaken process of winnowing, they engage in a process of dissemination with which they make their choices known.

It must be admitted that everyone in the diffusion chain (Rogers 1983) plays a gatekeeping role and helps to discourage or encourage the tastes of those who look to them for opinion leadership. Journalists are especially key in this process because they make their influence felt even before an innovation has passed to the "early adopters" (Baumgarten 1975; Meyersohn and Katz 1957; Polegato and Wall 1980).

When journalists have served to discriminate certain innovations from others, designers begin the task of drawing meaning into the mainstream and investing it in consumer goods. The designer differs from the advertising agency director insofar as he or she is transforming not just the symbolic properties of the consumer good but also its physical properties. Apart from fashion and trade shows through which only some potential consumers can be reached, the designer does not have a meaning-giving context like the advertisement into which he or she can insert the consumer good. Instead, the consumer good will leave the designer's hands and enter into any of the contexts the consumer chooses for it. So the designer must transform the object in such a way that the viewer/possessor can see that the object so designed possesses certain cultural meaning. The object must leave the designer's hands with its new symbolic properties plainly displayed in its new physical properties.

The designer, like the director, depends upon the viewer/possessor to supply the final act of association. The designer depends on the viewer/possessor to effect the transfer of meaning from world to good. But there is a special difficulty here. Unlike the director, the designer does not have the highly managed, rhetorical circumstances of the advertisement to encourage and direct this transfer. The designer cannot inform the viewer/possessor of the qualities intended for the good. These must be self-evident to the viewer/possessor. The viewer/possessor must be able to supply the new meaning for him or her self. It is therefore necessary that this viewer/possessor have access to the same sources of information about new fashions in meaning as the designer. The viewer/possessor must have been given prior acquaintance with new meaning so that he or she can identify the cultural significance of the physical properties of the new object. In short, the designer relies on the journalist at the beginning and then again at the very end of the meaning-transfer process. The journalist supplies new meaning to the designer as well as to the recipient of the designer's work.

In short, both advertising and the fashion system are instruments for the transfer of meaning from the culturally and historically constituted world to consumer goods. They are two of the means by which meaning is invested in the "object code." It is thanks to them that the objects of our world carry such a richness, variety, and versatility of meaning and can serve us so variously in acts of self-definition and social communication.[7]

LOCATIONS OF CULTURAL MEANING: CONSUMER GOODS

That consumer goods are the locus of cultural meaning is too well established a fact to need elaborate demonstration here. As Sahlins puts it with regard to one product category, clothing, "Considered as a whole, the system of American clothing amounts to a very complex scheme of cultural categories and the relations between them, a veritable map—it does not exaggerate to say—of the cultural universe" (1976:179).

What can be said of clothing can be said of virtually all other high involvement product categories and several low involvement ones. Clothing, transportation, food, housing exteriors and interiors, adornment, all serve as media for the expression of the cultural meaning according to which our world has been constituted.[8]

That goods possess cultural meaning is sometimes evident to the consumer and sometimes hidden. Certain kinds of this information, especially status, are a matter of self-conscious concern and manipulation. Just as often, however, individual consumers come to see the cultural meaning carried by their consumer goods only in exceptional circumstances. Those who have lost goods to burglary, sudden impoverishment, or the divestment that occurs with aging speak of the profound sense of loss and even mourning (Belk 1982:185). The rituals of possession to be discussed below also suggest that the meaningful properties of goods are not always conspicuously evident to the owner, however much they serve to inform and control his or her action.[9]

It was observed at the beginning of this chapter that the last decade has seen an outpouring of work on the cultural significance of consumer goods. Indeed the wealth of this literature reassures us that the study of the cultural meaning carried by goods is a flourishing academic enterprise. None of this literature, however, attends to the mobile quality of this meaning, and it may serve us well to make this an operative assumption in the field. It is time to ask, systematically and continually, whence this meaning comes, by what means it is delivered, for whom it is intended, and where it comes to rest.

INSTRUMENTS OF MEANING TRANSFER: GOOD-TO-CONSUMER

We have now tracked the movement of meaning from the culturally and historically constituted worlds into consumer goods, considering the role of two instruments in this process. It remains to observe how this meaning, now resident in consumer goods, can be moved again. It remains to observe how meaning is transferred from the consumer good to the consumer. In order to describe this process, reference must be made to another set of instruments of meaning transfer.

This second set of instruments moves meaning from the consumer good to the consumer. All of these instruments appear to qualify as special instances of "symbolic action" (Munn 1973; V. Turner 1969). Symbolic action, or "ritual," as it is more conventionally called, is a kind of social action devoted to the manipulation of the cultural meaning for purposes of collective and individual communication and categorization. Ritual is an opportunity to affirm, evoke, assign, or revise the conventional symbols and meanings of the cultural order. Ritual is to this extent a powerful and versatile tool for the manipulation of cultural meaning. In the form of a classic "rite of passage" it is used to move an individual from one cultural category of person to another, so that one set of symbolic properties can be given up (e.g., those of a "child") and another taken on (e.g., those of an "adult") (Van Gennep 1960; Turner 1967). Other forms of ritual are devoted to different social ends. Some forms are used to give "experiential reality" to certain cultural principles and concepts (Tambiah 1977). Others are used to create certain political contracts (McCracken 1984c). In short, ritual is put to diverse ends in its manipulation of cultural meaning.

In North America, ritual is used to transfer meaning from goods to individuals. It serves this purpose in four ways. There are exchange, possession, grooming, and divestment rituals. Each of these represents a different stage in a more general process in which meaning is moved from consumer good to individual consumer.

EXCHANGE RITUALS

Exchange rituals in contemporary North America, especially those of Christmas and birthdays, see the choice, purchase, and presentation of consumer goods by one party and their receipt by another (Caplow 1982; Cheal 1985, 1986). This movement of goods is potentially also a movement of meaningful properties. Often the gift-giver chooses a gift because it possesses the meaningful properties he or she wishes to see transferred to the gift-taker. Indeed, in much gift exchange the recipient of a gift is also the intended recipient of the symbolic properties that the gift contains. Thus, for instance, the woman who receives a particular kind of dress is also made the recipient of a particular concept of herself as a woman (Schwartz 1967). The dress contains this concept and the giver invites the recipient to define herself in its terms. Similarly, many of the continual gifts that flow between parent and children are motivated in precisely these terms. The gifts to the child contain symbolic properties that the parent would have the child absorb (Furby 1978:312–313).

The ritual of gift exchange establishes a potent means of interpersonal influence. It allows individuals to insinuate certain symbolic properties into the lives of a gift recipient. It allows them to initiate the possibility of meaning transfer. In more general terms, all consumers as gift-givers are made agents of meaning transfer to the extent that they selectively distribute certain goods with certain properties to recipients who may or may not otherwise have chosen them. The study of gift exchange, a well-established study in the social sciences (Davis 1972; Mauss 1970; McCracken 1983a; Sahlins 1972), is already under way in the field of consumption research (Belk 1979; Scammon, Shaw and Bamossy 1982) and deserves further study. Attention must be given to the process of choice by which the giver identifies the gift with the cultural meanings they seek to pass along to the recipient. Attention must also be given to the significance of wrapping and presentation as well as the domestic context (time and place) in which presentations are made. These aspects of the domestic ritual of gift giving are vitally important to the meaningful properties of the goods exchanged.

POSSESSION RITUALS

Consumers spend a good deal of time cleaning, discussing, comparing, reflecting, showing off, and even photographing many of their new possessions. Housewarming parties appear sometimes to give an opportunity for display, while the process of "personalization" (Hirschman 1982a:37–38; Kron 1983; Rapoport 1968, 1982) of homes especially serves as the occasion of much comparison, reflection, and discussion. While all of these activities have an overt functionality, they all appear to have the additional effect of allowing the consumer to claim the possession as his/her own. This process of claiming is not the simple assertion of territoriality through ownership. It is also an attempt to draw from the object the qualities that it has been given by the marketing forces of the world of goods. This process can be observed most plainly by its absence. Occasionally a consumer will claim that a possession such as a car, house, article of clothing, or other meaning-carrying good "never really seemed to belong to me." There are certain goods that the consumer never successfully lays claim to because the consumer never successfully lays claim to their symbolic properties. The good becomes a paradox: The consumer owns it without possessing it. Its symbolic properties remain immovable. Normally, however, the individual successfully deploys possession rituals and manages to extract the meaningful properties that have been invested in the consumer good. When this occurs they are able to use the goods as markers of time and space and occasion, and to draw on their ability to discriminate between cultural categories of class, status, gender, age, occupation, and lifestyle. Possession rituals allow the consumer to lay claim and assume a kind of ownership of the meaning of his or her consumer goods. They help complete the second stage of the trajectory of the movement of this meaning. As we have seen, advertising agencies and the fashion world move this meaning from the culturally and historically constituted world into the goods. With their possession rituals individuals move this meaning out of the goods into their lives.

It is worth observing that possession rituals, especially those devoted to "personalizing" the object, seem almost to enact on a small scale and for private purposes the activities of meaning transfer performed by the advertising agency. The act of personalizing is, in effect, an attempt to transfer meaning from the individual's own world to the newly obtained good. The new context in this case is the individual's complement of consumer goods, which has now assumed personal meanings as well as public ones. Indeed, it is perhaps chiefly in this way that an anonymous possession—manifestly the creation of a distant impersonal process of mass manufacture—is turned into a possession that belongs to someone and speaks for him or her. It is, perhaps, in this manner that individuals create a personal "world of goods" which reflects their own experience and concepts of self and world. The meaning that advertising transfers to goods is the meaning of the collectivity. The meaning that these personal gestures transfer to goods is the meaning of the collectivity as this meaning has been inflected by the particular experience of the individual consumer.

GROOMING RITUALS

It is clear that some of the meaning drawn from goods has a perishable nature. As a result, the consumer must draw this meaning out of his or her possessions on a repeated basis. When this continual process of transfer of meaning from goods to consumer is necessary, the consumer will likely resort to a grooming ritual. The purpose of this ritual is to take the special pains necessary to insure that special and perishable properties resident in certain clothes, certain hair styles, certain looks, are, as it were, "coaxed" out of their resident goods and made to live, however briefly and precariously, in the individual consumer. The "going out" rituals with which one prepares for "an evening out" are good examples here because they illustrate the time, patience, and anxiety with which an individual will prepare him or her self for the special public scrutiny of a gala evening or special dinner party. These rituals arm the individual who is "going out" with specially glamorous, exalted meaningful properties that exist in their "best" consumer goods. Once captured and made resident in the individual, this individual has new powers of confidence, aggression, and defense. The language with which advertisements describe certain make-up, hair styling goods, and clothing give tacit acknowledgment to the properties that can be got from goods through special grooming rituals.

Sometimes it is not the consumer but the good that must be groomed. In this case, it is the properties of the object that are perishable in nature and needful of constant maintenance. The extraordinary amounts of largely redundant time and energy that are lavished on certain automobiles is perhaps the best case in point here (Myers 1985:562). This grooming ritual "supercharges" the object, that it might, in turn, give special heightened properties to its owner. Here again the individual's role in meaning investment becomes evident. The continual attention to consumer goods that helps them render up their meaningful qualities is most strikingly highlighted by its absence. We see, for instance, aging individuals who have ceased this activity. Sherman and Newman report that the occupants of nursing homes who regard themselves as being "at the end of the line" engage in a process of "decathecting the significant objects in their lives" (1977–78:188).

In the field of consumer research, the study of ritual has been significantly advanced by Rook (1984, 1985) who has observed how much consumption is ritualized and the value of studying it from this perspective and by Rook and Levy

(1982) who have examined grooming ritual and grooming product symbolism.[10] It is clear that grooming rituals are one of the means by which individuals effect a transfer of symbolic properties. In the case of these rituals, the movement of meaning occurs between consumer goods and the consumer. Grooming rituals help draw the meaning out of these goods and invest it in the consumer.

Divestment Rituals

Individuals who draw meaning out of goods sometimes come to see these sources of meaning in personal terms. They come to associate the good with their own personal properties. This possible confusion between consumer and consumer good encourages the use of the *divestment ritual*. Divestment rituals are employed for two purposes. When the individual purchases a good that has been previously owned, such as a house or a car, the ritual is used to erase the meaning associated with the previous owner. The cleaning and redecorating of a newly purchased home, for instance, may be seen as an effort to remove the meaning created by the previous owner. This divestment allows the new owner to avoid contact with the meaningful properties of the previous owner and to "free up" the meaning properties of the possession and claim them for themselves. The second divestment ritual takes place when the individual is about to dispense with a good, either by giving it away or selling it. An attempt will be made to erase the meaning that has been invested in the good by association. Individuals in moments of candor will suggest that they feel "a little strange about someone else wearing my old coat." With still greater candor they confess that they fear the dispossession of personal meaning, a phenomenon that resembles the "merging of identities" that sometimes takes place between transplant donors and recipients (Simmons, Klein, and Simmons 1977:68). Both rituals suggest a concern that the meaning of goods can be transferred, obscured, confused, or even lost when goods change hands (Douglas 1966). The good therefore must be emptied of meaning before being passed along and cleared again of meaning when taken on. What looks like simple superstition is, in fact, an implicit acknowledgment of the movable quality of the meaning with which goods are invested.[11]

In sum, personal rituals are variously used to transfer the meaning contained in goods to individual consumers. Exchange rituals are used to direct goods charged with certain meaningful properties to individuals whom, the gift-giver supposes, are needful of these properties. In this case, the giver is inviting the receiver to partake of the properties possessed by the good. Possession rituals are undertaken by the owner of a good in order to establish access to its meaningful properties. These rituals are designed to accomplish the transfer properties of the good to the owner. Grooming rituals are used to effect the continual transfer of perishable properties, properties that are likely to fade when in the possession of the consumer. Grooming rituals allow the consumer to "freshen" the properties he or she draws from goods. These rituals can also be used to maintain and "brighten" certain of the meaningful properties resident in goods. Finally, divestment rituals are used to empty goods of meaning so that meaning-loss or meaning-contagion cannot take place. All of these rituals are a kind of microcosmic version of the instruments of meaning transfer that move meaning from world to goods. It is their responsibility to move meaning from goods to consumer.

LOCATIONS OF CULTURAL MEANING: INDIVIDUAL CONSUMERS

When meaning comes finally to rest in the consumer, it has completed its journey through the social world. This meaning is used to define and orient the individual in ways that we are only beginning to appreciate. It is clear that individuals in this culture have an enormous freedom in the meaning they seek to draw from goods. The first part of this chapter observes that contemporary North America leaves a great deal of the individual undefined. One of the ways individuals satisfy the freedom and responsibility of self-definition is through the systematic appropriation of the meaningful properties of goods.

Indeed it serves us well to see consumers as engaged in an ongoing enterprise of self-creation. Increasingly the social sciences treat the self and other cultural artifacts such as language and society as things that are "always in production, in process" (Bruner 1984:3; cf. Bakhtin 1981:270; Gergen and Davis 1985; Handler and Linnekin 1984; Kavanaugh 1978; Sapir 1931). According to this view, there is nothing fixed or given about cultural phenomena of this sort. The self, language, and society are all created and sustained only as a result of deliberate and continual efforts. It is time, perhaps, to observe the contribution made to this creative, performative, process by consumer goods and activities.

Let us, for instance, see the consumer as someone engaged in a "cultural project" (McCracken 1987a), the purpose of which is to complete the self. The consumer system supplies individuals with the cultural materials to realize their various and changing ideas of what it is to be a man or a woman, middle-aged or elderly, a parent, a citizen, or a professional. All of these cultural notions are concretized in goods, and it is through their possession and use that the individual realizes the notions in his own life. As Kavanaugh puts it, ". . . individuals in a society "create themselves" or define themselves culturally through the objectification of [a culture's] conceptual models in culturally prescribed phenomenal forms" (1978:67).

Plainly the task of self-completion through consumption is not an easy one, nor is it always successful. Many individuals seek kinds of meaning from goods that do not exist there. Others seek to appropriate kinds of meaning to which they are not by some sober sociological reckoning entitled. Still others attempt to constitute their lives only in terms of the meaning of goods. All of these consumer pathologies are evident in modern consumption and all of them illustrate how the process of meaning transfer can go wrong to the cost of the individual and the collectivity.[12] In normal situations, however, the individual uses goods in an unproblematical manner to constitute crucial parts of the self and world. The logic, imperatives, and details of this process of self- and world-construction through goods is enormously understudied and is only now drawing rigorous examination. Our culture, with a thoroughness and enthusiasm unheralded in the ethnographic record, has subjected its beliefs and practices to detailed study. It has with the same thoroughness and enthusiasm also made material possessions one of its most compelling preoccupations. It is therefore doubly odd and unfortunate that study of the use of goods in the construction of self and world should have suffered such prolonged and profound neglect.

CONCLUSION

It is only recently that the field of person-object relations has escaped the limitations imposed upon it by its founding father, Thorstein Veblen. The field has begun to recognize that the cultural meaning carried by consumer goods is enormously more various and complex than the Veblenian attention to status was capable of recognizing. But now that the field has made this advance, it might consider the possibility of another. It might begin to take account of the alienable, movable, manipulable quality of meaning. This chapter has sought to encourage this development by giving a theoretical account of the structure and movement of the cultural meaning of consumer goods. It has suggested that meaning resides in three locations: the culturally constituted world, the consumer good, and the individual consumer. It has identified advertising, the fashion system, and consumer rituals as the means by which meaning is drawn out of and transferred between these locations. Advertising and the fashion system move meaning from the culturally constituted world to consumer goods, while consumer rituals move meaning from the consumer good to the consumer. This is the trajectory of the movement of cultural meaning in modern, developed societies.

Part III

PRACTICE

The first two parts of this book are devoted to the history and the theory of the relationship between culture and consumption. This third part will treat the uses to which we put the cultural meaning in consumer goods. We will consider how the meaning of goods is used to preserve ideals (chapter 7), sustain and transform lifestyles (chapter 8), and resist and initiate social change (chapter 9). In chapter 6 we will consider how the meaning of goods enters into the definition and redefinition of gender.

SIX

Consumer Goods, Gender Construction, and a Rehabilitated Trickle-down Theory

THE TRICKLE-DOWN THEORY

The trickle-down theory, first stated by Simmel (1904), was an ingenious account of fashion change.[1] The theory holds that two conflicting principles act as a kind of engine or motive force for innovation. Subordinate social groups, following the principle of imitation, seek to establish new status claims by adopting the clothing of superordinate groups. Superordinate social groups, following the principle of differentiation, respond by adopting new fashions. Old status markers are forsaken, abandoned to the claims of subordinate groups, and new ones are embraced. In this way, the superordinate group continues to hold status markers peculiar to itself and to preserve the status difference these markers are meant to signify.

The theory holds that this process of imitation and differentiation has a progressive character. Eventually the new status markers devised by the superordinate group are themselves subject to subordinate appropriation, and still newer ones must be created. The behavior of superordinate and subordinate groups proves mutually provoking. It establishes a self-perpetuating cycle of change. It creates an engine which drives fashion forward in a continual process of innovation.

The theory also holds that the process of imitation and differentiation has a successive character. The superordinate and subordinate groups that engage in mutually provoking action are always proximate groups. They are always adjacent to one another in the larger social order. For example, a very subordinate group does not appropriate a superordinate style until the style has trickled down to the group that is its immediate superordinate.

The trickle-down theory has several strengths. First, it places fashion diffusion in a social context. It allows us to see how the movement of fashion articulates with the social system in which it takes place. The theory presupposes that this system will consist in the differential distribution of status, that it will be made up of social groups ranked high and low. It holds that fashion movement will be directed by the hierarchical nature of these social relations and the social interaction these relations create. In short, the trickle-down theory gives us an understanding of how the social context in which fashion movement occurs will determine its direction, tempo, and dynamics.

The trickle-down theory also allows us to see the fashion behavior of disparate social groups as expressions of the same underlying logic. It allows us to see that the two motives of fashion change act in concert because they are mutually presupposing. As long as there is imitation, the theory holds, there will be differentiation. As long as there is differentiation, there will be imitation. The trickle-down theory shows us that what is mutually presupposing in logical terms becomes mutually provoking in social ones.

There are two problems with this aspect of the theory. First, it is worth observing that the term "trickle-down" is, in fact, a misnomer or, at least, an error in metaphor. For what drives this diffusion dynamic is not the downward, gravitylike force that the term implies. What drives the dynamic is an upward "chase and flight" pattern created by a subordinate social group that "hunts" upper-class status markers and a superordinate social group that moves on in hasty flight to new ones. It is an upward movement, not a downward one, that drives this system of diffusion onward.

The second problem is that Simmel did not specify the operation of the trickle-down effect in its full detail and complexity. He failed to note that only two social groups in the social system have a single motive for their fashion behavior. The highest-ranking group acts solely for the purpose of differentiation (for they have no higher group to imitate). The lowest-ranking group acts solely for the purpose of imitation (for they have no lower group from whom they must differentiate themselves). But for all the intermediate groups in the system, the motives for fashion change are not so predictable. They may undertake fashion change for the purpose of imitation, differentiation, or both. These social groups are, after all, superordinate to one group and subordinate to another. They therefore have occasion to act sometimes as imitators and sometimes as differentiators. Any given act of fashion change may spring from the motive of imitation, the motive of differentiation, or the two together. Just which of these motives is at work in any particular act of fashion change cannot be specified in advance.

Simmel's failure to observe the duality of motive of intermediate groups left his theory insufficiently appreciative of some of the empirical realities for which it was meant to account. It discouraged a remarkable range of research opportunities by obscuring their existence. The duality of fashion motive raises several questions. Are there some social groups that are consistently more imitative than others and some that are consistently more differentiative? Are there aggressively imitative social groups that move upward so rapidly that they never feel the pressure of imitation from below? Do these groups create so much pressure on superordinates that this group must undertake fashion change always in a reactive, differentiating manner and never in an imitative one? In short, are there some social groups that drive upward by their own efforts, while other social groups are driven upward only by the pressure of those below (and never by a driving pressure of their own)? The questions by themselves are compelling ones. But they also raise larger questions that are equally compelling. How are social systems changed by these differences in fashion behavior? How do they react to the internal strains and pressures such behavior must put on a status hierarchy? These research opportunities have not been exploited by the fashion research community. This failure must be in part attributed to the insufficiency of the theory that guides it.

The third strength of the trickle-down theory is its ability to give the fashion observer early warning of fashion change. Simmel's theory allows the observer to predict a change in one group's fashion behavior from the moment there is a change in the behavior of a proximate group. As soon as a subordinate group begins to appropriate superordinate fashion, superordinate differentiation is set in train. Conversely, as soon as a superordinate group begins to differentiate itself from a subordinate group, this latter group will undertake further acts of appropriation. "Lag time" aside, the motive for fashion change is created for one group directly upon the change in the fashion behavior of another. The fashion observer may thus "read" from the present behavior of one group to the future behavior of another. As predictive theories go, this is very early warning indeed. Simmel's theory establishes a kind of early warning line for the study of fashion diffusion.

Possessed of these strengths, the trickle-down theory has found wide currency in the study of fashion in general and clothing fashion in particular. The theory has been used with particular profit for the historical study of fashion. Indeed it has been identified as a fundamental principle of explanation for this field of study (Brenninkmeyer 1963:51). The trickle-down theory has also been used with profit in the study of the sociological implications of contemporary fashion.[2]

Despite its heuristic value and widespread adoption, the trickle-down theory has met with increasing skepticism in recent years. It is not too much to say that the venerable model has been subject to attacks on all sides.

Horowitz (1975) has argued that elite fashion has been supplanted by mass fashion and that the latter involves little imitation of superordinates by subordinates (1975:291).[3] King (1963) delivered a more serious blow to the model by arguing that media exposure allowed simultaneous adoption of new styles at all levels of society. Each level, he argued, is led not by superordinate fashion behavior but by its own fashion innovators. The course of fashion diffusion is better represented, King argued, by a "trickle-across" model. The directionality of the model was still more fundamentally challenged by Field (1970) and Blumberg (1974) both of whom noted the "trickle-up" course of certain status symbols.[4]

Blumer (1969) suggested that fashion must be seen as a process of "collective selection" in which the trickle-down theory plays no significant part. Clothing does not take its prestige from the elite. Instead, "potential fashionableness" (1969:281) is determined by factors independent of the elite's control.

Blumer argues that Simmel's theory, while suitable for the study of sixteenth-, seventeenth-, and eighteenth-century European fashion, cannot account for the fashion of modern society (1969:278). King and Ring make a similar point on the grounds that "style differentiation" no longer distinguishes social classes (1980:14).

This sentiment appears to stand as a kind of consensus for the community of scholars concerned with the study of fashion diffusion. Modern research, following the discoveries of Katz and Lazarsfeld (1955) on opinion leadership, and the more particular work of King (1963) referred to above, is now in large part devoted to the identification of fashion leaders (e.g., Baumgarten 1957; King and Ring 1980; Polegato and Wall 1980; Sproles 1981; Summers 1970; and Tigert, King, and Ring 1980). Simmel's theory, once so central to the study of fashion diffusion, threatens to assume the status of a theoretical antique. It has been relegated to old textbooks, those museums of ideas once useful and now quaint.

One of the disadvantages of these new models of diffusion is that they do not possess the predictive power of the trickle-down theory. The model suggested by Blumer, "collective selection," gives little advance warning. To anticipate new fashion, the fashion observer must await the "convergence and marshaling" of taste in a particular direction (Blumer 1969:283). This is a process so variable and amorphous that prediction must almost always be premature. Once the process has resulted in a selection and a fashion is established, the theory specifies no inevitable fashion consequence. Subsequent fashion will emerge from a process as ill-defined as that which established present fashion. Blumer acknowledges that new fashions follow from old ones, but his theory establishes no grounds on which to account for this relationship (1969:283).

The "fashion life cycle" sketched by Sproles (1981:121–22) identifies the course of fashion diffusion and the factors that govern it. But Sprole's theory offers no provision for the prediction of a new fashion until after it has entered the life cycle, and even here prediction must grapple with the imponderables of leader adoption, historical continuity, marketing strategy, mass availability, social appropriateness, and the pressures of social conformity. Similarly, the fashion leader, or "change agent," who now receives so much attention gives us limited early warning. It is not until fashion leaders have begun to respond to new fashion that prediction becomes possible. The "status float" (Field 1970) and "subcultural leadership" phenomena (Blumberg 1975) are positively serendipitous from a predictive point of view. There is apparently no second guessing which of the symbols and styles that exist among subordinates will trickle up to superordinates.

None of these theories establishes a dynamic to enable the fashion observer to predict, at the moment of one innovation, the eventual appearance of a second, reactive innovation. This would appear to be one of the chief virtues of Simmel's concept, and one of the losses fashion diffusion theory will suffer if the trickle-down theory is allowed to fall into eclipse.

THE TRICKLE-DOWN THEORY REVISED

The trickle-down theory's fall from a position of explanatory preeminence does not perhaps invalidate it for all investigative purposes. It may still serve fashion investigators as one of the theories with which to consider the diverse and complicated body of data that constitutes the fashion world. In order to refashion the trickle-down theory for the study of contemporary fashion, however, it is necessary to refine and supplement the model in several ways. I have undertaken this theoretical revision in the light of a recent development in contemporary fashion, specifically the clothing behavior of women professionals in North America (see Dillon 1980; Douglas and Solomon 1983).

Changing concepts of women in the last twenty-five years have encouraged significant changes in the clothing of American women. Cassel (1974) notes that women's movement of the 1960s and 1970s produced several innovations, including the radical feminist "uniform" (1974:87) and the National Organization of Women's "resort look" (1974:88). Both of these created a new style of clothing for women: the first by erasing all of its "feminine" characteristics and the second by aggressively exaggerating them. More recently, we have seen a third style of clothing which, while very different from its predecessors, also reflects a changed concept of femaleness and the effort to represent this concept in a new and different manner of dress.

The professional woman's business outfit neither effaces femaleness nor exaggerates it. It seeks instead, according to John Molloy's charter statement, *The Woman's Dress for Success Book* (1977:35), to give businesswomen "a look of authority." The authoritative look for women's business wear is an attempt to isolate certain of the properties of male business clothing and incorporate them into female fashion. The object of this undertaking is to give businesswomen new credibility, presence, and authority in the business world.

It is possible to see in this attempt the same effort, driven by the same motive, that characterizes the subordinate described by Simmel. We find working women, like any subordinate group, appropriating the clothing of another group in order to claim new and equal status. Business dress, apparently, has trickled down.

It is doubtful whether at first glimpse Simmel would accept this phenomenon as an example of his theory. Certainly it is clear that the theory does not anticipate an application of this sort. For striking differences exist. First, the appropriating party is a group defined not by social location but by gender. Second, these groups are not differentiated by relative status. While occupational status of men and women may differ, their social status does not necessarily do so. Third, we see the trickle-down effect, not in a wholesale adoption of an article or style of clothing, but in the careful selection and adoption of certain properties only.

Still, Simmel's theory possesses a certain utility for a study of this phenomenon. Its application permits us to see at a stroke an essential similarity between this instance of clothing behavior and previous instances. The swift and nearly universal adoption of the business category of clothing may be seen not as an alien, peculiarly modern phenomenon but yet another manifestation of a familiar process. Second, it allows us to explain this new fashion phenomenon in terms of the imitative, assimilative, appropriative force posited by Simmel. And, third, it allows us to ask whether the appropriation of the business look by women will provoke a reaction from the party from whom the style has been appropriated. Indeed, it positively invites us to determine whether an engine of fashion change is being established here that will create further innovation.

If Simmel's theory is still useful, it nevertheless requires revision for modern-day application. Theoretical revisions of the trickle-down theory that must be made to accommodate the clothing of professional women are perhaps characteristic of those that must be made to adapt the theory to modern fashion in general. It is necessary perhaps to expect that the groups that assume superordinate and subordinate roles in the modern trickle-down process will not be defined as social strata. They may instead be drawn along one or several other demographic dimensions (gender, age, and ethnicity). It is also perhaps necessary to expect that these groups will not be distinguished by relative social status. While some status difference will exist, this difference will not necessarily be defined in terms of social position. Third, the imitation that occurs may be expected to be not the wholesale appropriation of a symbol or a style, but a selective borrowing that works to preserve some of the qualities of the subordinate group even as it allows them to claim the status of the superordinate group from whom the borrowing occurs.

But these are not the only revisions that are required to adapt the trickle-down theory to modern circumstances. It is also necessary to have some theoretical idea of the cultural context in which imitation and differentiation take place. Simmel's theory presently lacks an appreciation of this context. It therefore fails to give us a more detailed understanding of the particular motives and ends that inspire fashion change. It fails to give us the logic and substance of the changes it treats. The theoretical supplementation of Simmel's theory that enables it to supply an account of the cultural context of fashion change requires a brief treatment of recent advances in the study of fashion symbolism.

It is widely noted that clothing serves a communicative, cultural function in large part through its ability to express distinct categories within status, age, gender, class, occupation, marital status, religion, and politics (Bogatyrev 1971; Kuper 1973a; Messing 1960; Murphy 1964; Neich 1982; Wolf 1970).[5] Clothing represents these cultural categories through a process of correspondence. In the language of structuralism, clothing forms a "system of material difference" that corresponds to and so communicates a "system of conceptual difference."[6] It is thus that clothing allows a community to distinguish the superordinate from the subordinate, the young from the old, the married from the unmarried, believers from nonbelievers, and so on.

It is also widely noted that the expressive code supplied by clothing for this communicative purpose will have a peculiar symbolic aptness (Kuper 1973b; McCracken 1983a; Schwarz 1979). Clothing signs, it is argued, do not merely distinguish one cultural category from another. They also demonstrate in a symbolic manner how the two categories are held to differ from one another. In short, clothing not only marks the difference between cultural categories, it also specifies the nature of the difference that exists between them.

This model of the cultural, symbolic nature of clothing gives us a more exacting perspective from which to view the trickle-down phenomenon that the clothing of professional women represents. Let us look first of all at the way in which clothing has been used in America to represent the distinction between the categories "male" and "female." Table 1 provides this data in summary form. This chart gives us in broad terms the system of material difference that corresponds to and so represents the system of conceptual difference that distinguishes the cultural categories male and female. It specifies how the distinction between men and women is expressed by the symbolic characteristics of their clothing.

TABLE I
CLOTHING SYMBOLISM AND GENDER DIFFERENTIATION

	Women	*Men*
Line	Nontailored	Tailored
Fabric	Soft, fine	Coarse, stiff
	Light	Heavy
Color	Lighter	Darker
	Polychromatic	Monochromatic
Shape	Curved, rounded	Squared
	Flowing, fluffy	Angled
Style	Elaborate	Plain

Source: Adapted from Sahlins (1976:190–91).

These symbolic distinctions do not merely discriminate one category from another. They also communicate what we have conventionally taken to be the nature of the difference of men and women. From this stereotypic (and now properly disputed) point of view, it is seen to be peculiarly apt that men should dress in more tailored clothing; coarse, heavy fabrics; dark, more monochromatic colors; angular lines; and, finally, less elaborate style. For these are the qualities of clothing that are supposed to represent most aptly the culturally assigned character of men. Men, especially at work, are supposed to be disciplined, sober, stable, and grave. The objective characteristics of this wardrobe therefore encode the supposed characteristics of the North American male. And it is, from this same stereotypical and spurious point of view, considered apt that women should dress in less tailored clothing; light fabrics; light, polychromatic colors; curved lines; and with greater elaborateness. These material, objective characteristics of clothing most aptly represent their supposed interior qualities. Women, especially at work, are supposed to be undisciplined, insubstantial, delicate, whimsical, expressive, and changeable. In short, clothing gives a symbolic rendering of the cultural categories it distinguishes.

In the workplace, the symbolic character of men's and women's clothing assumes a special significance. Women, as a subordinate group, find themselves assigned a wardrobe that expresses qualities that disqualify them from active, equal participation in the workplace. Their clothing announces a lack of resourcefulness, competence, and trustworthiness. Men, as the superordinate group, possess, by contradistinction, a wardrobe that proclaims and justifies their superordinate position in the workplace. Their clothing is expressive of ability, discipline, and reliability, the very qualities most useful to their occupational roles.

This symbolic account of clothing is essential to a proper understanding of the trickle-down effect. It provides the cultural context in which imitation and differentiation takes place—a context just as important as the social one that Simmel insisted on. The virtue of this cultural context is that it allows us to see in greater detail and depth what the trickle-down effect consists in. In the case of professional women it allows us to see that the process of imitation undertaken by a subordinate group is set in train by motives more particular, and the pursuit of ends more purposeful, than Simmel's theory allows.

Women as a subordinate group in the world of work do not imitate the superordinate group in response to some vague general force for imitation. Nor do they imitate in the simple pursuit of greater prestige and status. Their motive is a more particular and strategic one: It is, first of all, to escape the damning symbolic character of their present style of dress. Simmel's theory treats change as the effort to achieve the new; it does not treat it as an effort to escape the old. But this act of differentiation is, I would argue, the first moment of the imitative process. The negative act of disassociation is what precedes the act of imitation. It is in order to move away from one style of dress and its pejorative symbolic connotations that change is contemplated and imitation undertaken.

If the *motive* of imitation is left unspecified by Simmel's theory, so is the *end* to which imitation is devoted. Women have adopted the clothing of male colleagues in the workplace in order to appropriate its expressive qualities. They imitate in pursuit of a social object: acceptance as a competent and equal partner in the world of work. Imitation is devoted to acquiring the symbolic complements in which competence and equality are expressed. Imitation then is not the simple pursuit of prestige nor the work of some generalized force; it is a culturally purposeful activity motivated by an appreciation of the symbolic liabilities of one style of dress, and the symbolic advantages implicit in another.

PREDICTION AND
THE TRICKLE-DOWN THEORY

If Simmel's theory fails to see the cultural context of imitation, it also gives an inadequate account of differentiation. Here, too, the theory posits a vague and general force when a very much more particular mechanism can be identified. The insufficiency of the theory in this regard is especially grave, for it is with the process of differentiation that the theory's predictive power comes into play. As long as differentiation is characterized in vague and general terms, prediction must have the same imprecise quality. As it stands, the theory allows us to say only that the superordinate group will undertake differentiation upon the discovery that a subordinate group has undertaken imitation. It does not allow us to specify in what this change will consist. The provision of a cultural context permits a more exacting prediction.

According to Simmel's theory the imitation by women as a subordinate party should provoke an act of differentiation by the superordinate party. The theory suggests that the process will be undertaken by superordinates in order to reestablish status markers that are distinctly their own. A culturally more sophisticated rendering of the trickle-down theory allows us to go a step further. We have established that the process of imitation is symbolically purposeful and designed not only to effect an identity of dress with superordinates but also to appropriate their badges of power and authority. This understanding allows us to predict not only that men will seek a new style of clothing but also that they will seek a style in which power and authority are reestablished. As a superordinate group, men will seek to accomplish an act of differentiation that will do more than recreate an exclusive male clothing style. They will also seek to recreate an exclusive look of authority. Acting as every superordinate group has done, they will seek to preserve not only their markers of higher status but also their markers of higher power. In other words, a trickle-down theory that supplies a cultural context can predict not only that superordinate change take place but also the symbolic properties the new style will seek. It can predict not only the fact but also the direction of change.

To illustrate, let me note a recent development in men's fashion in which the process of differentiation appears to be under way. The fall collection of men's clothing presented by the September 1983 issue of *Esquire* magazine heralded the emergence of a "Return to Heroic Elegance" for men. This development was described by *Esquire* writer Vincent Boucher (1983:38) as a return to "refinement," "grace," "polish," and "richness." Indeed the wardrobe was remarkably rich. It employed luxurious fabrics, distinctive detail, French cuffs, elaborate cuff links, waistcoats, and striking accessories of several kinds. The object of the wardrobe, Boucher (1983:38) suggested, was to express the "heroism" of the wearer; it was meant to bring him "admiration." The assumption guiding this style was that "the impulse to dress richly and with authority is a traditional male prerogative that has never gone out of style." In short, the look of "heroic elegance" described by Boucher is designed to have overt political significance; it is explicitly a statement of power.

This development in men's fashion is remarkable not least because it defies the conventions that had long governed men's clothing. The "heroic" look deliberately breaks with the subdued, conservative, and understated symbolism of men's clothing. But should this radical departure from the clothing code surprise us? Not at all. Indeed, Simmel's theory predicts it. The imitation of men by women has blurred a cultural distinction that the clothing code was meant to represent. It is therefore fully to be expected that men as the superordinate group would seek to reestablish the distinction and (and the code) with a fashion innovation of their own.

Supplemented by symbolic theory and new attention to the cultural context of fashion change, Simmel's theory goes a step further. Observing that women as the subordinate group have appropriated the "authority look" of male clothing, it suggests that it is the recovery of this symbolic advantage that will be the particular object of new male fashion innovation.

Certainly the "return to heroic elegance" that emerged in the pages of *Esquire* and the fashion industry appears to be a straightforward effort to restate the "authority look" in new male terms. In Boucher's words, it allows a man to "dress richly and with authority"; it seeks "admiration." With its rich fabrics, elegant styling, and unabashed ornamentation, the heroic look is deliberately overstated where conventional male dress is understated. It is extravagant where conventional male dress is conservative and sober. This clothing look is, apparently, designed to be self-advertising and visually coercive. It seeks, in the manner of the Renaissance courtier, to preempt all competing visual claims to status. The heroic look is an act of symbolic aggression which uses its qualities of richness, expense, and sumptuousness as instruments of interpersonal politics. There can be little doubt that the heroic style seeks to create a new authority look of particularly daunting proportions.

It is my contention that the emergence of this new style in men's fashions could have been foreseen well in advance of its appearance. From the moment that women began to appropriate the "authority look," it was possible to predict that a corresponding development in men's clothing would seek to reclaim this look. Clearly, the exact details of this development were not foreseeable; that men would adopt "heroic elegance" rather than another authority look could not be anticipated. But it was possible to anticipate the appearance of a style of similar character and intent. In short, a culturally sophisticated trickle-down theory allows the observer to anticipate new fashion and to judge new styles according to a highly explicit set of expectations. Informed of the symbolic motive and end of previous imitative fashions, the observer is made prescient in the anticipation of future, differentiative ones.

This predictive power is an improvement on the power of Simmel's theory. The early warning of fashion innovation established by the trickle-down theory was limited: It could predict the fact but not the character of change. Supplemented by a symbolic theory of clothing symbolism, the theory becomes more accurate. It can specify with rough accuracy the direction of change and some of its symbolic properties. Taken together, these predictive capacities provide the fashion observer with an early warning line of some sophistication.

This is considerably greater predictive power than present diffusion theories can provide. As I have noted, these theories are incapable of relating disparate acts of fashion behavior in causal terms. At best they can predict fashion adoption in one group from the fashion behavior of another group's fashion leaders. They cannot predict the change of one group by the change in another group. Nor can they identify the motives or symbolic strategies of these groups. These deficiencies preclude the prediction of the direction and properties of fashion change.

CONCLUSION

This chapter has sought to demonstrate that Simmel's trickle-down theory can be recovered from its present neglect and made useful for the study of some instances of fashion change in contemporary society. This rehabilitation requires several theoretic adjustments. First of all, the focus of the theory must be changed. Groups must be defined not only in terms of hierarchical social status but also in terms of status difference established by sex, age, and ethnicity. These groups must also be seen to engage in selective appropriation rather than outright borrowing.

Still more significant changes must be made in the emphasis of the theory. It is not enough to emphasize the social context that concerned Simmel. The theory must also attend to the cultural context of fashion innovation and diffusion. The provision of a cultural context enables the theory to account for the symbolic motives and ends of social groups engaged in fashion behavior. This in turn allows for a more penetrating analysis of the acts of imitation and differentiation in which the trickle-down effect consists. And this in turn frees the theory from its present limitations. It is no longer necessary or useful to account for imitation and differentiation in the general psychological and social terms that Simmel supplied. Recourse to symbolic theory enables us to account for these acts in rather more exacting terms.

The provision of a cultural sensitivity for the trickle-down theory gives it new relevance for the study of contemporary fashion behavior. It also gives the theory a more sophisticated predictive ability. At a time when theories of diffusion suffer a certain predictive insufficiency, this rehabilitation of Simmel's theory has something to recommend it. It permits us to restore a venerable theory to a position of investigative utility and to something of its former status.

SEVEN

The Evocative Power of Things

Consumer Goods and the Preservation of Hopes and Ideals

This chapter examines another pragmatic use of consumer goods. In this case, we are concerned not with the redefinition of gender but with the cultivation of hopes and ideals. Consumer goods are bridges to these hopes and ideals. We use them to recover this displaced cultural meaning, to cultivate what is otherwise beyond our grasp. In this capacity, consumer goods are also a way of perpetually renewing our consumer expectations. The dark side of this aspect of consumption is that it helps to enlarge our consumer appetites so that we can never reach a "sufficiency" of goods and declare "I have enough." This aspect of consumption also helps illuminate some of the irrational, fantastic, escapist attachments we have to consumer goods. Treating goods as bridges to displaced meaning helps to make these issues more intelligible.

DISPLACED MEANING AND CONSUMER GOODS

This chapter gives a theoretical account of a little studied category of cultural meaning.[1] This category is here called "displaced meaning" because it consists in cultural meaning that has deliberately been removed from the daily life of a community and relocated in a distant cultural domain. The chapter also seeks to give a theoretical account of the role of consumption in the evocation of this meaning. Consumption is one of the means by which a culture reestablishes access to the cultural meaning it has displaced. In sum, this chapter is designed to show what "displaced meaning" is and how this meaning is represented and manipulated through the consumer system.

The topic of "displaced meaning" has not been widely studied in the social sciences. The topics of "ideals" and "values" have been considered (e.g., Kluckhohn 1962; Rokeach 1979; Silverman 1969) but these studies do not treat the strategic "displaced" nature of this kind of cultural meaning. This is so common and useful a practice for human communities that it is odd that there should be so few theoretical concepts to deal with it. It is the purpose of this chapter to supply such a concept.

If the study of displaced meaning has not been abundant, the role of inanimate objects in the representation and recovery of cultural meaning is much better understood. In anthropology, the subdisciplines of structuralism and material culture have both examined this topic (Douglas and Isherwood 1978; McCracken 1986a, 1986b; Reynolds and Stott 1986; Sahlins 1976). American studies, a field that also uses the title "material culture," has made this topic the object of intense and sophisticated research (Prown 1982; Quimby 1978; Schlereth 1982). In the field of consumer behavior, a long-standing interest in the topic has been sharpened by new approaches to its study (Belk 1982; Hirschman and Holbrook 1981; Holman 1980; Levy 1981; Mason 1981, 1984; Solomon 1983). Psychology is also the host of new research in this area (Csikszentmihalyi and Rochberg-Halton 1981; Furby 1978; Graumann 1974–75). Sociology, following a period of intense interest in the 1950s (e.g., Goffman 1951; J. Davis 1956, 1958) appears to be returning to this topic (Lauman and House 1970; Nicosia and Mayer 1976; F. Davis 1985). The field of history is also beginning to devote itself to this question (Fox and Lears 1983; Lears 1981; McCracken 1985; McKendrick 1982). For all of its breadth and penetration, this work has also failed to consider the category of meaning here called "displaced meaning."[2]

A clearer understanding of the role of consumer goods in the representation and recovery of displaced meaning promises several contributions to scholarship. First, it will help clarify one of the ways in which objects carry meaning. This in turn will help advance the present effort in the social sciences to understand how objects serve as a medium of nonlinguistic communication. To glimpse the role of goods in the recovery of displaced meaning is also to gain new insight into the systematic properties of consumption that are now dismissed as "irrational," "fantastic," or "escapist." When goods serve as bridges to displaced meaning they help perpetually to enlarge the individual's tastes and preferences and prevent the attainment of a "sufficiency" of goods. They are, to this extent, an essential part of the Western consumer system and the reluctance of this system ever to allow that "enough is enough." A proper understanding of displaced meaning promises insight into aspects of consumption now obscure.

DISPLACED MEANING

The gap between the "real" and the "ideal" in social life is one of the most pressing problems a culture must deal with. There is no simple solution. Those who retreat into naive optimism must eventually accept that the gap is a permanent feature of social life. Those who move, instead, to open cynicism and a formal acceptance of the gap must contend with the unmanageable prospect of a life without larger goals and hope. The discrepancy between the realities and the moral imperatives of a community has no obvious remedy.

There are, however, several strategies at the disposal of a culture in its treatment of this chronic aspect of social life. This chapter is concerned with only one of them. It is concerned with what may be called the "displaced meaning" strategy.

Confronted with the recognition that reality is impervious to cultural ideals, a community may displace these ideals. It will remove them from daily life and transport them to another cultural universe, there to be kept within reach but out of danger. The displaced meaning strategy allows a culture to remove its ideals from harm's way.

But the strategy does more than shelter cultural ideals. It also helps to give them a sort of empirical demonstration. When they are transported to a distant cultural domain, ideals are made to seem practicable realities. What is otherwise unsubstantiated and potentially improbable in the present world is now validated, somehow "proven," by its existence in another, distant one. With ideals displaced, the gap between the real and the ideal can be put down to particular, local difficulties. It reflects contingent rather than necessary circumstances. The strategy of displaced meaning contends with the discrepancy between the real and the ideal by the clever expedient of removing the ideal from the fray.

LOCATIONS FOR DISPLACED MEANING

The culture that resorts to the "displaced meaning" strategy must find a place for its ideals. There are many alternatives here. Ideals can be removed to an almost infinite number of locations on the continua of time and place. The continuum of time is, for instance, often made the location of a "golden age." Putatively, this golden age is always a historical period for which documentation and evidence exists in reassuring abundance. In fact, the period is a largely fictional moment in which social life is imagined to have conformed perfectly to cultural ideals. A version of this notion appears in Ovid's *Metamorphoses.*

> Golden was that first age, which, with no one to compel, without a law, of its own will, kept faith and did the right. There was no fear of punishment, no threatening words were to be read on brazen tablets; no suppliant throng gazed fearfully upon its judge's face; but without judges lived secure. (Ovid 1960:9)

The "golden age" tradition is especially active in the West where from Hesiodic and Platonic origins it has proven itself continually useful as a safe haven for cherished ideals (Nisbet 1969:51). Von Grunebaum called this confidence in a perfect past "cultural classicism." He makes it plain that this strategy of meaning displacement has existed not only in the West but in several oriental traditions as well (1964).[3]

Sometimes it is not a glorious past that becomes the location of unfulfilled ideals but a glorious future. The Western tradition has given ample demonstration of this location as well. Christian theologians have posited "the other world" as a fundamental tenet of faith. Even the eighteenth-century philosophers who took issue with this Christian concept of the future created their own version of it in order to have a place to keep tenets safe from empirical test (Becker 1932:150). The future is a versatile location with many alternative possibilities: an anarchist's commune that has no law and no property, the perfect democracy in which all people are fully equal and free, the perfect socialist state that advances a common good over individual interest, the perfect laissez-faire society in which economic individualism decides all collective matters. Some of these may be realistic possibilities. They are, more important, also temporal locations in which ideals can find protection from the possibility of contradiction.

The future is, in some respects, more accommodating than the past as a refuge for displaced meaning. It is, after all, more unconstrained by historical record or demonstrable fact. The future has no limitation but the imagination that contemplates it. It is a tabula rasa while the past has certain, sometimes inconvenient, notation already in place. There is, as a result, perhaps some principle of meaning displacement here that says that the choice of the past and future as a location will be constrained by the degree of implausibility of the ideal to be displaced. The more extreme the degree of this implausibility the more likely is it to be transported to the future.

But the "unspecified" character of the future is not only an advantage but also a weakness. A golden past can give credibility to cultural ideals by "demonstrating" that these ideals were once extant. Future periods can establish no such illusion. They establish no grounds for the argument that ideals are practicable because once practiced. Apparently, however, the "true believer" still finds a future location of ideals compelling evidence for their plausibility. The utopian vision, apparently, has its own facticity. It exists in the mind of the believer with such vividness and authority that it has the force of demonstrable fact. Ideals displaced to a future location can be their own proof. They are validated by the imagination, verified in the act of thinking. The act of thinking can be an act of faith (Manuel and Manuel 1979:27). In sum, the future is a somewhat more accommodating location for displaced meaning than the past, but it is also marginally less authoritative.

It is also possible to transport one's ideals across the continuum of space. Somewhere in the present day, a society can be found that appears to live a life in which "all keep faith and do the right." Ideally, this society is sufficiently distant to ensure that thorough scrutiny is not easily undertaken, for this scrutiny is almost always disappointing. With this condition, displacement in space works just as effectively as displacement in time. The imperfections of a given society can now be dismissed as local aberrations. Ideals have found a place of safety.

There are some systematic properties to the displacement of ideal knowledge in space. Colonized countries tend to regard the "mother country" or the "fatherland" as the perfect fulfillment of local ideals. This misconception is encouraged especially by the propagandistic efforts in which all colonizers engage. It is also true that societies tend to favor their structural opposites when seeking out new locations. Industrial societies tend toward a certain fondness for pastoral societies. Pastoral societies look forward to the opportunities for perfection that development will bring. Similarly, traditional societies admire modern ones, and they, in turn, return the compliment. Somewhere on the spatial continuum there is always a perfect "other" in terms of which locally unobtainable ideals can be cast.

The culture that seeks to contend with the discrepancy between real and ideal through the strategy of displaced meaning will never be disappointed. The continua of space and time are endlessly hospitable. They represent a vast ethnographic experiment in which recognizably human elements are combined and recombined in richly various configurations. Some one of these experiments must surely serve as a reasonable facsimile of what one wishes for one's own time and place. Thus can a culture protect itself from the grueling possibility that local failure to realize ideals is a necessary and universal condition.

The displacement strategy is clearly more than an idle fiction, a game cultures play for their own amusement. It is indeed one of history's most powerful engines. Some significant part of the richness of the ethnographic and historical record follows precisely from the effort to realize distant ideals in the "here and now." The "displaced meaning" strategy is therefore a vital source of historical transformation. Whatever success has been enjoyed in this pursuit of displaced ideals, it is also true that it has given rise to an astonishing collection of misadventures and calamities. It is a measure of the essential strength of the displacement strategy that this catalogue of disaster has not discouraged it. That the recovery of displaced meaning has brought tragedy and despair to virtually every culture has done nothing to discredit the strategy and nothing at all to dim the enthusiasm with which it is still pursued. Of all of the strategies with which a culture may contend with the discrepancy between the real and the ideal, displaced meaning should perhaps be regarded as a characteristically reckless "species favorite."

DISPLACED MEANING WRIT SMALL

What occurs on this grand scale, for nations and cultures, also occurs on a much smaller one, for individuals. Like cultures, individuals display a characteristic refusal to attribute the failure of ideals to the ideals themselves. Like cultures, individuals prefer to displace their ideals, removing them from the "here and now" to the relative safety of another time or place. Individuals, like cultures, find the displaced-meaning strategy a useful sleight of hand, one that sustains hope in the face of impressive grounds for pessimism.

The strategies evoked by individuals resemble those evoked by cultures. They seek out locations on the continua of time and place for their ideals. They "discover" a personal "golden age" in which life conformed to their fondest expectations or noblest ideals: the happy years of childhood or perhaps merely a single summer holiday. With ideals displaced to this largely fictional location, present difficulties and disappointments are rendered inert and hope allowed to sustain itself.

For individuals who cannot find a satisfactory location in the past, the future proves more accommodating. As noted above, the future is unspecified and therefore without constraints. What kind of future will prove a satisfactory location for ideals is often specified by convention. Conventional locations include "when I get married . . . ," "when I finally have my degree . . . ," "when opportunity comes aknockin'. . . ." These desirable futures are collective inventions and subject to changing fashion. A favorite Victorian future began "when I am acknowl-edged . . ." and was especially popular among domestic servants who awaited the discovery that they were the illegitimate offspring of ancient, childless, and stag-geringly rich aristocrats.

Again, it is apparently true that the unspecified nature of the future does not prevent it from having great powers of persuasion. The individual believer can make a future location just as convincing a source of optimism as a past location. The fact that it has never been extant does not diminish it as a source of validation for ideals.

What cannot be found in a personal past or future can be sought out on the continuum of space. Individuals are constantly engaged in the study of the lives of others for proof that their personal ideals have been realized. This tendency is exploited for political purposes in "cults of personality" and for commercial ones in the Hollywood "star system." In both cases the willingness to transport one's ideals to a location outside of one's own life is used to persuasive effect. This phenomenon has been well studied under "distant reference group," "status em-ulation," and "diffusion" theories in several of the social sciences without the recognition of the displacement process.

For both groups and individuals quite astonishingly unhappy situations can be made tolerable through the judicious displacement of certain hopes and ideals. The displacement strategy has enabled both individuals and groups to suffer circum-stances created by poverty, racism, and dispossessed statuses of all kinds. So im-portant is the role of displaced meaning in these lives that it cannot be forsaken without dramatic consequences. The individuals and groups who give up their displaced meaning are promptly moved either to consuming despair or fierce re-bellion. It is, however, a measure of displaced meaning's terrible power that it can prevail unchallenged and unforsaken through generations of unhappiness.

THE EVOCATIVE POWER OF OBJECTS

It has been suggested that each culture must contend with a universal discrepancy between the real and the ideal and that one of the ways of doing so is the strategy of displaced meaning. It must now be observed that this strategy creates a difficulty. How does the culture reestablish access to the meaning it has displaced? This section of the chapter will argue that it is partly through inanimate objects and consumer goods that this problem is addressed. Goods serve both individuals and cultures as bridges to displaced meaning. They are one of the devices that can be used to help in the recovery of this meaning.

The question of recovery is a delicate one. The process of meaning displace-ment is undertaken in the first place in order to establish a kind of epistemological immunity for ideas. When an attempt is made to recover this meaning, care must be taken to see that this immunity is not compromised. Recovery must be accom-plished in such a way that displaced meaning is brought into the "here and now" without having to take up all of the responsibilities of full residence. When displaced meaning is recovered from its temporal or spatial location, it must not be exposed to the possibility of disproof. In other words, access must not be allowed to undo the work of displacement.

Let us examine just how consumer goods help to accomplish this delicate task. The discussion to follow is divided into two parts. The first part will examine how goods can serve as bridges before the act of purchase when they are no more than a gleam in the individual's eye. The second part will consider how goods serve as bridges when they have entered the individual's possession.

Goods serve as bridges when they are not yet owned but merely coveted. Well before purchase an object can serve to connect the would-be owner with displaced meaning. The individual anticipates the possession of the good and, with this good, the possession of certain ideal circumstances that exist now only in a distant location.

In this case, goods help the individual contemplate the possession of an emotional condition, a social circumstance, even an entire style of life, by somehow concretizing these things in themselves. They become a bridge to displaced meaning and an idealized version of life as it should be lived. When called to mind, these objects allow the individual to rehearse a much larger set of possessions, attitudes, circumstances, and opportunities. A simple example of this is the use of a "rose-covered cottage." The individual reflects on the eventual possession of such a cottage and in the process reflects upon the possession of an entire way of life that specifies more or less explicitly a certain kind of livelihood, spouse, domestic arrangement, and so on. The cottage becomes the "objective correlative" of this diverse package of displaced meaning.[4] How goods serve as the correlatives of displaced meaning will be discussed in greater detail below.

The striking thing about the use of goods as bridges is their ability to establish access without undoing the work of displacement. They can accomplish both halves of the displacement strategy without compromising either. When goods become the "objective correlative" of certain cultural meanings, they give the individual a kind of access to displaced meaning that would otherwise be inaccessible to them. They allow the individual to participate in this meaning, even in a sense to take possession of it. But goods accomplish this semiotic miracle without actually bringing displaced meaning into the withering light of the real world. In this capacity, the good makes displaced meaning accessible without also making it vulnerable to empirical test or compromising its diplomatic status.

Objects can be future-oriented as in the case of the "rose-covered cottage," or they can be past-oriented as when an object comes to represent a happier time. Here, too, an object comes to concretize a much larger set of attitudes, relationships, and circumstances, all of which are summoned to memory and rehearsed in fantasy when the individual calls the object to mind.

A good example here is the "rosebud" insignia that adorns a childhood sled in the movie *Citizen Kane*. This movie may be taken as a study in displaced meaning and consumption. The picture deliberately exploits the tragic and ironic implications of the protagonist's failure to see that it is his past (real or imagined) that he seeks so desperately and that the word "rosebud" that so powerfully evokes this state of happiness is indeed the name of his childhood sled. This object, a potential bridge to displaced meaning, has got lost in Kane's priceless collection of objects, no one of which can serve as the bridge he seeks so urgently.

The tragedy of *Citizen Kane* follows from the fact that its protagonist has lost touch not only with his past but also with the bridge that allowed him to gain access to this past. A popular interpretation of the movie finds a "anti-materialistic" message in the movie. Poor, misguided Kane seeks his happiness in things, in a pathology of consumption. But the real nature of Kane's difficulty is not that he seeks his happiness in things. The displacement strategy moves all of us to similiar attempts. The real nature of his difficulty is that he is unable to determine in which of his possessions this happiness is really (or apparently) resident.

These two examples illustrate the use of objects as a bridge to displaced meaning in personal terms only. It is also true that groups make objects the "objective correlative" of ideals that have been transposed to the past and future. These objects can be the flags of courts in exile, the national costume of a subjugated country, the sacred objects of a religion that awaits the millennium, or the emblem of any group that looks forward to the realization of ideals that are now unfulfilled (Firth 1973). The "log cabin," as the symbol of former civic virtues, serves one nation as a place to keep certain of its political ideals. The examples here are endless. Collective displaced meanings can be got to through consumer goods just as readily as private ones.

Thus far we have discussed objects that are coveted, not owned, by the individual. But ownership is not incompatible with the use of a good as a bridge to displaced meaning. Individuals can take possession of objects without destroying their strategic value. Normally, however, when the individual chooses a good to be a bridge to displaced meaning, he chooses something that is well beyond his purchasing power. There is no point in longing for what is readily within one's reach. Or, more accurately, desire rarely matures into longing when the object of desire is at hand. In most cases, then, the bridge to meaning is as inaccessible as the meaning itself. It does not admit of ready purchase. So when the individual does buy the good it is almost always as an exceptional purchase. It outstrips in value and/or character the scale of the consumer package presently in the consumer's possession.

The motivation for the exceptional purchase is usually anticipatory. It arrives as a "front runner." The good is purchased in anticipation of the eventual purchase of a much larger package of goods, attitudes, and circumstances of which it is a piece. These purchases are long contemplated and looked forward to. Usually they include "high involvement" goods such as a car, a watch, an article of clothing, a perfume, a special foodstuff.[5] Individuals buy them in order to take possession of a small concrete part of the style of life to which they aspire. These bridges serve as proof of the existence of this style of life and even as proof of the individual's ability to lay claim to it.

Normally the purchase of the good does not violate the displacement rule. It does not summon the larger system of which it is a part and so expose it to empirical scrutiny and proof. What is being bought is not the whole bridge but a small part of it. Indeed the purchase has a quality of rehearsal to it. It is consumption in training. The individual clearly understands that he or she is not laying claim to the whole parcel of displaced meaning that has been transported to another time and place, but merely a small, anticipatory part of it. This gives another virtue for the concrete and discrete nature of the good. It can be broken off and used to anticipate the larger purchase.

But when the purchase does evoke the displaced system of meaning, there is another solution. The individual simply discredits the object obtained as a bridge to displaced meaning and transfers this role to an object not yet in his or her possession. The consumer looks forward to a life that is, finally, fulfilled, satisfied, replete. But no sooner is this purchase made than the consumer transfers anticipation to another object. What has been long sought is swiftly devalued and the individual moves on to another bridge, so that displaced meaning can remain displaced. The process of "trading up" is often driven in just this manner.

There is another solution to this problem. It takes the form of simple avoidance. It has been suggested that living rooms are the sites of a family "on its best behavior." Living rooms are places where a family lives to a higher standard, according to more exacting ideals. Having invested the living room with this displaced meaning, the family fastidiously avoids it.

> Decorating folklore brims with tales of velvet ropes across the doorways of middle-class living rooms; sofas protected between social calls with clear plastic slipcovers; families spending evenings in living-room avoidance, and silent agreement among middle-class consumers that certain objects are inappropriate in the living room—TV sets, telephones, recliners, trophies. Some people even feel books don't belong there. All to protect the immaculate concept of the living room, an ironic name for a room no one lives in. (Kron 1983:93–94)

But the possession of objects that serve as bridges to displaced meaning is perilous. Once possessed these objects can begin to collapse the distance between an individual and his or her ideals. When a "bridge" is purchased, the owner has begun to run the risk of putting the displaced meaning to empirical test. Once the car that has for so long stood as a representative of "what my life will be like some day" is in fact part of the individual's life, then displaced meaning is no longer fully displaced. It is now an incipient part of the "here and now" and to this extent vulnerable to contradiction. The possession of an object that has served as a bridge to displaced meaning presents a clear and present danger to the individual's ideals.

The most striking illustration of this occurs from time to time when individuals unexpectedly receive wealth sufficient to buy any and every object they have ever used as a bridge. Purchase behavior of this order effectively makes every bridge and every location suddenly accessible. One's displaced meaning is no longer safely out of reach. A Canadian woman recently won $900,000 in a provincial lottery and then succeeded in spending nearly half of this amount in a three-week period. A reporter talked to her toward the end of this riot of consumer activity, and she confided in him: "A lot of fun is taken out of life when you just go out and buy whatever you want. It is not as wonderful as you think it will be before you win. I don't think you can ever get back to the way it was before" (Rickwood 1984:A14).

Indeed when one purchases all of the things that have served as bridges to displaced meaning and discovers that one's ideals remain unrealized, life is changed irrevocably.

The difficulty faced by the lottery winner is faced by any individual who enjoys great wealth. Great wealth enables the individual to buy virtually any and every thing he or she might want. As a result, the consumer devalues the purchase and transfers "bridge" status to another object not yet owned. When anything can be bought on whim, there can be no location in space or time that can be used as a refuge of personal ideals. Never can they say, "if I could only have a rose-covered cottage, then . . ." There are no happiness or fulfillment contingencies in the lives of the very rich.

There is, however, a way out of this dilemma as well. It is to buy what is scarce and rare; it is to collect. The virtue of pursuing collectibles rather than merely consumer goods is precisely that they have their own special scarcity. Collectibles are not available to any one with means. Their availability is constrained by the fact that they are no longer made (as in the case of antiques) or that they are not the products of mass manufacture and can therefore claim to be unique (as in the case of art). Not even a vast purchasing power will bring these objects into reach. Collectibles, unique or very rare, must be hunted down, brought out of hiding, won away from other collectors. When goods have this special elusiveness, they can once again become bridges. It is now possible for the individual to treat them as things to which certain displaced meanings adhere. They have the all-important quality of being beyond one's grasp and can therefore serve as bridges to displaced meaning. The individual can now pretend that there is a distant location for his or her personal ideals and that these ideals will be realized when the bridge to them is obtained. In short, collectibles make it possible once again to dream. One can look forward to that magic day in which one owns every Renoir outside of public collection.[6]

Let us now take up the precise mechanics of the process by which goods serve as bridges. How do they succeed in giving us conditional access to our displaced meaning? The answer to this question rests in the physical, economic, and structural characteristics of goods and the contribution these characteristics make to nonlinguistic communication. There are four aspects of goods that give them special efficacy in the expression of displaced meaning.

First, unlike the signs of other media of communication (e.g., spoken language, music, etc.), these signs are concrete and enduring.[7] This gives them a special advantage in the representation and recovery of displaced meaning. Displaced meaning is by its very nature insubstantial. It has been very deliberately removed from the "here and now" and made remote. As a result, access is established best when this displaced meaning can be given substance and facticity. Goods have the virtue of suggesting, even demonstrating, this substance, through their own substance. In more theoretical terms, it may be suggested that the property of concreteness passes from the signifying object to the signified meaning. The rose-covered cottage, for instance, gives to the abstract conditions, circumstances, and opportunities for which it stands something of its own squat, colorful, immovable substance. Suddenly the abstract notion of a perfectly happy life, spent with the perfect spouse, engaged in perfect circumstances, takes on a substance. In the peculiar epistemology of common sense, this substance has several striking implications. It suggests with new force the plausibility of the imagined circumstance. It suggests with new plausibility the possession of these circumstances. Finally, it stands as a kind of experiential proof of the existence of displaced meaning. These concrete signs help encourage the fiction that the intangibles for which they stand are indeed substantial and that they can be possessed concretely. They create a kind of concreteness that stands emotionally as a kind of "proof" of the displaced meaning.

Second, these signs have the advantage of appearing to exploit a rhetoric trope well known for its persuasive powers. This trope is the "synecdoche," a figure of speech in which a part is used to represent the whole (Sapir 1977). The classic synecdoche appears in the expression "all hands on deck," in which part "hands" stands for the whole "sailors." When an object represents displaced meaning, it appears to do so in precisely this part-for-whole manner. The individual's concept of his or her future somehow comes to center on a material piece of this future. To return to our example, it is the "rose-covered cottage" that represents a large and diverse bundle of emotional conditions and social circumstances. Similarly, it is the imagined wedding ring that becomes the symbol of the perfect bliss of matrimony the individual looks forward to. The part represents the whole.

Third, the economic value of these objects helps give them symbolic value. The desired object stands beyond the individual's purchasing power as this is conventionally deployed. It is nearly or entirely unobtainable. It is to this extent scarce and to this extent desirable. But these, interestingly, are precisely the properties of displaced meaning. This meaning is itself scarce and desirable. For its own somewhat different reasons, it has been put beyond the individual's grasp and made correspondingly more desirable. In other words, the economic character of the desired objects makes them peculiarly well suited to stand for displaced meaning. The logical similarity between them makes for a special bond between signifier and signified.

The fourth quality that gives goods a special efficacy in the representation of displaced meaning is their plenitude. Goods in modern consumer cultures make up a vast array of objects which show a very considerable and finely differentiated range in their scarcity and cost. As a result, for most consumers there is always another, higher level of consumption to which they might aspire. These higher levels serve as a guarantee of safe refuge for displaced meaning. Should one level eventually be achieved by the individual, there will always be a still greater one to which ideal meaning can be displaced.

In sum, when ideals have been removed to new locations in time and space, goods can serve as bridges to them. The goods enable individuals and groups to recover displaced meaning without bringing it fully into the demanding circumstances of the "here and now." Goods serve so well in this capacity because they succeed in making abstract and disembodied meaning extant, plausible, possessable, and, above all, concrete. They represent displaced meaning by serving as synecdoches of this meaning. They represent this meaning by reproducing its value and scarcity through their own. Finally, they represent this meaning by creating a series of almost infinitely expandable locations through finely articulated diversity.

"Bridge" goods normally serve in this capacity when they are merely anticipated purchases. Inevitably some of them find their way into the individual's possession. When this occurs the individual must swiftly transfer "bridge" status from the purchased object to one that is not now owned. Thus does displaced meaning remain displaced. Great wealth, however, frustrates this strategy by putting any and all objects within one's reach. The appropriate substitute strategy here is collecting. The uniqueness or great scarcity of collectibles allow them to serve as objects beyond one's reach and bridges to the displaced meaning.

IMPLICATIONS OF THE DISPLACEMENT EFFECT

The use of goods to recover displaced meaning is one of the engines of consumption in modern society. It helps perpetuate consumer appetite. It helps declare certain purchases obsolete (when they can no longer serve as bridges) and demands the purchase of new goods. The pursuit of displaced meaning through goods makes the consumer sharply attentive to luxury categories of goods and to product innovation. It induces a willingness to violate the normal constraints of income and to make the exceptional purchase. It works constantly to whet appetite and to enlarge demand.

All of these things are plainly good for a sound economy. They are, just as plainly, serious impediments to the creation of a society in which tastes and preferences have internal limits, in which a sufficiency of goods becomes a consumer reality. Without these limits, without this sufficiency, there can be no reapportionment of resources within Western economies nor between the economies of the first and third worlds. The use of goods to recover displaced meaning commits us to consumption that exceeds physical and most ordinary cultural needs. It commits us to a consumer system in which the individual always achieves sufficiency as a temporary condition, no sooner established than repudiated. The displacement effect prevents Western economies from controlling the impulses that drive them and from taking control of the motive forces from which they draw their social energy. Hitherto, these aspects of consumption have been dismissed as simple greed and irrationality. According to the usual account, consumers buy luxury goods because they are the prisoners of extravagance. They are the captives of irrational appetites.

Thus speaks the traditional view. In point of fact, the matter is more complicated and, perhaps, somewhat less unworthy. Our taste for luxuries, for goods beyond our conventional buying power, is not simply greed, not only self-indulgence. It is also attributable to our need, as groups and as individuals, to re-establish access to the ideals we have displaced to distant locations in time or space. This cultural and psychological phenomenon has its own peculiar rationality. It is at once more complicated, more systematic, and more curious than we have previously recognized.

The account of displaced meaning proposed here will perhaps also help us to understand certain less macroscopic issues in the field of consumer behavior. For instance, to know that goods are bridges to displaced meaning helps illuminate certain instances of "consumer pathology" as Schlereth (1982) calls them. An individual's moments of compulsive, irrational, insupportable consumption may spring from a desperate effort to lay claim to certain meanings that they have displaced. It is also easy to see that a nasty, self-perpetuating logic can establish itself in which the desperate individual buys an exceptional good in search of displaced meaning, finds it incapable of delivering this meaning, and is then forced to buy another, still more expensive, good. More common and straightforward consumer actions may also be illuminated. Might the "post-purchase dissonance" so often referred to in the literature (Cummings and Venkatesan 1976) follow in some cases from precisely the unhappy discovery that the purchase of a "bridge" does not indeed give one access to displaced meaning? Might the use of goods as a way of altering moods (as in the case of a purchase to "cheer one up") also find explanation here? Certainly, the notion of goods as bridges to displaced meaning has been thoroughly domesticated and exploited by advertising professionals. This group consistently suggests through its advertisements that goods are bridges and that their purchases will give the consumer access to displaced ideals.

DISPLACED MEANING AND THE NATURE OF HOPE IN A CONSUMER SOCIETY

One of the things this chapter means to bring to light is the intimate connection between consumer goods and hope in consumer societies. Displaced meaning helps us to resist the pessimistic conclusions that unhappy personal or collective affairs threaten to force upon us. It allows us to suppose that while things may not presently conform to ideal expectations, there is a time or a place in which they do. The displacement of meaning allows us to take heart, to sustain hope. Goods also help to sustain hope by suggesting that displaced meaning can be recovered and realized in the "here and now." It is however absolutely essential for us never to receive what it is we want. It is necessary for us always to be denied the goods that would give us access to distant ideals. This requires the constant expansion of our wants. The things we want must always be beyond us, always just out of reach. For goods to serve the cause of hope, they must be inexhaustible in supply. We must always have new goods to make our bridges if hope is to spring eternal.

CONCLUSION

Hannah Arendt (1958) suggested that meaningful objects prevent the "drift" and deterioration of our ideas of self and world. They help in this chief mnemonic capacity to remind us of who and what we are. This chapter has made another, contrary claim. It has suggested that goods are bridges to displaced meaning and to this extent objects that tell us not who we are, but who we wish we were. It has suggested that the displacement of meaning is a fundamental strategy cultures and individuals use to deal with discrepancy between the "real" and the "ideal." When meaning is relocated in space or time, it is protected from empirical test but also removed from ready access. Consumer goods are bridges that allow groups and individuals to reestablish a limited kind of access to this meaning. Through goods we are able to entertain the eventual possession of ideals that present circumstances now deny us. Of all the kinds of meaning that consumer goods carry, displaced meaning is perhaps the least understood. This chapter has suggested one of the ways in which we might begin our study of it.

EIGHT

Diderot Unities and the Diderot Effect
Neglected Cultural Aspects of Consumption

"Diderot unities" are highly consistent complements of consumer goods. The "Diderot effect" is a coercive force that maintains them. The unity and the effect, named here for the French Enlightenment philosopher Denis Diderot, are key instruments with which culture controls consumption. The Diderot effect is especially interesting because it can operate in two quite different ways. It can constrain the consumer to stay within his or her existing patterns of consumption. But, in a second mode, it can force the consumer to transform these patterns of consumption beyond all recognition. Like the preceding chapter, the present one details how consumption is driven and constrained by fully cultural considerations. In this case, the cultural factor is not the displacement of meaning but the government of its consistency right across the range of the individual's purchasing behavior. This chapter looks at Diderot unities, the Diderot effect, and the implications of the unities and the effect for our understanding of advertising, lifestyle, and the engines of consumer demand.

THE DIDEROT UNITY AND EFFECT: FIRST SIGHTING

The first person to document the unity and the effect considered here was Denis Diderot (1713–1784). As chief editor and author of the *Encyclopedie*, Diderot was an important contributor to the codification and advancement of knowledge in eighteenth-century France. The Philosophe tradition and Diderot's own temperament moved him to treat weighty issues in a witty, lighthearted manner (Bowen 1964:viii). It is therefore characteristic of both the scholar and his time that Diderot should have presented the momentous discovery with which we are concerned here in a good-natured little essay entitled, "Regrets on Parting with My Old Dressing Gown."

This essay begins with Diderot sitting in his study bemused and melancholic. Somehow this study has undergone a transformation. It was once crowded, humble, chaotic, and happy. It is now elegant, organized, beautifully appointed, and a little grim. Diderot suspects the cause of the transformation is his new dressing gown.

This transformation, Diderot tells us, took place gradually and by stages. First, the dressing gown arrived, a gift from a friend. Delighted with his new possession, Diderot allowed it to displace his "ragged, humble, comfortable old wrapper." This proved the first step in a complicated and ultimately distressing process. A week or two after the arrival of the dressing gown, Diderot began to think that his desk was not quite up to standard and he replaced it. Then the tapestry on the study wall seemed a little threadbare, and a new one had to be found. Gradually, the entire study, including its chairs, engravings, bookshelf and clock were judged, found wanting, and replaced.

All of this, Diderot concludes, is the work of an "imperious scarlet robe [which] forced everything else to conform with its own elegant tone" (1964: 311). Diderot looks back with fondness and regret to his old dressing gown, and its "perfect accord with the rest of the poor bric-a-brac that filled my room." He has lost his dressing gown, the bric-a-brac, and, most important, the accord itself. "Now the harmony is destroyed. Now there is no more consistency, no more unity, and no more beauty" (1964:311). This unhappy revelation constitutes what is likely the first formal recognition of a cultural phenomenon here called the "Diderot unity" and the "Diderot effect."[1]

DIDEROT UNITY AND THE MEANING OF THINGS

Diderot's troubled observations help to suggest that the consumer goods in any complement are linked by some commonality or unity. They suggest that these things have a kind of harmony or consistency and therefore somehow "go together." We shall call these patterns of consistency "product complements" and, in honor of their observer, "Diderot unities."

Diderot unities are well known to and daily exploited by advertisers, designers of all kinds, and, of course, the individual consumer, but they are less well understood by social scientists. As Solomon and Assael (1986) point out, much more attention has been paid to the substitutability of products than to their complementarity. According to microeconomic theory, for instance, the product has value in isolation (its bundle of utilities) and it can be replaced by other products (which represent bundles of more or less comparable utilities).[2]

Solomon and Assael, taking a "gestalt" approach to symbolic consistency, are among the few social scientists to address this issue directly.[3] They suggest that product constellations occur because the products so unified all carry role information. Following Solomon's important previous work (1983) on this question, they suggest that goods are used to ensure success in societal role playing and that this success is not possible unless the goods are used in their proper configuration. Constellations exist, they argue, because individuals must use entire complements of products to play the parts assigned them in the drama of social life. Useful as this argument is, it begs the question of why there are product constellations or Diderot unities in the first place.[4] On this point, Solomon and Assael assert only that the consumers "read" the meaning of a particular product from its companion products.

Let us examine why it is that some consumer goods appear to "go together." Let us consider why certain complements of these goods have a cultural consistency. There are three related aspects to this question. The cultural consistency of consumer goods reflects (1) the nature of the meaning that is contained in things, (2) the way in which this meaning enters into things, (3) the manner in which the meaning of things is communicated by the "object code."

As was noted in chapter 5, the meaning of consumer goods stems from their place in a system of goods and the relationship of this system to a system of cultural categories. For example, the Rolex watch takes its meaning from its relationship to all the other extant brands of watches and the way in which this product set corresponds to (and therefore represents) cultural categories of person, place, time, and occasion. The Rolex is associated with particular cultural categories of class, sex, age, and occasion because of the overall correspondence between the system of watches and the system of cultural categories.[5]

It is this correspondence between cultural categories and consumer goods that helps determine which goods will go together. All product categories are organized in order to correspond to the same set of cultural categories. This means, perforce, that all product categories must also correspond to one another. It is therefore possible to take each product category and line it up with every other product category, so that their internal distinctions exist in parallel. When this is done, the structural equivalent of a brand in one category becomes evident in all others. It becomes possible to match, for example, the system of watches to the system of cars and to determine, in a general way, which watch "goes" with which car. When the product set of watches is matched to that of cars, it appears that the Rolex and BMW are structural equivalents. They occupy the same relative position in their product category. They have, to this extent, a roughly comparable meaning. The system of correspondences that organizes the relationship between culture and consumer goods establishes a scheme in which the Rolex and the BMW appear as structural equivalents and to this extent to "go" together.

The second part of the answer to the mystery of the Diderot unity stems from how meaning gets into things. One of the ways in which meaning gets into things is through the advertising and fashion system.[6] In order to get meaning into things, creative directors and fashion/product designers discover structural equivalents and draw them together in the compass of an advertisement to demonstrate that the meaning that inheres in the advertisement also inheres in the product in question. We are the careful students of these commercial messages and, as a result, we are constantly being instructed in both the correspondences between product categories and the unities that issue from them. In this way the advertising and the fashion system first draw from, and then contribute to, the consistencies of the object code. They are constantly instructing us in what things go together.

A second and, in some ways, more interesting aspect of the meaning assignment process is the role played by innovative groups. Groups such as hippies, yuppies, and punks inevitably engage in the creative acts of consumer selection and combination when they ransack the consumer world for their own, highly characteristic, complement of consumer goods. When they do so they help create new patterns of product consistency.

Before yuppies, there was no compelling connection between the Rolex and the BMW. In the general system of correspondences, they appeared as roughly comparable locations in the correspondence between goods and cultural categories of class. Accordingly, while they could be said to go together, there was, nevertheless, no sense of their inevitable association, no sense that they were especially mutually presupposing. Yuppies (and, ironically, the media that have so routinely mocked them) have given the Rolex and BMW this mutuality and brought them together into a special product complement. By dint of yuppie and media efforts, the Rolex and the BMW are now goods that go together with special intimacy.[7]

The final part of the answer to the cultural consistency of consumer complements is to be found in the nature of material culture communication. As chapter 4 notes, material cultural messages are most successful when they are made up of "highly redundant, mutually presupposing elements" and less successful when they consist in novel combinations. This is in the very nature of nonlinguistic communication, according to Jakobson (1971), and applies equally to clothing, housing, cars, and all consumer goods. It appears to be the case that consumer goods do not communicate well when they exist in isolation or in heterogeneous groups. The meaning of a good is best (and sometimes only) communicated when this good is surrounded by a complement of goods that carry the same significance. Within this complement, there is sufficient redundancy to allow the observer to identify the meaning of the good. In other words, the symbolic properties of material culture are such that things must mean together if they are to mean at all. Product complements create the associations that supply the companion products for any particular good that help to make its meaning clear. The nature of product communication is therefore another factor that encourages things to go together.[8]

There are, then, at least three good reasons why there should be complements of consumer goods unified by a cultural consistency. The nature, the origins, and the communication of the cultural meaning of consumer goods all help to encourage this consistency. Goods "go together" in large part because their symbolic properties bring them together. It is the cultural, meaningful aspects of goods that help to give them their secret harmonies. It remains to consider the cultural force that help to preserve these harmonies in individual lives. The following sections will consider the logic of the Diderot effect and its implications for life in consumer society.

DIDEROT UNITIES AND THE LIFESTYLE CONCEPT

The lifestyle concept has been provocative and unproductive in almost equal proportions. As Kassarjian and Sheffet (1975) observed in the mid-seventies, the concept has generated a vast amount of work but much of this languished in working paper and unpublished manuscript form. A decade later, Anderson and Golden put the point more strongly, observing (after Talarsk) that if all of the people doing lifestyle research were laid end to end, they would (a) never reach a conclusion and (b) point in all directions at once (1984:406).

The appeal of the idea in consumer research is clear enough. Here was an idea that promised to improve upon the insufficiency of market segmentation. It was also a way of dealing with an apparently "class"-driven phenomenon without having to wrestle with the very considerable definitional and operational problems that plagued this notion (e.g., Myers and Gutman 1974: Rainwater, Coleman, and Handel 1959). Third, it was a way of pursuing "personality" issues without having to embrace all of the assumptions of the personality model (e.g., Wells 1974). Finally, it was a way of capturing certain ethnographic detail that the positivist and quantitative paradigm tended to push out of account (e.g., Plummer 1971).

Perhaps the most powerfully appealing aspect of the idea was that it allowed the observer to conceive of consumption as an "interrelated patterned phenomenon" (Wells and Cosmas 1977:301). This was central. Lazer (1964), Levy (1963), Moore (1963), and Plummer (1971) all recognized that the lifestyle concept permitted the observer to draw together data that were normally treated disparately and to glimpse patterns of interrelationship otherwise unseen. There was a strong conviction that this more global view and only this more global view could capture fundamental truths about consumption. And a still more ambitious hope was harbored here. Lazer wondered whether "life-style studies could foster the unification of findings and theories related to consumption" (Lazer 1963:132).

Why then should the concept have proven so unproductive? We have been given a glimpse of a paradise in which all data are interconnected and all theory integrated, but the road to this paradise is still far from clear.[9] Part of the problem is plainly that we do not have the necessary theoretical tools with which to handle the nature and the complexity of lifestyle data. More particularly, we do not have the necessary theory with which to capture the interrelated nature of lifestyle phenomena.

It can, in fact, be argued that much of the methodology and theory designed to study lifestyle has stood as a positive barrier to understanding the interrelated nature of lifestyle phenomena. Conventional theory and method has had the ironic effect of neglecting and often even fragmenting the unity of the data. This is precisely the effect, for instance, of the AIO (i.e., Attitudes, Interests, and Opinions) methodology that is still extensively used. A hundred details on the respondent's life and experience are caught in the AIO net, but the method makes it impossible to judge their interconnection and relative weight. The pieces of the lifestyle are recovered in a form that insures that their unity will be utterly obscured from view. Typically, it is the analyst who attempts to piece together disparate pieces of data by speculating on the principles that unify them.

It does appear that certain important methodological tools to capture lifestyle unities are now being developed and more extensively embraced in the field of consumer research.[10] What is not so obvious is whether the necessary theoretical work has been undertaken. With the distinguished exceptions of scholars such as Assael, Holbrook, Moore, and Solomon, there is virtually no work being accomplished in this area. This is especially odd when it is understood that it was precisely to capture unified patterns of data that the lifestyle concept was developed in the first place.

Let us begin this research with the understanding that lifestyle unities are, in part at least, Diderot unities. We may capture them using structural theories of meaning. Things go together because of their internal cultural consistency. Products travel in complements because culture gives them the same symbolic properties. These theories of culture can be used then to understand the interrelatedness of a lifestyle. An understanding of Diderot unities helps to clarify the building blocks of a lifestyle. An understanding of the Diderot effect helps to clarify how these building blocks maintain their internal consistency.

As it is presently conducted, the consumer study of lifestyle is almost purely empirical. We observe that there are bundles of attitudes, activities, consumer goods, and family patterns, and we are prepared to label and describe these bundles as styles of life. But we have no systematic way of understanding why the contents of these bundles go together because we have no theory of the nature of unity and no sense of the Diderot principle that appears to protect them. There is perhaps something to learn from the speculation of the splendidly adorned M. Diderot.

THE DIDEROT EFFECT: HOW IT WORKS

For formal purposes, the Diderot effect may be defined as "a force that encourages the individual to maintain a cultural consistency in his/her complement of consumer goods." In his "Dressing Gown" essay, Diderot gives us the Diderot effect in a novel and therefore especially conspicuous form. On this occasion, it forced Diderot to take the cultural meaning of a *new* good (i.e., the dressing gown) as the carrier of privileged meaning and make all the rest of his possessions consistent with it. Normally, however, the Diderot effect works to preserve the cultural significance of the *existing* set of goods and to bar the entry of goods like Diderot's "scarlet intruder." Indeed, if Diderot had been ruled by the conventional operation of the Diderot effect, he would never have worn the new dressing gown, written "Regrets on Parting with My Old Dressing Gown," or had his name used for present nominal purposes.

What then is the Diderot effect? It operates in three ways. In its most straightforward manifestation, it works to prevent an existing stock of consumer goods from giving entry to an object that carries cultural significance that is inconsistent with that of the whole. In a second, radical, mode, it operates as it did in the case of Diderot's dressing gown, to force the creation of an entirely new set of consumer goods. In a third capacity, the Diderot effect is deliberately manipulated, exploited by the individual to symbolic purpose. Let us look at each of these in turn.

THE DIDEROT EFFECT:
IMPLICATIONS FOR CONTINUITY

In its conventional mode, the Diderot effect protects individuals from the intrusion of destabilizing objects into their lives. It protects them from any object that brings radically new ideas into their experience and threatens to reshape this experience according to its own blueprint. To this extent, the Diderot effect contributes to the maintenance of cultural consistencies of the material world and, indirectly, to continuities of the experience and self-concept of the individual.

The possessions that belong to an individual make up the objective correlative of his or her emotional world. They stand as a substantiation of this world, proof of its veracity, demonstration of its actuality. As Robert Hass puts it in a poem entitled "House":

> I am conscious of being
>   myself the inhabitant
> of certain premises:
>   coffee & bacon & Handel
> & upstairs asleep my wife.
> (1973:54–55)

Hass is right to suggest that the premises of one's existence are inevitably the premises of one's existence (and vice versa). Surrounded by our things, we are constantly instructed in who we are and what we aspire to. Surrounded by our things, we are rooted in and visually continuous with our pasts. Surrounded by our things, we are sheltered from the many forces that would deflect us into new concepts, practices, and experiences. These forces include our own acts of imagination, the constructions of others, the shock of personal tragedy, and simple forgetfulness. As Arendt has suggested, things are our ballast. They stabilize us by reminding us of our past, by making this past a virtual, substantial part of our present.

The Diderot effect serves to preserve the continuity-making function of things by seeing to it that no interloper, no naysayer, no rhetorician of other meanings, is allowed to slip into one's experience and suggest new possibilities as Diderot's dressing gown did to him. The Diderot effect helps to protect us from virulent arrivals who can infect the domestic economy with new and dangerous notions. It helps to protect us from the "Trojan horse" gift that brings into our lives seditious meanings that will assume control by stealth and cunning. If the things of an individual's life help constantly to return this life to itself, to turn it back upon itself, then it is the Diderot effect that works to keep it capable of doing so, of ensuring that only the purest, cleanest signal comes from our possessions.

THE DIDEROT EFFECT AND THE TRANSFORMATION OF PRODUCT COMPLEMENTS

When the Diderot effect works as it did in Diderot's case, in its radical mode, it has very different consequences. Here it has the power totally to transform one's existence. From the moment of introduction, a new good begins to demand new companion goods. The individual who assents to the first demand finds that it is followed by a hundred others. The drive for consistency that is the motive force of the Diderot effect is insatiable. It is not satisfied until all of the companion goods around it are replaced with new ones that speak as it speaks, "yes men," as it were, who honor their master by parroting him.

There is of course a puzzle here. How is it that the force that normally preserves a complement of products suddenly turns into the agent of its transformation? Why does the Diderot effect change from a conservative force into an innovative one?

The answer to this question centers on the special nature of certain acts of purchase and certain product categories. There are apparently certain acts of purchase in which individuals make what is sometimes called an "impulse" purchase (Kollat and Willett 1967; Rook and Hoch 1985). This concept has proved to be a troublesome concept around which several unanswered questions still revolve. Some define the impulse purchase as one that is not planned. The difficulty with this definition is that it is possible to argue that planning has indeed taken place, but that it did so beneath the threshold of conscious awareness. Another definition of the impulse purchase treats it as the purchase that does not exhibit the usual calculation of cost and benefit. According to this scheme, the consumer normally acts with perfect rationality, carefully calculating what will be gained and lost in each transaction. When this rationality is suddenly "abandoned" (as in the purchase of a sports car when a station wagon was sought), the purchase is declared an "impulse" purchase.[11] But this definition is subject to a similar objection: that the impulse decision is a rational decision processed at a sufficiently deep level that we cannot see what makes it systematic and predictable. In either case, there are grounds to doubt whether there is anything genuinely "impulsive" about the impulse purchase and so to vitiate the concept.

It is perhaps more useful, for present purposes, to call this category of action the "departure purchase." To identify the departure purchase, one need only determine that the consumer has departed from the usual pattern of consumption, the incumbent Diderot unity. Any purchase that has no precedent in the existing complement of consumer goods qualifies as an act of departure purchase. The question then arises as to what it is that moves a consumer to make a departure purchase.

Factors such as sophisticated advertising, merchandising, product development, and design can serve as prompts to the departure purchase (Rook and Hoch 1985). Plainly the machinery of marketing works constantly to encourage "departure purchases" and this is a point to which we will turn below. But it is also true that the displacement effect discussed in the previous chapter has the effect of encouraging this category of purchases. When the individual is looking for safe hiding for his or her ideals, the appropriate consumer good will frequently be one that does not exist in the present product complement. An individual can also be moved to the departure purchase by new circumstances and events. Progress through the life cycle, movement from job to job, divorce, personal loss, and dislocation of all kinds can serve as new contexts in which the departure purchase seems plausible and perhaps even compelling.

But one of the greatest opportunities for the creation of a radical Diderot effect is the receipt of a gift. This is of course precisely what took place in the life of Diderot. The radically destabilizing dressing gown was not purchased but received. "Departure gifts" are therefore an important category for consideration here. It is now argued (McCracken 1983a; Schwartz 1967) that gifts are often given with the witting or unwitting purpose of manipulating the recipient. The gift-giver intends the gift to act as a Trojan horse in the life of the gift recipient. The gift is intended to carry new meanings into the recipient's product complement, there to act surreptitiously as the new standard of consumption. The gift-giver hopes that the transformation of the complement will work a transformation of its owner. The gift-giver hopes that a radical Diderot effect will sweep through the life of the recipient.

As a final point, it is worth asking whether there are special categories of goods that are especially provocative departure opportunities. Are some categories of consumer good especially good at slipping through the defenses of the Diderot effect into the product complement and leading an internal revolt? Do cars, clothing, entertainment equipment, furnishings, or cosmetics have special ability in this area? Do some goods have more radical Diderot potential than others? Do some social groups tend to adopt certain goods, or more particularly, certain brands, as their departure good of choice? There is no research in this area.[12]

THE DIDEROT EFFECT AND PERSONAL EXPERIMENTATION

In *Lucky Jim*, Kingsley Amis describes a man called "Beesley" and his "curved nickel-banded pipe round which he was trying to train his personality, like a creeper up a trellis" (1954:33). This is a novelistic observation of the third way in which the Diderot effect operates in certain lives. Apparently, some individuals happily violate the Diderot effect and constantly seek out consumer goods in which potentially disruptive meanings lay. They do so as part a process of personal experimentation in which new concepts of the self and world are contemplated, tried on, adopted, or disposed of. For these individuals the departure purchase is the experimental one, an opportunity to take momentary leave of the charter co-ordinates of one's experience and to contemplate quite different ones. Others go beyond simple contemplation and make departure purchases in the hope that these new goods will set in train a thoroughgoing transformation of their product complements and lives. These individuals are the bricoleurs of the consumer world, constantly taking the meaning elements made available to them and drawing them into new configurations. They hope that a new purchase—a pipe, a watch, or a car—will lead a revolt within their product complement. Their hope is that this revolt will transform the material world and the self, giving entirely new symbolic properties to both. In a culture that believes that there is a "whole new me" to be discovered in untried consumer options, this deliberate attempt to exploit the Diderot effect is a powerfully appealing one. It is some measure of the individualism and the oddity of modern Western societies that we should voluntarily set in train in our own lives so powerfully transformative and potentially alienating a force.

THE DIDEROT EFFECT AND THE UPWARD MOVEMENT OF CONSUMER EXPECTATION

It is possible that there is a "rolling" version of the Diderot effect. In this version, the effect works by increments, pressing the level of expenditure constantly upward. The rolling Diderot effect has the following characteristics. When an individual makes a new purchase in any product category, they find themselves (when income allows) buying at the very top of, and perhaps just beyond, their product complement. (Constrained by the Diderot effect in its conventional mode, they stay within their existing complement, but driven by marketing stimulus they reach just beyond it.) The good so purchased may then act according to the Diderot effect in its radical mode, forcing the things around it to conform to its higher tone. The departure good exerts a kind of gravitational pull on the complement so that when the next purchase is made, it is chosen to match the tone of the previous purchase. In this way, the entire product complement, as it is replaced piece by piece, comes to match the first purchase. Once this stage is achieved a new departure purchase can be made and the cycle started again.

This is the rolling Diderot effect in its stepwise mode. There may however be a still more dynamic, "spiral," version of the rolling Diderot effect. In its spiral mode, the Diderot effect works on *each* purchase, drawing the complements ever upward. In this version, each new purchase is set higher than the last, so that there is never a period in which the entire complement can "catch up" to the first departure purchase. In this pattern each purchase sets a new standard which is repudiated by the purchase to follow, and the consumer is locked into an ever-ascending spiral of consumption.

THE DIDEROT EFFECT AND THE RATCHET EFFECT

In its radical and rolling modes, the Diderot effect has clear "ratchet" implications for consumer expenditure. It helps to move the standard of consumption upward and prevent backward movement. It is this ratchet power that helps to explain the common complaint among consumers that patterns of consumption seem always to exceed purchasing power, even when this power continues to rise steeply. We complain there is no satisfaction in obtaining a level of consumption which just a year or two before we assumed would make us blissfully content. No sooner do we establish this level than we find ourselves looking forward to a still higher level.

Scitovsky (1976:152) has explained this process as an artifact of our confusion between comfort and pleasure. Higher and higher levels of consumption are seen as the loci of pleasure where in fact they offer only dulling, boring comfort. Inevitably we are unhappy, and seek the new pleasures promised by more consumption, only once again to be disappointed. This brilliant account must explain some of the dissatisfactions and the ratchet pattern of the "joyless economy," but it is perhaps also true that we are inclined to consumer dissatisfactions because we are the captives of the Diderot effect. This effect in its radical and rolling modes prohibits the attainment of consumer satisfaction. It insists that there is no such thing as a sufficiency of goods, a complement of possessions which once obtained can be considered complete. Sometimes it is dressing gowns, sometimes a new car, sometimes a new pipe, but continually we admit objects into our lives that will radically change the whole of our product complements and force us onto new levels of expenditure. Sometimes we will achieve in the process a level of expenditure that brings us new happiness. But just as often we are likely to end, as Diderot did, surrounded by a new complement of goods that bears no necessary relationship to our concepts of the self and world. The Diderot effect, in its radical and rolling modes, can alienate us from ourselves.

CONCLUSION

The Diderot unity and effect are curious cultural phenomena. For the individual consumer, they have both conservative and radical implications. They can help conserve a life, protecting it from change and disruption. They do this by substantiating interior thoughts and emotions and providing ballast. This is a very good thing when the individual is the victim of personal tragedy and suddenly vulnerable to new definitions of the self. But it is plainly rather less good when the individual finds him or herself the member of an ethnic, racial, religious, or gender group that has had forced upon it a set of stereotypic and subordinating self-definitions. For this individual the continuity creation of the Diderot unity and effect helps imprison him and frustrate his efforts to redefine himself. For those who find their subordinate status played out in their material world, the Diderot unity and effect can serve as jailers of a kind.

But Diderot unities and effects can also be the engine that helps transform a life beyond recognition. They do this when they work, like Diderot's new dressing gown, to demand that every consumer good in the product complement be replaced with another. This too has oddly opposite implications. When one wishes, as Diderot did, merely to be left to one's present definition of the world, to one's familiar sense of things, the radical Diderot effect is disruptive and alienating. However, for those who feel themselves imprisoned (or merely limited) by their mainstream and their own self-concepts, the Diderot effect is a kind of gift, a way of creating the self-definitions for which one yearns. At its most benign, the Diderot effect carries the potential for continuity in the face of disruption and liberation in the face of oppression. At its least, it carries the potential for the disruption of the familiar and the containment of the oppressed.

For the marketing system, the implications are also striking and again dualistic. The Diderot unity and effect can serve as an opportunity to change tastes and preferences and create new patterns of consumption. Once the consumer has been persuaded to make an initial departure purchase, an entire set of purchases may well follow. The marketing efforts of the 1950s, for instance, appeared to have created patterns of consumption in which each purchase exceeded the last and the consumer moved deliriously away from a familiar sense of things with each new purchase.

But it is also true that the Diderot effect can work to insulate the consumer from marketing influences. This occurs when Diderot unities and effects encourage a consistent, unchanging pattern of consumption. The individual fully governed by the Diderot effect, fully the captive of Diderot unities, is safe from even the most cunning and sophisticated attempts to encourage new patterns of purchase. This individual, witting or not, is simply impenetrable.

In sum, the revelations of Diderot's study have a certain usefulness for the study of consumption. They suggest that the possessions of each individual have an internal consistency that follows from their cultural meaning. They suggest further that product complements are governed by an effect which serves either to preserve their existing meaning or to transform it radically. Diderot unities and the Diderot effect deserve a place in the inventory of ideas that we now use to make sense of the cultural properties of consumption. They promise to cast their illumination well beyond the study of M. Diderot.

NINE

Consumption, Change, and Continuity

CONSUMER GOODS AND HISTORY

Consumer goods and behavior have played unexpected and diverse roles in the ongoing transformation of the modern world. Indeed, it has been suggested that the West's early and decisive commitment to continual change followed partly from its fondness for changing consumer tastes.

> Can it have been merely by coincidence that the future was to belong to the societies fickle enough to care about changing the colors, materials and shapes of costume, as well as the social order and the map of the world—societies, that is, which were ready to break with their traditions? There is a connection. (Braudel 1973:323)

If consumer goods were important in the modern origins and development of Western society, they remain important to its present structure and operation. Consumer goods, charged with meaning, are signal objects in the process of self-transformation to which the West is committed. They are important and ubiquitous agents of change and continuity. Nevertheless, the scholarship that looks at the relationship between consumer goods and change is scarce. Still more problematically, a theoretical scheme that provides a general perspective from which to study this relationship is non-existent. It is the object of the present chapter to begin to construct such a scheme.

In chapter 5 of this book, I have sought to describe the origins, structure, and movement of the cultural meaning that is carried by consumer goods. It remains here to show the dynamic quality of this meaning. Goods are a versatile instrument of meaning manipulation and one of the ways this society both initiates and survives the social change to which it is by necessity and design committed.

There is, however, something more at issue here than the further understanding of the cultural and communicative properties of consumer goods. The study of the relationship between consumer goods and social change will also contribute to a long neglected inquiry into the full structural complexity of the North American social system. Braudel suggests that the modern West may have originated in a peculiar attitude toward consumer goods. This chapter is prepared to suggest that this relationships continues to hold in the present day. It can be argued that what sustains the West in its extraordinary experiment with constant social change may in part consist in its use of consumer goods as instruments of change and continuity. The very objects that Braudel suggests helped launch us on the career of reckless and constant change may indeed be important instruments in the processes by which we survive this change.

Western, developed societies have distinguished themselves as an ethnographic oddity by their willingness to submit to continual change. Unlike "traditional" worlds, the modern West has made itself, in the words of Lévi-Strauss, a "hot" society, one committed by ideological principle to its own transformation through continual change (1966:233). It has not been asked often enough just how it is that the modern West manages so successfully to defy ethnographic precedent and survive in the face of this continual change. Nor is it often wondered how the West sustains its commitment to change when conservative forces appear to predominate with such authority elsewhere in the human community.

Some part of the answers to both these questions rests in the relationship between the consumer goods with which the modern West is so preoccupied and the continual change with which it must continually contend. Goods are in Sahlins's words an "object-code" (1976:178). They establish a medium in which cultural meaning can be variously manipulated. Goods establish an opportunity for a community to express and contemplate cultural meaning in a medium other than language, and to do so in a way that positively aids both the reform and the preservation of this meaning. Goods, as Sahlins's "object-code," allow meaning to be made visible and they allow for its use as an agent of change and continuity. It is in these capacities that goods serve as a means by which the continual change of developed Western societies is both encouraged and endured.

GOODS AS AN INSTRUMENT OF CONTINUITY

As an instrument of continuity, goods serve in two capacities. One of these is the "ballast" that they create when they serve as a concrete, public record of the existing categories and principles that make up culture. The other is the way in which goods create an "object-code" that absorbs change and helps to configure it according to the existing terms sanctioned by culture. Let us develop these below.

Consumer objects are part of what Douglas and Isherwood call the "visible part" of culture (1978:66). They help to give the ideas of culture, which are by their very nature intangible, a certain concreteness. When culture is concretized in the form of consumer objects, it is more stable and consistent. It has, in the words of Miles Richardson, been removed "from the drift and flow of opinions, attitudes, and ideas" and given a new substance and authority (1974:4). In other words, goods create a kind of ballast that works against cultural drift. It is with this aspect of goods that Arendt was concerned when she noted that "the things of the world have the function of stabilizing human life" (1958:137).[1]

Consumer goods are able to accomplish this miracle for culture because, as we have noted in chapter 5, they capture the categories and principles of culture in a form that makes them ever present and newly convincing. When culture exists in goods, it is played out everywhere in the material world. Everywhere one looks, every man-made thing one touches, everything one sees is fashioned according to cultural categories and principles. In goods, culture makes itself ubiquitous.

But goods are something more than a mere diacritic of culture. They do more than merely exhibit it. They are indeed very like an advertisement. They seek not only to describe but also to persuade. When culture appears in objects, it seeks to make itself appear inevitable, as the only sensible terms in which anyone can constitute their world. Culture uses objects to convince.

Groups who wish to reform society, to change culture, are often powerless in the face of this conservative aspect of goods. Radical groups may successfully dispute the political and social principles on which their society is founded. But it proves much more difficult to root out old ideas from their most secure and perhaps more persuasive loci, the physical objects of the material world. For instance, it is surely in part because of the thoroughness with which this society has inscribed the cultural categories and principles of "maleness" and "femaleness" in the object code and material world, that it is so difficult to contend with the problem of sexism. If sexism persists and indeed even continues to flourish it must be to some extent because, as Goffman in *Gender Advertisements* (1979) so brilliantly noted, sexist stereotypes are thoroughly grounded in even the subtlest details of everyday life and the object code. It is in this capacity that the meaning in goods assumes a hegemonic significance.

Material cultural makes culture material. It makes it palpable, present, and ubiquitous. To borrow the phrasing of the poet Hass, when culture is insinuated into our physical landscape, our housing, and its furnishing, the premises of our existence are also the premises of our existence. Ideology and the material world are one.

It is this powerfully persuasive link between idea and reality that explains our difficulty in grasping the realities of our ancestors. Even the nearby 1950s now seem a profoundly different and, in many respects, an almost unimaginable time. Part of our difficulty is simply that we do not live in the world of pushbuttons, delta-winged cars, asymmetrical ashtrays, and Tupperware sociality (Hine 1986). This collection of objects gave off and took in the meanings of this now deeply alien period. In the process, they gave the culture of the 1950s some of its taken-for-grantedness, some of its claim to being the only sensible way of seeing the world. If we were daily surrounded by these things, the peculiar world of the 1950s would begin to seem as plausible now as it was plausible then. We would have concrete, sensual proof of what are now only frail and improbable ideas.

So consumer goods serve culture in a perfectly conservative way. Some of their power in this regard stems from the nature of their symbolism. As we have noted in the fourth chapter of this book, objects are unlike language insofar as they bear a "motivated" and "non-arbitrary" relationship to the things they signify. Linguistic signs are founded on simple difference and bear so little resemblance to the things they signify that we speak of them as being "unmotivated" and "arbitrary." But consumer objects allow us to glimpse the basis of their signification.

They display the principles according to which they were constituted. They come appended with a record of the cultural co-ordinates according to which they and the concepts they signify were formed.[2]

This feature of objects gives them an extraordinary significance for the study of the world of goods. To know that goods carry these cultural principles is to begin to understand how it is that goods serve as a kind of tableau in which the meaning of this cultural universe is written. Goods possessed of principles have a performative capacity (Austin 1963; Tambiah 1977). They are capable of creating or enacting cultural assumptions and beliefs. They give them a reality, a facticity, what Douglas and Isherwood would call a concreteness that they would not otherwise have. The performative character of goods means that they can body forth certain tenets of culture. Here too goods may be seen to assume a "hegemonic" significance (Thompson 1974:387). They can enter as meaning carriers into the rhetoric of persuasion with which one group wins the obedience of another.

This significance is increased by the fact that goods communicate their meaning *sotto voce*. This makes them an especially effective and stealthy means for the communication of certain potentially controversial political messages. Communicated through goods, these messages are largely hidden from the conscious awareness of the recipient (McCracken 1982b). They do nevertheless enter into consciousness, there to take up residence and exert their influence. For instance, messages that are communicated in this surreptitious manner can persuade an underclass of its "unworthiness" without once presenting itself to the light of full scrutiny. The messages carried by consumer goods help diminish the possibility of close scrutiny, conscious understanding, and counterassertion.

In the second capacity, goods serve as a stabilizing "object-code" through their ability to "disarm" certain innovations and diminish their potential as agents of change. The use of clothing and household furnishings to fashion and announce a new social identity by dissatisfied social groups is the most striking case in point here. In seeking redefinition, these groups are potentially the agents of highly destabilizing social change. They defy the conventions according to which cultural categories of person are defined. However, it is usually the case that these groups give voice to their protest through the strategic deployment of the symbolic properties of consumer goods. Ironically it is just this piece of social protest that helps to undo the potential for destabilization. The object-code serves as a dynamic, open set that can be rearranged to accommodate the creative product symbolism of emergent social groups. As Sahlins puts it, ". . . the object-code works as an open set, responsive to events which it both orchestrates and assimilates to produce expanded versions of itself" (1976:184).

When "hippies," "punks," "gays," "feminists," "young republicans," and other radical groups use consumer goods to declare their difference, the code they use renders them comprehensible to the rest of society and assimilable within a larger set of cultural categories. Radical groups may express their protest in the language of goods but in doing so they inevitably create messages that all can read. The act of protest is finally an act of participation in a set of shared symbols and meanings. Embraced by culture and its media of communication, the "act" of protest becomes an act of rhetorical conformity. The use of the object-code by radical social groups has the unintended effect of finding them a place in the larger cultural system.

Plainly the object-code has profoundly conservative powers. It is capable of encompassing even its own departures. It can render even these intelligible. When radical groups use goods to express their dissatisfaction and their new identity, they invite the object-code to create an expanded version of itself. When it does so, radical, marginal, anomalous groups are assimilated into the system.

Plainly, the change that threatens cultural categories and their representation in goods is not always the work of a self-conscious social group. It is sometimes the result of social forces that are beyond the control and understanding of social actors. A change of this order occurred when North America found itself quite suddenly in possession of a new cultural category of age: adolescence. In this case the object-code helped a society come to terms with this new phenomena by finding means for its expression in the symbolism of goods. This opportunity to open up the symbolic code helped in the process of opening up the set of cultural categories.

When adolescence emerged as a plausible unit in the categorization of age (Gillis 1981:133), it required signs for its signification. The object-code in which existing age-categories were encoded responded by simply expanding to incorporate it. A change in cultural categories was accepted in such a way that the larger system of categories continued to be represented without loss or disruption of meaning. Consumer goods helped to announce and fashion this new cultural category of age and to give it a coherent place in a larger set of categories. Clothing in particular was an opportunity to declare this existence of this new category in a way that demonstrated the fact and the nature of the relationship to the larger set of categories. Clothing served as a collective medium of expression in which a society took note of and then made adjustment to a fundamental cultural change.

Sometimes it is not the categories that are under the pressure of change but the signs that represent them. Here too the object-code exhibits a certain fluidity and the ability to persist in the communication of important cultural distinctions. The use of cigarettes to signify cultural categories of gender is perhaps the best case in point (Schudson 1984). At the beginning of the present century the cultural distinction between men and women was expressed through the object-code distinction between smokers (male) and nonsmokers (female). As women began to smoke, this symbolism was compromised. The object-code soon reestablished the distinction between men and women in the form of a new distinction between nonfilter users, who were male, and filter users who were female. Concerns for health prompted men to move to filters and the new symbolic distinction was compromised as well. The object-code responded with the distinction between "strong" cigarettes for men and "weak" cigarettes for women. This distinction was itself compromised when men began to move to light cigarettes. With this development physical properties no longer could be used to differentiate cigarettes according to gender and the object-code resorted to image-differences alone.

In this case, social change, in the form of shifting health concerns, continually erased signs that were intended to express a distinction between cultural categories. The cigarettes used to communicate the difference between men and women was repeatedly rendered inappropriate. We see however that the object-code succeeded continually in reinventing this symbolism. This apparently endless ingenuity and versatility is an important aspect of the conservative power of the object-code. It helps the object-code to serve as an instrument of continuity. It puts at the disposal of culture a semiotic device that gives familiar cultural co-ordinates to a novel situation.

GOODS AS AN INSTRUMENT OF CHANGE

Goods serve as an instrument of change in two capacities as well. In one of these capacities, they serve as an opportunity to fashion a new cultural concept through the selective use, novel combination, and premeditated innovation of existing cultural meanings. In this case, goods are a creative medium in which invention can take place through experimentation with existing cultural meanings. In the other, goods serve as an opportunity for a group to engage in an internal and external dialogue in which changes are contemplated, debated, and then announced. In the first case, goods are used as an opportunity for creativity and experimentation. In the second, they are used as a means of the internal and external reflection and disclosure which help shape and formalize the creative process.[3]

Goods serve in the first capacity when they help a group to create a new definition of itself and a revision of the cultural category to which it belongs. The meaning present in goods allows the group to engage in a process of definition that is sometimes parallel to and sometimes independent of the linguistic discourse with which they contemplate their self-definition. The object-code becomes a source of new meaning and a new vocabulary. Goods are a means with which the group can rethink itself.

Goods aid in this process of invention because they carry a record of cultural categories and cultural principles. The first act of the innovatively minded group is to dispense with the consumer goods that carries their conventional definition. The second is to begin to adopt the goods of other groups, so to experiment with and perhaps to take possession of the meaningful properties that exist therein. For instance, radical feminists in the 1960s deliberately disassociated themselves from the clothing that gave voice to conventional cultural categories of gender and the cultural principles on which this distinction was founded. This group then sought out clothing in which other cultural concepts were resident. They settled finally on the clothing worn by working-class men, thereby moving across cultural categories of both gender and class in pursuit of an appropriate set of symbols (Cassel 1974).

Meaning manipulation through goods resembles the activity of the bricoleur described by Lévi-Strauss in *The Savage Mind* (1966) in one respect and departs from it in another. Like the bricoleur, the meaning innovator must use the bits and pieces of a previous system to create a novel message. But unlike the bricoleur, the meaning innovator is, in the famous phrase with which Lévi-Strauss characterizes the conduct of the scientist,

> . . . always on the look out for *that other message* which might be wrested from an interlocutor in spite of his reticence in pronouncing on questions whose answers have not been rehearsed. (1966:20, emphasis in original)

Novel messages are sought through the recombination of familiar material in unconventional ways. Combination and recombination take place until a concept and an aesthetic emerge that help give substance to a group's wish to differentiate itself from the mainstream. To use a phrase well known to anthropologists, goods "are good to think" (Tambiah 1969). Especially in this dynamic context, they serve the innovatively minded group as a medium for the contemplation of new configurations of meaning.

Examples of the use of goods in this creative capacity are abundant. The case best known to the present author is the use of clothing and especially clothing color by Elizabethan courtiers and counselors as a means of defining new groups at the court of Elizabeth (McCracken 1985a). In this case, the careful deployment of color symbolism allowed these two groups to define themselves as an interest group in the court, a client of the monarch, and an opponent of their opposite number. Here cultural categories of age were created through the rearrangement and novel combination of cultural principles. An example closer to the modern day can be found in the manner in which women of the nineteenth and twentieth centuries have used clothing to fashion a new concept of themselves as women, mothers, workers, and spouses. Clothing has provided a medium in which experimental notions could be created and contemplated. "Bloomers" are one such experiment; the "authority look" is another more recent one (Cassel 1974; Roach 1979).

In its second capacity, as an instrument of change, consumer goods serve as an opportunity for discourse both within the innovative group and between the innovative group and the larger society. Innovative groups use goods to inform members of the group of possible further innovations and the present consensus. In this use, goods serve as a kind of bulletin board. The "members" of the club are kept informed. They post messages to one another and the collectivity and these messages change continually. Gradually a consensus is established and the messages grow fewer and less controversial. When goods are used to address a larger society we may speak of their use not as a bulletin board, but as a kind of billboard. In this case, the group announces to a much more general public its dissatisfaction with existing conventions and indicates in the language of goods just which alternate ideas and values it intends to champion. Public reaction (usually in the form of a hue and cry) returns to the radical group to inform the process of self-definition. Goods, then, are two media of communication: both bulletin boards for internal messages and billboards for external ones.

These two uses of goods as an instrument of change can be seen in sequence. In the first capacity, goods are a way of devising a new concept of the group, and in the second, they are a way of giving notice of the undertaking and its outcome.

But it is also true that there is a more complicated relationship here in which one use of goods as an instrument of change is constantly interacting with the other. Speaking strictly, experimentation and its public declaration can only be separated for heuristic purposes.

CONCLUSION: THE STRUCTURAL IMPLICATIONS OF THE RELATIONSHIP BETWEEN CONSUMER GOODS AND CULTURAL MEANING

The role goods play in the negotiation of constant social change is as fundamental as it is unexamined. It is no exaggeration to say that goods and the object-code are one of the ways this society continues in the face of quite overwhelming ethnographic odds. Committed to continual change, this is a society in which the center should not hold, in which order should steadily fall apart. That it does not do so is due in some part to the role played by goods in allowing structure a relatively consistent expression in the face of the disruptive potential of radical social changes and due also to its ability to contribute to this change as this becomes necessary in the face of unavoidable structural change.

Paradoxically, the object-code serves as a means by which a society both encourages and endures change. It helps social groups establish alternative ways of seeing themselves that are outside of and contrary to existing cultural definitions. But it also serves to help a society incorporate these changes into the existing cultural framework and to diffuse their destabilizing potential. The object-code is Janus-faced. It looks away from innovation and toward it. It looks away from tradition and toward it. It serves both as an instrument of change and an instrument of continuity.

The contribution made by goods to social change is not well understood. This chapter does no more than suggest one of the theoretical approaches that might be taken in its study. It remains now to undertake this study in the form of empirical investigations in all of the fields that are currently concerned with "person-object" relations. All of the social sciences (and especially those subfields concerned with "meaning" and "culture"), the material culture arm of American studies, and the product symbolism field of consumer behavior have a contribution to make. It is worth emphasizing that there is something more at stake here than a clearer understanding of the communicative and cultural properties of consumer goods, though this is itself no small academic objective. What can also be accomplished by this omnibus study is an understanding of one of the means by which this society survives as one of the most astonishing oddities in the ethnographic record: a society that makes change its constant, and radical transformation its rule of thumb. What Braudel suggests was decisive to the origins of this very peculiar historical experiment remain decisive now in the present day. Goods enter into the historical process of modern life as vital agents of continuity and change. Between goods and the dynamic character of the modern world there is, as Braudel would say, a "connection."

NOTES

INTRODUCTION

1. The architects responsible for this broadening of the field are too many to list exhaustively. A partial list includes: Anderson (1986), Bagozzi (1975), Belk (1984b, 1986b), Bloch (1982), Block and Bruce (1984), Deshpande (1983), Firat (1985), Friedman (1985b), Gardner (1985), Hirschman (1985), Hirschman and Holbrook (1980), Holbrook (1985), Holbrook and Hirschman (1982), Holman (1980a), Kassarjian (1986), Kehret-Ward (1985), Kehret-Ward and Yalch (1984), Levy (1981), Mayer (1978), Mick (1986), Nicosia and Mayer (1976), Pollay (1986), Rook (1985), Sherry (1985), Solomon (1983), Sommers (1983) Wallendorf and Reilly (1983), and Wells (1986). More particular acknowledgment of the contribution of these and other authors appears in the chapters to follow.

2. Again only a partial list of those who have contributed to this reclamation of anthropology for the study of consumption and contemporary society is possible here: Appadurai (1986), Barthes (1972), Basso (1984), Baudrillard (1968, 1970), Boon (1973), Bourdieu (1984), Bruner (1984), Cedrenius (1983), Dominguez (1986), Douglas and Isherwood (1978), Gillin (1957), Glassie (1973), Greenhouse (1985), Lewis (1969), Mertz and Permentier (1985), Messerschmidt (1981), Miner (1956), Rathje (1978), Reynolds and Stott (1986), Rodman and Philibert (1985), Sahlins (1976, 1977), Schneider (1968), Shweder and LeVine (1984), Silverstein (1976), and Singer (1984).

ONE. THE MAKING OF MODERN CONSUMPTION

1. "Consumption" refers here (as it does throughout this book) to the processes by which consumer goods and services are created, bought, and used. This definition broadens the traditional view. It adds to the traditional emphasis on the act of purchase, the *product development* that must precede purchase and the *product use* that must follow it.

2. The review to follow takes up the key monographic contributors to the history of consumption. For a broader review of the literature, see McCracken 1987b.

3. For a treatment of this and other methodological issues in the history of consumption, see McCracken 1985c and 1987b.

4. Spufford (1984:4) has also suggested that McKendrick misjudges the importance of the eighteenth century in the history of consumption, observing that what he attributes to this century is already apparent in the previous one.

5. This point is explored in chapter 6.

6. The attempts of social commentators, scholars, clergymen, and political theorists to comprehend the consumer revolution are not pursued here, but they are well treated by Appleby (1976, 1978), Hirschman (1977, 1982b), Hont and Ignatieff (1983), Horowitz (1985), Shi (1985), Stone (1984), Thirsk (1978), Vichert (1971) and Wiener (1981).

7. On this point, see Hexter (1961), James (1974, 1978), Kelso (1929), and Marston (1973).

8. For other recent treatments of Weber's thesis, see Marshall (1980, 1982) and Poggi (1983).

9. A more particular example of competition between high-standing Elizabethans and their use of consumer goods to negotiate this competition may be found in McCracken (1985a). The more conventional use of the symbolism of consumer goods in the Elizabethan period to express cultural categories and contend with the conflict of cultural principles is discussed in McCracken (1982a).

10. On marketing and its historical origins, see Dixon (1980, 1981), Fullerton (1984), Hollander and Rassuli (1985), and Hollander and Savitt (1983).

11. Advertising has systematically cultivated one medium after another, capturing a larger and larger volume of public space in the process. McKendrick's account may be supplemented with studies of advertising in the form of signboards (Hendon and Muhs, 1985), newspapers (Presbry, 1968), catalogues (Boorstin, 1973:128), trade cards (Welch, 1986), and magazines (Pollay, 1985). The full sociological and cultural significance of this historical development is now the subject of intense debate. See, for instance, Belk and Pollay (1985), Cowan (1982), Ewen (1976), Leiss, Kline, and Jhally (1986), Marchand (1985), Pollay (1986), Pope (1983), and Schudson (1984), to name just a few of the recent contributors to this vital debate.

12. The transformation of domestic space in the course of the consumer revolution is an important one. It represents the study of how changes in material culture drive changes in patterns of sociality (e.g., concerns for privacy) and how these changes work back upon material culture, forcing its continual transformation. This topic has been considered in the context of twentieth century America by C. Clark (1986), Cohn (1979), Hayden (1981), Jackson (1976), West (1976), and Wright (1980).

13. Barriers to full participation in the form of sumptuary legislation in England ceased to be written in the sixteenth century (Baldwin 1926; Hollander 1984; Hooper 1915; Phillips and Staley 1961). It is a modern irony that we now pass laws to protect consumers' rights, not curtail them (Herrmann 1974, 1980). Ironies aside, differential income distribution makes equal participation in consumption one of the most distant and improbable objectives of the "consumer society" (Firat 1986).

14. Schlereth in two brilliant pieces of review and conceptualization (1982, 1983) has surveyed the historical literature on the cultural properties of homes, home furnishings, clothing, toys, food, tools, and a range of other product categories.

15. A full treatment of dandy consumption has yet to be written. Existing scholarship (Moers 1960; Smith 1974) demonstrates that this is a key episode in the history of consumption and that its further study will substantially advance our understanding of the historical interaction of culture and consumption.

16. The intimate relationship between motion pictures and new patterns of consumption is also discussed by O'Guinn, Faber, and Rice (1985). While there is no equivalent study for the relationship between consumption and literature, Harris (1981), Friedman (1985a, 1985b), and Shell (1978, 1982) establish interesting points of departure. For the relationship between consumption and art, see the provocative work of Barrell (1984) and Berger (1972).

17. Highly sophisticated work of this character has been accomplished by other scholars, especially in the American studies tradition (e.g., Ames 1982; Prown 1980, 1982; Quimby 1978; and Schlereth, 1982, 1983, 1984, 1985) but none of the scholars in this remarkable group has, to my knowledge, taken up this approach on a monographic scale. Two monographs have appeared since this essay was written to challenge Miller's position here. Forty's (1986) superb study provides new depth to our understanding of the symbolic character of the material culture of the bourgeoisie in late nineteenth-century and early twentieth-century England, and the still more recent study by Hine (1986) brilliantly illuminates the possibilities for such a study in 1950s America. A third contender for this distinction is the impressive work on the cultural properties of clothing by Valerie Steele (1985).

18. For a brilliant study of the conjunction of culture and consumption in twentieth-century America, see Allen's (1983) extraordinary examination of how the Container Corporation used culture to market products, and products to market culture. A variation on this theme may be found in Harris's (1978) treatment of the borrowing and competition that took place between American museums, expositions, and the retail sector in the twentieth century.

TWO. "EVER DEARER IN OUR THOUGHTS"

1. A still earlier strategy represents what may be the perfect solution to the problem. The nobilities of ancient China, Egypt and the Mayan Peninsula marked their children with physical deformities that could not be counterfeited. The West has not resorted to this strategy and has chosen instead to make physical possessions and social characteristics the tell-tale marks of high standing.

2. I do not wish to imply that patina as an icon is wholly natural in its symbolism. Even in the case of iconic symbols, it remains necessary for the signaling community to decide and to formalize just what information will be inferred from them. The meaning of icons must be "culturally constituted" to serve a communicative purpose.

3. In noting how few merchant families sustained their county seats and gentle status for more than a single generation, Stone and Stone cast doubt upon the degree of mobility that existed at the very top of English society. This chapter is concerned with mobility throughout the upper stratum of society, the existence of which is relatively well established. As Stone and Stone note, if there is reason to doubt the existence of an "open elite," there are rather fewer grounds for skepticism on the issue of an "open gentry" (1984:404).

4. Five generations was the maximum period required and some argued that the transformation required only four or three generations.

5. See Dumont's *Homo Hierarchicus* (1972) for a discussion of a hierarchical society that was unable to keep wealth and status consistent.

6. McKendrick conscientiously turned to his colleagues in the social sciences for the conceptual tools with which to understand the remarkable developments of the eighteenth century. He found there Veblen's notion of conspicous consumption and Simmel's notion of competitive consumption and has used them to good effect. He did not find a theory of patina.

7. This concept and the trickle-down theory are discussed in Chapter 6.

8. Steiner and Weiss (1951) suggest that another of the strategies into which high-standing individuals were forced by the usurpation of their status markers was the cultivation of a more "subdued" style of consumption (which helped "trap" pretenders by making their efforts appear conspicuous). I would argue that this subdued style is indeed a companion and a consequence of the patina strategy. Goods with patina are inevitably less obvious, "showy," and attention-seeking than those without.

9. It is not clear that it was taken seriously even in 1930s America. The high-standing individual who reported this act of status misrepresentation dismissed it by saying "What could you expect?" The implication here is that the Starr family was of low standing and had demonstrated this by their bid for high-standing material culture in a gauche and self-defeating manner. Still, Warner and Lunt note that the upper-upper class in Yankee City made concerted efforts to keep their status trophies from falling into the hands of the "mobile lower-upper group." This suggests that high-standing groups were indeed afraid that low-standing ones could derive some status advantage from objects with patina (1941:109).

10. This is only one of the misreadings that Pratt makes in an otherwise extremely capable piece of work. She also fails to see that the Shaughnessy devotion to voluntary work is motivated by the long-standing association of community service and high status. Pratt suggests that Shaughnessy women are devoted to their community work for reasons of altruism only.

11. Barber and Loebel (1953) also noted the existence of two high-status groups of women and use an "old money/new money" distinction to differentiate them. They too note that the old money group insists on classical British fashions while the new money group inclines toward Parisian fashions.

THREE. LOIS ROGET: CURATORIAL CONSUMER IN A MODERN WORLD

1. The research on which this case study is based was funded by the Gerontology Research Centre of the University of Guelph and the Social Sciences and Humanities Research Council of Canada. The project is described in detail in McCracken (1987c). This particular case study is based on six hours of interviews I conducted with an individual we shall call Lois Roget in her home in Gresham, Ontario, in late May of 1985.

2. Lois Roget was at the time of this interview seventy-eight years of age. She was born into a farm family and raised in a small farm community in southern Ontario. She was educated at local schools and at a local university where she took an undergraduate degree in the health sciences. She has two children, both of whom are in their forties. Her husband is a highly educated professional and now retired. They have been married for well over forty years and lived in Gresham for this entire period. Gresham is a town of 100,000 inhabitants in southern Ontario. Lois and her husband have lived an entirely urban, middle-class, and professional existence, despite their strong ties to the farming tradition and communities from which they both spring.

FOUR. CLOTHING AS LANGUAGE

1. A version of this paper was presented in session E-26 (Material Culture) of the 11th International Congress of Anthropology and Ethnological Sciences, Vancouver, British Columbia, 24 August 1983. Thanks are due to my colleagues at the University of British Columbia with whom I have discussed the paper: Peter Ashmore, Ron Goldman, Anne Lewison, Marg Meikle, Judy Robertson, and Cathy Tyhurst. Finally, thanks are due to the Killam Trust and the Department of Anthropology and Sociology for their support during my tenure as a Killam Post-Doctoral Fellow at the University of British Columbia during which time the research for this paper was conducted.

2. A more detailed treatment of the concept "cultural categories" is given in the next chapter. A much broader range of consumer goods is also referred to there.

3. It is worth noting that Bogatyrev's treatment of the expressive character of clothing is undercut by his use of the term and concept "function." While most of the functions that Bogatyrev identifies in Moravian folk costume have a genuine semiotic import, two of them, the "practical" function, and the "aesthetic" function, have no semiotic value at all. They do not represent cultural categories. Imprecision on this point diminishes the value of Bogatyrev's work as a theoretical guide to the study of clothing and its representation of cultural categories. The work remains, however, a valuable example of what can be done in this area from an ethnographic point of view. I have chosen to discuss this example in the terminology of a later structuralism.

4. The concept of "cultural principles" is also developed in more detail in chapter 5.

5. This aspect of material culture and consumer goods is explored in chapter 9.

6. For an example of the comparison of another instance of material culture and language, see Forge (1973).

7. The pre-test consisted in the collection of a group of forty slides. Each of these slides pictured an instance of clothing worn by an individual in the streets of downtown Vancouver in the fall of 1982. Individuals were photographed in situ and without special framing. The forty slides were shown to a sample of ten subjects in individual interviews. The following question was asked of each subject for each slide: "What can you tell me about this person on the basis of their clothing?" Subjects were encouraged to give an exhaustive response to this question and left to do so without the interviewer's intervention. "Prompts" (e.g., "What

about that coat?'') were introduced after the subject had completed their initial response. Interviews were long. None was under two and a half hours. An unrehearsed, non-directed, detailed, and spontaneous response was sought.

8. This second project has been completed since the writing of this paper (McCracken and Roth 1986). This study was quantitative, controlled by a more rigorous research instrument, and more comprehensive (n = 360) than the pilot reported here. Its results are, however, substantially the same, and suggest that individuals engage in a "decoding" process for clothing that is very different from the one they use for language.

9. It should be noted that this source of evidence is problematical as a basis for the consideration of the principles of selection and combination in two respects. First, it considers communicative activity not at the moment of encoding, or creating the message, but at the moment of decoding the message. There are several methodological advantages to this choice of evidence, and it is also true that what is true of the process of encoding should hold for the process of decoding as well. Second, it is not at all certain that what was elicited in this interview situation bears any necessary relation to what occurs in the minds of informants when they decode clothing in other more spontaneous social situations.

FIVE. MEANING MANUFACTURE AND MOVEMENT IN THE WORLD OF GOODS

1. This treatment of culture departs from the conventional one in consumer research which treats culture as values (e.g., Henry 1976). "Values" as a concept are included in this present formulation but they are subsumed in the discussion "cultural principles."

2. See chapter 6 for more on this point.

3. See Bryson (1983) for a nice treatment of the Western ideology of naturalism.

4. A superb recent study of the cultural principles reflected in consumer goods may be found in Forty's (1986) Objects of Desire, especially chapter 4, "Differentiation in Design."

5. This point is developed at length in chapter 6.

6. This issue is explored in chapter 9.

7. Three other treatments of the meaning movement system can be found in Gottdiener (1985), Hirschman (1986a) and Wernick (1984).

8. One of the product categories that is likely to reward cultural study is that of cars (Belasco 1979; Flink 1975; Lewis and Goldstein 1983; Moorhouse 1983; Rae 1971).

9. It would appear that this culture is systematic in its suppression of the individual's awareness of the cultural properties of his or her possessions. The explosive difficulties that routinely attend divorce settlements and estate inheritance attest to how modest and unsystematic this awareness is.

10. The study of ritual and consumption has been advanced recently by the work of Kehret-Ward (1985) and Kehret-Ward and Golden (1986).

11. Recent research of my own suggests that certain families feel an obligation to store possessions for a period of a year or two in the basement of their homes before allowing them to go to a Salvation Army depot. This represents a kind of "cooling" period in which the object gives up its special meanings and associations. Objects that are so charged with meaning that they cannot "cool" (and be disposed of) are in some families given permanent storage in the attic.

12. The study of consumer pathologies has yet to be undertaken in a systematic way. Pioneering work has come from Benjamin (1969), Goldberg (1985), Gronmo (1984), Marcus (1985), McCracken (1986b), O'Guinn, Faber, and Krych (1987), and Pittman (1985).

SIX. CONSUMER GOODS, GENDER CONSTRUCTION, AND A REHABILITATED TRICKLE-DOWN THEORY

1. This treatment of the trickle-down theory ignores the influence of Tarde (1961) and Spencer (1897) and Veblen (1912).

2. See Barber and Lobel (1953) and Fallers (1961). It is a measure perhaps of how widely Simmel's theory has diffused in academic circles that neither Barber and Lobel nor Fallers acknowledged his contribution.

3. Horowitz contradicts this claim in a later part of the paper (1975:293).

4. Goffman in a prescient and characteristically brilliant piece of work doubted whether borrowed subordinate symbols are used by superordinates as status symbols (1951:303n1). It may also be noted that Field gives us only half of the trickle dynamic. He does not tell us whether subordinates change their fashions when these are adopted by superordinates. Peter York (1980) suggests that this does occur in some cases.

5. This point is developed at length in chapters 4 and 5.

6. The topic of clothing symbolism in general is treated in Brooks (1981), Cordwell and Schwarz (1979), Holman (1980b, 1980c, 1981), McCracken (1983b), and Roach and Eicher (1965).

SEVEN. THE EVOCATIVE POWER OF THINGS

1. This paper originated in research funded by the Killam Trust and the Social Sciences and Humanities Research Council of Canada. Their assistance is gratefully acknowledged here. The paper has profited from comments by Russell Belk, Mary Ellen Roach Higgins, and my colleagues at the University of Guelph, Victor Roth and Montrose Sommers.

2. Indeed the present author's own effort to account for the meaning possessed by goods (McCracken 1986a) fails to take account of this category of cultural meaning.

3. The practice of inventing the past to serve the needs of the present has a long and distinguished history; see Handler and Linnekin (1984) and Hobsbawm and Ranger (1983).

4. A striking example of this kind of meaning-bridge emerged in research conducted at the University of Guelph in the summer of 1985. One respondent spoke of the Caribbean sailboat he was sure he would own one day. The purchase of this boat held for him the promise of certain qualities that were now missing from his life. The long and detailed interview demonstrated, however, that these were qualities that the respondent was not, realistically, likely ever to realize in his life. "Transported to a boat in the Caribbean, these meanings (of autonomy, self-reliance, complete mobility and merciful isolation) are now within his grasp but well beyond his reach" (McCracken 1986c:63).

5. The term "high involvement" is taken from the consumer behavior literature and applies to possessions which have marked cultural significance as well as utilitarian value. This definition conforms roughly to the one defined as "ego involvement" in Muncy and Hunt (1984:193).

6. Collecting is a topic of new interest in the social sciences and consumption; see Belk (1982), Benjamin (1969), and Danet (1986).

7. The importance of an object's concreteness to its ability to serve as a symbol has been observed in several places in the literature: Basso (1984:44–45), Forty(1985:66), and Richardson (1974:4), to name a few.

EIGHT. DIDEROT UNITIES AND THE
DIDEROT EFFECT

1. A more recent example of the Diderot effect is reported here to suggest that the effect operates to constrain modern consumption as much as it did the consumption of the eighteenth century. In casual conversation, a professor at the University of Chicago told me that he drove a Volvo for the most practical reasons. I suggested that there were, perhaps, cultural, symbolic reasons for his choice. To prove my point I suggested as an alternative to his Volvo a car that I would purchase, insure, and maintain so that it cost him nothing at all to use. He readily agreed that this choice would be the most rational one for him to make. I then insisted on small cosmetic changes to the car, changes that would affect its appearance but not its utility. These included his initials on panel between back and side windows, fur lining for the seats and dashboard, a hood ornament that showed a rampant horse, and dice for the rear view mirror. After a moment's reflection he agreed that these superficial changes rendered the car "less useful to me" and declined my hypothetical offer. Product complement consistency and the Diderot effect are two of the things that prohibit University of Chicago professors from accepting gifts of this sort.

2. The shift away from the definition of product significance on the basis of a one-to-one relationship between products and their meaning resembles the development in linguistics set in train by Saussure who insisted that meaning comes not from the one-to-one relationship between signifier and signified but from the systems of relations in which these terms exist. Solomon and Assael mistake this point and claim that the semiotic tradition looks at the relationship between the sign and its symbolism.

3. See Holbrook and Moore (1981a, 1981b) and Holbrook and Dixon (1985) for other important contributions to the study of the study of products in combination. See especially Holbrook and Moore (1981b) for the review of salient psychological literature.

4. There are perhaps also some logical problems here. It is well known that an individual's social roles are often not consistent and that the individual is sometimes caught between them. It has been suggested that single products can be used to protect the individual from this role conflict (Murphy 1964), but Solomon and Assael give no indication just how *product constellations* reflect and accommodate these role conflicts.

5. This point is made in more complete detail in Chapter 4.

6. This point is also treated in detail in Chapter 4.

7. This begs a question of its own: Why did yuppies choose these particular goods and not others to create their product complement? The answer appears to be that yuppies were driven by their preoccupation with particular cultural principles (see chapter 4 for a definition and exposition of this term) such as conservative tradition, old money status, professional success, "refined" taste, and body cultivation, and therefore chose goods that best gave voice to these principles. Status preoccupation led them to the category of high-priced watches, but the particular choice of a Rolex was encouraged by its association with sports and physical accomplishment. The same preoccupation took them to a certain section of the car set, but it was a concern for taste and elegance that prompted them to choose the BMW. See Belk (1986a) for another account of the relationship between the yuppie style of life and consumer complement.

8. This contention has the support of recent research by McCracken and Roth (1986). It is worth observing that Solomon and Assael (1986) also contend that the meaning of products depends on the presence of companion products. This assertion follows from social psychological principles rather than the structural linguistic/anthropological ones and gives interdisciplinary foundation for the argument.

9. Some might argue that the work of the Stanford Research Institute and its VALS

project (Mitchell 1983) is the flower (and a vindication) of the lifestyle approach but this cannot be ascertained as long as substantial portions of research findings remain proprietary and inaccessible to scholarly examination. There is the further problem created by the moral objectives of this undertaking (Atlas 1984) and its lifestyle typology, which do something to diminish its ethnographic veracity.

10. In the field of consumer research, new interest and methods are evident in the work of Anderson (1986), Hirschman (1986b), and McCracken (1987d), among others.

11. I leave aside any observation of how this concept has the special advantage of dismissing anomalous data that the rational man model would otherwise find problematical.

12. This research may well have some very strange conclusions. The "departure purchase" vital to the eventual purchase of a Rolex may prove to be the BMW. It is indeed conceivable (if a little counterintuitive) that it is more useful for Rolex to advertise for BMW than for itself.

NINE. CONSUMPTION, CHANGE, AND CONTINUITY

1. It is this "storage" capacity of consumer goods that make them such an important opportunity for historical study, as Schlereth has noted so well (1982, 1983, 1985.) Consumer goods are a very precise record of contemporary society as it moves through successive stages of development. This makes especially unfortunate the disinclination of North America museums to follow the lead of the Swedish SAMDOK project and collect consumer goods as historical artifacts (Cedrenius 1983, Conradson 1980, Schlereth 1984, Rubenstein 1985).

2. Impressive historical treatments of cultural principles and consumer objects appear in Forty (1986) and Cohen (1982).

3. The Birmingham Group has been especially active in exploring the ways in which certain social groups use objects to political purpose. See, for instance, Clarke (1975), Clarke et al. (1975), and Jefferson (1975).

REFERENCES

Adams, Marie Jeanne (1973), "Structural Aspects of a Village Art," *American Anthropologist*, 75 (February), 265–279.

Allen, James Sloan (1983), *The Romance of Commerce and Culture: Capitalism, Modernism, and the Chicago-Aspen Crusade for Culture Reform*, Chicago: University of Chicago Press.

Allison, Neil K., Linda L. Golden, Gary M. Mullet, and Donna Coogan (1980), "Sex-Typed Product Images: The Effects of Sex, Sex Role Self-Concept and Measurement Implications," in *Advances in Consumer Research*, Vol. 7, ed. Jerry C. Olson, Ann Arbor, MI: Association for Consumer Research, 604–609.

Ames, Kenneth L., (1982) "Meaning in Artifacts: Hall Furnishings in Victorian America," in *Material Culture Studies in America*, ed. Thomas J. Schlereth, Nashville, TN: The American Association for State and Local History, 206–221

Amis, Kingsley (1954), *Lucky Jim*, New York: Penguin Books.

Anderson, Paul F. (1986), "On Method in Consumer Research: A Critical Relativist Perspective," *Journal of Consumer Research*, 13 (2 September), 155–173.

Anderson, W. Thomas and Linda L. Golden (1984), "Lifestyle and Psychographics: A Critical Review and Recommendation," in *Advances in Consumer Research*, Vol. 11, ed. Thomas C. Kinnear, Provo, UT.: Association for Consumer Research, 405–411.

Anonymous (1579), *Cyvile and Uncyvile. A Discourse Very Profitable*, London.

Appadurai, Arjun (1981), "Gastro-Politics in Hindu South Asia," *American Ethnologist*, 8 (3 August), 494–511.

———, ed. (1986), *The Social Life of Things: Commodities in Cultural Perspective*, Cambridge: Cambridge University Press.

Appleby, Joyce O. (1976), "Ideology and Theory: The Tension between Political and Economic Liberalism in Seventeenth-Century England," *American Historical Review*, 81 (3 June), 499–515.

——— (1978), *Economic Thought and Ideology in Seventeenth-Century England*, Princeton: Princeton University Press.

Arendt, Hannah (1958), *The Human Condition*, Chicago: University of Chicago Press.

Arlen, Michael J. (1980), *Thirty Seconds*, New York: Farrar, Straus and Giroux.

Arnould, Eric J. and Richard E. Wilk (1984), "Why Do The Natives Wear Adidas?" in *Advances in Consumer Research*, Vol. 11, ed. Thomas C. Kinnear, Provo, UT.: Association for Consumer Research, 748–752.

Atlas, James (1984), "Beyond Demographics: How Madison Avenue Knows Who You Are and What You Want," *The Atlantic Monthly*, 254 (4 October), 49–58.

Austin, J. L. (1965), *How To Do Things With Words*, New York: Oxford University Press.

Bagozzi, Richard P. (1975), "Marketing as Exchange," *Journal of Marketing*, 39 (4 October), 32–39.

Bakhtin, Mikhail M. (1981), *The Dialogic Imagination: Four Essays by Mikhail M. Bakhtin*, ed. Michael Holquist, trans. Caryl Emerson and Michael Holquist, Austin: University of Texas Press.

Baldwin, Frances E. (1926), "Sumptuary Legislation and Personal Regulation in England," *John Hopkins University Studies in Historical and Political Sciences*, 44 (1), 1–282.

Barber, Bernard and Lyle Lobel (1953), " 'Fashion' in Women's Clothes and the American Social System," in *Class, Status and Power*, eds. Reinhard Bendix and Seymour Martin Lipset, New York: The Free Press, 323–332.

Barrell, John (1984), "The Transcendence of Property," *Times Literary Supplement*, 9 November 1984, 1285.

Barthes, Roland (1967), *Elements of Semiology*, trans. Annette Lavers and Colin Smith, London: Jonathan Cape.
—— (1972), *Mythologies*, trans. Annette Lavers, London: Jonathan Cape.
—— (1983), *The Fashion System*, trans. Matthew Ward and Richard Howard, New York: Hill and Wang.
Basso, Keith H. (1984), " 'Stalking With Stories': Names, Places and Moral Narratives among the Western Apache," in *Text, Play and Story: The Construction and Reconstruction of Self and Society*, eds. Stuart Plattner and Edward Bruner, Washington, D.C.: American Ethnological Society, 19–55.
Baudrillard, Jean (1968), *Le système des objets*, Paris: Gallimard.
—— (1970), *La société de consommation*, Paris: Gallimard.
Baumgarten, Steven A. (1975), "The Innovative Communicator in the Diffusion Process," *Journal of Marketing Research*, 12 (1 February), 12–18.
Becker, Carl L. (1932), *The Heavenly City of the Eighteenth-Century Philosophers*, New Haven: Yale University Press.
Becker, Howard S. (1982), *Art Worlds*, Berkeley: University of California Press.
Belasco, James (1979), *Americans on the Road*, Cambridge: M.I.T. Press.
Belk, Russell W. (1979), "Gift-Giving Behavior," in *Research in Marketing*, Vol. 2, ed. Jagdish N. Sheth, Greenwich, CT: JAI Press, 95–126.
—— (1982), "Acquiring, Possessing, and Collecting: Fundamental Processes in Consumer Behavior," in *Marketing Theory: Philosophy of Science Perspectives*, eds. Ronald F. Bush and Shelby D. Hunt, Chicago: American Marketing Association, 185–190.
—— (1984a), "Cultural and Historical Differences in Concepts of Self and their Effects on Attitudes Toward Having and Giving," in *Advances in Consumer Research*, Vol. 11, ed. Thomas C. Kinnear, Provo, UT: Association for Consumer Research, 753–760.
—— (1984b), "Manifesto for a Consumer Behavior of Consumer Behavior," *1984 AMA Winter Educators' Conference: Scientific Method in Marketing*, eds. Paul F. Anderson and Michael J. Ryan, Chicago: American Marketing Association, 163–167.
—— (1985), "Materialism: Trait Aspects of Living in the Material World," *Journal of Consumer Behavior*, 12 (3 December), 265–280.
—— (1986a), "Yuppies as Arbiters of the Emerging Consumption Style," in *Advances in Consumer Research*, Vol. 13, ed. Richard J. Lutz, Provo, UT: Association for Consumer Research, 514–519.
—— (1986b), "What Should ACR Want To Be When It Grows Up?" in *Advances in Consumer Research*, Vol. 13, ed. Richard J. Lutz, Provo, UT: Association for Consumer Research, 423–424.
——, Robert Mayer, and Kenneth Bahn (1981), "The Eye of the Beholder: Individual Differences in Perceptions of Consumption Symbolism," in *Advances in Consumer Research*, Vol. 9, ed. Andrew Mitchell, Ann Arbor, MI: Association for Consumer Research, 523–530.
—— and Richard W. Pollay (1985), "Images of Ourselves: The Good Life in Twentieth Century Advertising," *Journal of Consumer Research*, 11 (4 March), 887–897.
Benjamin, Walter (1969), *Illuminations: Essays and Reflections*, trans. Harry Zohn, New York: Schocken Books.
Berger, John (1972), *Ways of Seeing*, London: British Broadcasting Corporation.
Bernstein, Basil (1975), *Class, Codes and Control*, New York: Schocken Books.
Birnbach, Lisa, ed. (1980), *The Official Preppy Handbook*, New York: Workman Publishing.
Bloch, Peter H. (1982), "Involvement Beyond the Purchase Process: Conceptual Issues and Empirical Investigation," in *Advances in Consumer Research*, Vol. 9, ed. Andrew Mitchell, Ann Arbor, MI: Association for Consumer Research, 413–417.
—— and Grady D. Bruce (1984), "Product Involvement as Leisure Behavior," in *Advances in Consumer Behavior*, Vol. 11, ed. Thomas C. Kinnear, Provo, UT: Association for Consumer Research, 197–202.

Blumberg, Paul (1974), "The Decline and Fall of the Status Symbol: Some Thoughts on Status in a Post-Industrial Society," *Social Problems*, 21 (4 April), 480–498.

Blumer, Herbert (1969), "Fashion: From Class Differentiation to Collective Selection," *Sociological Quarterly*, 10 (3), 275–291.

Bogatyrev, Peter (1971), *The Functions of Folk Costume in Moravian Slovakia*, trans. Richard G. Crum, The Hague: Mouton.

Boon, James A. (1973), "Further Operations of Culture in Anthropology: A Synthesis of and for Debate," in *The Idea of Culture in the Social Sciences*, eds. Louis Schneider and Charles Bonjean, Cambridge: Cambridge University Press, 1–32.

Boorstin, Daniel J. (1973), *The Americans: The Democratic Experience*, New York: Random House.

Boucher, Vincent (1983), "The Return of Heroic Elegance," *Esquire*, Fall.

Bourdieu, Pierre (1973), "The Berber House," in *Rules and Meanings*, ed. Mary Douglas, Harmondsworth: Penguin Books, 98–110.

—— (1984), *Distinction: A Social Critique of the Judgement of Taste*, trans. Richard Nice, Cambridge: Harvard University Press.

Bowen, Ralph H. (1956), "Introduction," in *Rameau's Nephew and Other Works by Denis Diderot*, trans. Jacques Barzun and Ralph Bowen, New York: Bobbs-Merrill, vii–xviii.

Braudel, Fernand (1973), *Capitalism and Material Life 1400–1800*, trans. Miriam Kochan, London: Weidenfeld and Nicolson.

Brenninkmeyer, Ingrid (1963), *The Sociology of Fashion*, Paris: Librairie du Recueil Sirey.

Bronner, Simon J. (1983), " 'Visible Proofs': Material Culture Study in American Folkloristics," *American Quarterly*, 35 (3), 316–338.

Brooks, John (1981), *Showing Off in America: From Conspicuous Consumption to Parody Display*, Boston: Little, Brown and Co.

Bruner, Edward M. (1984), "Introduction: The Opening Up of Anthropology," in *Text, Play and Story: The Construction and Reconstruction of Self and Society*. eds. Edward M. Bruner and Stuart Plattner, Washington: American Ethnological Society, 1–16.

Bryson, Norman (1983), *Vision and Painting: The Logic of the Gaze*, New Haven: Yale University Press.

Burghley, Lord (Sir William Cecil) (1930), as quoted in 9th Earl of Northumberland (Henry Percy), *Advice to his Son*, ed. G. B. Harrison, London: Ernest Benn.

Campbell, Colin (1983), "Romanticism and The Consumer Ethic: Intimations of a Weberstyle Thesis," *Sociological Analysis*, 44 (4), 279–295.

Caplow, Theodore (1982), "Christmas Gifts and Kin Networks," *American Sociological Review*, 47 (3 June), 383–392.

Carlisle, Susan G. (1982), "French Homes and French Character," *Landscape*, 26 (3), 13–23.

Carrithers, Michael, Steven Collins, and Steven Lukes, eds. (1985), *The Category of the Person*, Cambridge: Cambridge University Press.

Carroll, Michael P. (1982), "The Logic of Anglo-American Meals," *Journal of American Culture*, 5, 36–45.

Cassell, Joan (1974), "Externalities of Change: Deference and Demeanor in Contemporary Feminism," *Human Organization*, 33 (1 Spring), 85–94.

Cedrenius, Gunilla (1983), "The Creation of Contemporary Collections of Relevance," paper presented at the 13th General Conference of the International Council of Museums, 24 July–2 August 1983.

Cheal, David (1985), "Moral Economy: Gift Giving in an Urban Economy," Winnipeg Area Study Report No. 5, Institute for Social and Economic Research, University of Manitoba, Winnipeg, Manitoba.

—— (1986), "The Social Dimensions of Gift Behavior," *Journal of Social and Personal Relationships*, 3, 423–439.

Clark, Clifford E., Jr. (1976), "Domestic Architecture as an Index to Social History: The

Romantic Revival and the Cult of Domesticity in America, 1840–1870," *Journal of Interdisciplinary History*, 7 (1 Summer), 33–56.

———— (1986), *The American Family Home, 1800–1960*, Chapel Hill: University of North Carolina Press.

Clark, Grahame (1986), *Symbols of Excellence: Precious Materials as Expressions of Status*, Cambridge: Cambridge University Press.

Clarke, John (1975), "Style," in *Resistance Through Rituals: Youth Subcultures in Post-war Britain*, eds. Stuart Hall and Tony Jefferson, London: Hutchinson and Co., 175–191.

————, Stuart Hall, Tony Jefferson, and Brian Roberts (1975), "Subcultures, Cultures and Class," in *Resistance Through Rituals: Youth Subcultures in Post-war Britain*, eds. Stuart Hall and Tony Jefferson, London: Hutchinson and Co., 9–79.

Cohen, Lizabeth A. (1982), "Embellishing a Life of Labour: An Interpretation of the Material Culture of American Working-Class Homes, 1885–1915," in *Material Culture Studies in America*, ed. Thomas J. Schlereth, Nashville, TN: The American Association for State and Local History, 289–305.

Cohn, Jan (1979), *The Palace or the Poorhouse: The American House as Cultural Symbol*, East Lansing: Michigan State University Press.

Coleman, Richard P. (1983), "The Continuing Significance of Social Class to Marketing," *Journal of Consumer Research*, 10 (3 December), 265–280.

Conradson, Birgitta (1980), "Swedish Museums in Our Times and Their Achievement in Documenting the Present," *Current Sweden*, 257 (7 September), 2–6.

Cooper, J. P. (1970), *The Decline of Spain and the Thirty Years War*, Cambridge: Cambridge University Press.

Cordwell, Justine and Ronald A. Schwarz, eds. (1979), *The Fabrics of Culture*, The Hague: Mouton.

Cowan, Ruth Schwartz (1982), "The 'Industrial Revolution' in the Home: Household Technology and Social Change in the Twentieth Century," in *Material Culture Studies in America*, ed. Thomas J. Schlereth, Nashville, TN: The American Association for State and Local History, 222–236.

Csikszentmihalyi, Mihaly and Eugene Rochberg-Halton (1981), *The Meaning of Things: Domestic Symbols and the Self*, New York: Cambridge University Press.

Culler, Jonathan (1975), *Structuralist Poetics*, London: Routledge and Kegan Paul.

Cummings, William H. and M. Venkatesan (1976), "Cognitive Dissonance and Consumer Behavior: A Review of the Evidence," *Journal of Marketing*, 13 (August), 303–308.

Cunningham, Clark E. (1973), "Order in the Atoni House," in *Right and Left: Essays on Dual Classification*, ed. Rodney Needham, Chicago: University of Chicago Press, 204–238.

Danet, Brenda (1986), "Books, Butterflies, Botticellis: A Sociological Analysis of the 'Madness' of Collecting," paper given at the 6th International Conference on Culture and Communication, Temple University, Philadelphia, 9 October 1986.

Davis, Fred (1985), "Clothing and Fashion as Communication," in *The Psychology of Fashion*, ed. Michael R. Solomon, Lexington, MA.: Lexington Books, 15–27.

Davis, J. (1972), "Gifts and the U.K. Economy," *Man*, new series, 7 (3 September), 408–429.

Davis, James A. (1956), "Status Symbols and the Measurement of Status Perception," *Sociometry*, 19 (3 September), 154–165.

———— (1958), "Cultural Factors in the Perception of Status Symbols," *The Midwest Sociologist*, 21 (1 December), 1–11.

Deshpande, Rohit (1983), " 'Paradigms Lost': On Theory and Method in Research in Marketing," *Journal of Marketing*, 47 (4 Fall), 101–110.

Diderot, Denis (1964), "Regrets on Parting with My Old Dressing Gown," in *Rameau's*

Nephew and Other Works by Denis Diderot, trans. Jacques Barzun and Ralph H. Bowen, New York: Bobbs-Merrill, 309–317.

Dillon, Linda S. (1980), "Business Dress for Women Corporate Professionals," *Home Economics Research Journal*, 9 (2 December), 124–129.

Disman, Milada (1984), "Domestic Possessions as Manifestations of Elderly Immigrants' Identity," paper presented at the 13th Annual Meeting of the Canadian Association on Gerontology, Vancouver, B.C.

Dixon, Donald F. (1980), "Medieval Macromarketing Thought," in *Macromarketing: Evolution of Thought*, eds. George Fisk, Robert W. Nason, and Phillip D. White, Boulder: Graduate School of Business Adminstration, University of Colorado, 59–69.

——— (1981), "The Role of Marketing in Early Theories of Economic Development," *Journal of Macromarketing*, 1 (2 Fall), 19–27.

Dominguez, Virginia R. (1986), "The Marketing of Heritage," *American Ethnologist*, 13 (3 August), 546–555.

Douglas, Mary (1966), *Purity and Danger: An Analysis of Concepts of Pollution and Taboo*, Harmondsworth: Penguin Books.

——— (1971), "Deciphering a Meal," in *Myth, Symbol, and Culture*, ed. Clifford Geertz, New York: W.W Norton and Co., 61–81.

——— and Baron Isherwood (1978), *The World of Goods: Towards an Anthropology of Consumption*, New York: W. W. Norton and Co.

Douglas, Susan P. and Michael R. Solomon (1983), "Clothing the Female Executive: Fashion or Fortune?" in *1983 AMA Winter Educators' Conference: Proceedings*, Series No. 49, eds. Patrick E. Murphy et al., Chicago: American Marketing Association, 127–132.

Doxtater, Dennis (1984), "Spatial Opposition In Non-Discursive Expression: Architecture as Ritual Process," *Canadian Journal of Anthropology*, 4 (1 Summer), 1–17.

Drewal, Henry John (1983), "Body Art as an Expression of Aesthetics and Ontology Among the Yoruba of West Africa," paper presented in session E-023 of the 11th International Congress of Anthropological and Ethnological Sciences, Vancouver, B.C., 21 August, 1983.

Dumont, Louis (1972), *Homo Hierarchicus: The Caste System and Its Implications*, London: Paladin.

Durkheim, Emile and Marcel Mauss (1963), *Primitive Classification*, trans. Rodney Needham, Chicago: University of Chicago Press.

Dyer, Gillian (1982), *Advertising as Communication*, New York: Methuen.

Elias, Norbert (1978), *The History of Manners. The Civilizing Process*, Vol. 1, trans. Edmund Jephcott, New York: Pantheon Books.

Elyot, Sir Thomas (1907), *The Boke Named the Governour*, London: J. M. Dent.

Ewen, Stuart (1976), *Captains of Consciousness: Advertising and the Social Roots of the Consumer Culture*, New York: McGraw-Hill.

Fairholt, Frederick W. (1885), *Costume in England*, London: George Bell.

Fallers, Lloyd A. (1961), "A Note on the 'Trickle Effect'," in *Sociology: Progress of a Decade*, eds. Seymour Lipset and Neil Smelser, Englewood Cliffs, NJ: Prentice-Hall, 501–506.

Felson, Marcus (1976), "The Differentiation of Material Life Styles: 1925 to 1966," *Social Indicators Research*, 3, 397–421.

Fernandez, James W. (1966), "Principles of Opposition and Vitality in Fang Aesthetics," *Journal of Aesthetics and Art Criticism*, 25 (Fall), 53–64.

——— (1977), "The Performance of Ritual Metaphors," in *The Social Use of Metaphor*, eds. J. David Sapir and J. Christopher Crocker, Philadelphia: University of Pennsylvania Press, 100–131.

Ferne, John (1586), *The Blazon of Gentrie*, London: n.p.

Field, George A. (1970), "The Status Float Phenomenon: The Upward Diffusion of Innovation," *Business Horizons*, 13 (4 August), 45–52.

Firat, A. Fuat (1985), "A Critique of the Orientations in Theory Development in Consumer Behavior: Suggestions for the Future," in *Advances in Consumer Research*, Vol. 12, eds. Elizabeth C. Hirschman and Morris B. Holbrook, Provo, UT: Association for Consumer Research, 3–6.

———— (1986), "A Macro Theory in Marketing: The Social Construction of Consumption Patterns," in *Philosophical and Radical Thought in Marketing*, eds. Richard P. Bagozzi, Nikhilesh Dholakia, and A. Fuat Firat, forthcoming.

———— and Nikhilesh Dholakia (1982), "Consumption Choices at the Macro Level," *Journal of Macromarketing*, 2 (2 Fall), 6–15.

Firth, Raymond W. (1973), "Symbolism of Flags," in *Symbols: Public and Private*, by Raymond W. Firth, Ithaca: Cornell University Press, 328–368.

Flink, James J. (1975), *The Car Culture*, Cambridge: M.I.T. Press.

Forge, Anthony (1970), "Learning to See in New Guinea," in *Socialization: The Approach from Social Anthropology*, ed. Philip Mayer, London: Tavistock, 269–291.

———— (1973), "Style and Meaning in Sepik Art," in *Primitive Art and Society*, ed. Anthony Forge, London: Oxford University Press, 169–192.

Form, William H. and Gregory P. Stone (1957), "Urbanism, Anonymity and Status Symbolism," *American Journal of Sociology*, 62 (5 March), 504–514.

Forty, Adrian (1986), *Objects of Desire: Design and Society from Wedgwood to IBM*, New York: Pantheon Books.

Fox, Richard Wightman and T. J. Jackson Lears, eds. (1983), *The Culture of Consumption: Critical Essays in American History, 1880–1980*, New York: Pantheon Books.

Fraser, Kennedy (1981), *The Fashionable Mind*, New York: Knopf.

Fraser, W. Hamish (1981), *The Coming of the Mass Market, 1850–1914*, Hamden, CT: Archon Books.

Friedman, Monroe (1985a), "Commercial Influences in Popular Literature: An American Historical Perspective," in *Historical Perspective in Consumer Research: National and International Perspectives*, eds. Chin Tiong Tan and Jagdish N. Sheth, Singapore: National University of Singapore, 307–308.

———— (1985b), "The Changing Language of a Consumer Society: Brand Name Usage in Popular American Novels in the Postwar Era," *Journal of Consumer Research*, 11 (4 March), 927–938.

Fullerton, Ronald A. (1984), "Capitalism and the Shaping of Marketing: Marketing as a World-Historical Force," paper presented at the 9th Macromarketing Seminar, Vancouver, B.C.

Furby, Lita (1978), "Possessions: Toward a Theory of Their Meaning and Function throughout the Life Cycle," in *Lifespan Development and Behavior*, ed. Paul B. Baltes, New York: Academic Press, 297–336.

Gardner, Meryl Paula (1985), "Mood States and Consumer Behavior: A Critical Review," *Journal of Consumer Behavior*, 12 (3 December), 281–300.

Garfinkle, Andrew D. (1978), "A Sociolinguistic Analysis of the Language of Advertising," unpublished dissertation, Department of Linguistics, Georgetown University, Washington, D.C. 20057.

Gennep, Arnold Van (1960), *The Rites of Passage*, trans. Monika B. Vizedom and Gabrielle L. Caffee, London: Routledge and Kegan Paul.

Gergen, Kenneth J. and Keith E. Davis, eds. (1985), *The Social Construction of the Person*, New York: Springer-Verlag.

Gibbins, Keith (1971), "Social Psychological Theories of Fashion," *Journal of the Home Economics Association of Australia*, 3, 3–18.

———— and Tonya K. Gwynn (1975), "A New Theory of Fashion Change: A Test of Some Predictions," *The British Journal of Social and Clinical Psychology*, 14 (1), 1–9.

———— and Anthony Schneider (1980), "Meaning of Garments," *Perceptual and Motor Skills*, 51, 287–291.

Gillin, John (1957), "The Application of Anthropological Knowledge to Modern Mass Society," *Human Organization*, 15 (4 Winter), 24–29.

Gillis, John R. (1981), *Youth and History: Tradition and Change in European Age Relations, 1770–Present*, New York: Academic Press.

Givens, D. B. (1977), "Shoulder Shrugging: A Densely Communicative Expressive Behavior," *Semiotica*, 19, 13–28.

Glassie, Henry (1973), "Structure and Function, Folklore and the Artifact," *Semiotica*, 7 (4), 313–351.

Goffman, Erving (1951), "Symbols of Class Status," *British Journal of Sociology*, 2 (December), 294–304.

———— (1979), *Gender Advertisements*, Cambridge: Harvard University Press.

Goldberg, Jim (1985), *Rich and Poor*, New York: Random House.

Gottdiener, M. (1985), "Hegemony and Mass Culture: A Semiotic Approach," *American Journal of Sociology*, 90 (5), 979–1001.

Gordon, Jean and Jan McArthur (1985), "American Women and Domestic Consumption, 1800–1920: Four Interpretive Themes," *Journal of American Culture*, 8 (3), 35–46.

Graumann, Carl F. (1974–75), "Psychology and the World of Things," *Journal of Phenomenological Psychology*, 4 (1), 389–404.

Greenberg, Laura J. (1975), "Art as a Structural System: A Study of Hopi Pottery Designs," *Studies in the Anthropology of Visual Communication*, 2 (1), 33–50.

Greenhouse, Carol J. (1985), "Anthropology at Home: Whose Home?" *Human Organization*, 44 (3 Fall), 261–264.

Gronmo, Sigmund (1984), "Compensatory Consumer Behavior: Theoretical Perspectives, Empirical Examples and Methodological Challenges," *1984 AMA Winter Educators' Conference: Scientific Method in Marketing*, eds. Paul F. Anderson and Michael J. Ryan, Chicago: American Marketing Association, 184–188.

von Grunebaum, Gustave E. (1962), *Modern Islam: The Search for Cultural Identity*, New York: Vintage Books.

Hall, Edward T. (1983), *The Dance of Life: The Other Dimension of Time*, Garden City, NY: Anchor Press/Doubleday.

Handler, Richard and Jocelyn Linnekin (1984), "Tradition, Genuine or Spurious," *Journal of American Folklore*, 97 (385), 273–290.

Harris, Neil (1978), "Museums, Merchandising, and Popular Taste: The Struggle for Influence," in *Material Culture and the Study of American Life*, ed. Ian M. G. Quimby, New York: W. W. Norton and Co.

———— (1981), "The Drama of Consumer Desire," in *Yankee Enterprise: The Rise of the American System of Manufacturers*, eds. Otto Mayr and Robert C. Post, Washington: Smithsonian Institution Press, 189–216.

Hass, Robert (1973), *Field Guide*, New Haven: Yale University Press.

Hayden, Dolores (1981), *The Grand Domestic Revolution: A History of Feminist Designs for American Homes, Neighborhoods and Cities*, Cambridge: M.I.T. Press.

Heal, Felicity (1984), "The Idea of Hospitality in Early Modern England," *Past and Present*, 102 (February), 66–93.

Hebdige, Dick (1979), *Subculture: The Meaning of Style*, London: Methuen.

Hendon, Donald W. and William F. Muhs (1985), "Origins and Early Development of Outdoor Advertising in the United States," in *Historical Perspective in Consumer Research: National and International Perspectives*, eds. Chin Tiong Tan and Jagdish N. Sheth, Singapore: National University of Singapore, 309–313.

Henry, Walter A. (1976), "Cultural Values Do Correlate with Consumer Behavior," *Journal of Marketing Research*, 13 (2 May), 121–127.

Herrmann, Robert O. (1974), "The Consumer Movement in Historical Perspective," *Consumerism: Search for the Consumer Interest*, eds. David A. Aaker and George S. Day, New York: The Free Press, 10–18.

—— (1980), "Consumer Protection: Yesterday, Today and Tomorrow," *Current History*, 78 (457), 193–196, 226–227.

Hexter, Jack H. (1961), "The Education of the Aristocracy in the Renaissance," in *Reappraisals in History*, by Jack H. Hexter, London: Longmans, 45–70.

Hine, Thomas (1986), *Populuxe*, New York: Knopf.

Hirsch, Paul M. (1972), "Processing Fads and Fashions: An Organization-Set Analysis of Cultural Industry Systems," *American Journal of Sociology*, 77 (4 January), 639–659.

Hirschman, Albert O. (1977), *The Passions and the Interests: Political Arguments for Capitalism before Its Triumph*, Princeton: Princeton University Press.

—— (1982a), *Shifting Involvements: Private Interests and Public Action*, Princeton: Princeton University Press.

—— (1982b), "Rival Interpretations of Market Society: Civilizing, Destructive, or Feeble?" *Journal of Economic Literature*, 20 (December), 1463–1484.

Hirschman, Elizabeth C. (1981), "Comprehending Symbolic Consumption," in *Symbolic Consumer Behavior*, eds. Elizabeth C. Hirschman and Morris B. Holbrook, Ann Arbor, MI: Association for Consumer Research, 4–6.

—— (1984), "Leisure Motives and Sex Roles," *Journal of Leisure Research*, 16 (3), 209–223.

—— (1985), "Primitive Aspects of Consumption in Modern American Society," *Journal of Consumer Research*, 12 (2 September), 142–154.

—— (1986a), "The Creation of Product Symbolism," in *Advances in Consumer Research*, Vol. 13, ed. Richard J. Lutz, Provo, UT: Association for Consumer Research, 327–331.

—— (1986b), "Humanistic Inquiry in Marketing Research: Philosophy, Method, and Criteria," *Journal of Marketing Research*, 23 (3 August), 237–249.

—— and Morris B. Holbrook, eds., (1981), *Symbolic Consumer Behavior: Proceedings of the Conference on Consumer Esthetics and Symbolic Consumption*, Ann Arbor: Association for Consumer Research.

Hobsbawm, Eric and Terence Ranger, eds., (1983), *The Invention of Tradition*, Cambridge: Cambridge University Press.

Holbrook, Morris B. (1985), "Why Business is Bad for Consumer Research: The Three Bears Revisited," in *Advances in Consumer Research*, Vol. 12, eds. Elizabeth C. Hirschman and Morris B. Holbrook, Provo, UT: Association for Consumer Research, 145–156.

—— and William L. Moore (1981a), "Feature Interactions in Consumer Judgments of Verbal versus Pictorial Presentations," *Journal of Consumer Research*, 8 (1 June), 103–113.

—— and William L. Moore (1981b), "Cue Configurality in Esthetic Responses," in *Symbolic Consumer Behavior*, eds. Elizabeth C. Hirschman and Morris B. Holbrook, Ann Arbor, MI: Association for Consumer Research, 16–25.

—— and Elizabeth C. Hirschman (1982), "The Experiential Aspects of Consumption: Consumer Fantasies, Feelings, and Fun," *Journal of Consumer Research*, 9 (2 September), 132–140.

—— and Glenn Dixon (1985), "Mapping the Market for Fashion: Complementarity in Consumer Preferences," in *The Psychology of Fashion*, ed. Michael R. Solomon, Lexington, MA: Lexington Books, 109–126.

Hollander, Stanley C. (1984), "Sumptuary Legislation: Demarketing by Edict," *Journal of Macromarketing*, 4 (1 Spring), 4–16.

—— and Kathleen M. Rassuli (1985), "Desire: Induced, Innate, Insatiable? Historians' Views of Consumer Motivation and Behavior in the 18th, 19th and 20th Centuries," Working paper, Department of Marketing and Transportation, Michigan State University, East Lansing, MI, 48824–1121.

—— and Ronald Savitt, eds. (1983), *First North American Workshop on Historical Re-*

search in Marketing: Proceedings, East Lansing: Department of Marketing and Transportation, Michigan State University.

Holman, Rebecca (1980a), "Product Use as Communication: A Fresh Appraisal of a Venerable Topic," in *Review of Marketing*, eds. Ben M. Enis and Kenneth J. Roering, Chicago: American Marketing Association, 250–272.

——— (1980b), "A Transcription and Analysis System for the Study of Women's Clothing Behavior," *Semiotica*, 32 (1–2), 11–34.

——— (1980c), "Clothing as Communication: An Empirical Investigation," in *Advances in Consumer Research*, Vol. 7, ed. Jerry C. Olson, Ann Arbor, MI: Association for Consumer Research, 372–377.

——— (1981), "Apparel as Communication," in *Symbolic Consumer Behavior*, eds. Elizabeth C. Hirschman and Morris B. Holbrook, Ann Arbor, MI: Association for Consumer Research, 7–15.

Hont, Istvan and Michael Ignatieff (1983), *Wealth and Virtue: The Shaping of Political Economy in the Scottish Enlightenment*, Cambridge: Cambridge University Press.

Hooper, Wilfred (1915), "The Tudor Sumptuary Laws," *The English Historical Review*, 30, 433–449.

Horowitz, Daniel (1985), *The Morality of Spending: Attitudes toward the Consumer Society in America, 1875–1940*, Baltimore: Johns Hopkins University Press.

Horowitz, R. Tamar (1975), "From Elite Fashion to Mass Fashion," *Archives Européennes de Sociologie*, 16 (2), 283–295.

Hoskins, W. G. (1953), "The Rebuilding of Rural England 1570–1640," *Past and Present*, 4, 44–59.

Jackson, J. B. (1976), "The Domestication of the Garage," *Landscape*, 20 (2 Winter): 11–19.

Jakobson, Roman (1971), "Language in Relation to Other Communication Systems," *Selected Writings of Roman Jakobson*, Vol. 2, The Hague: Mouton, 697–708.

——— and Morris Halle (1956), "Two Aspects of Language," in *Fundamentals of Language*, Janua Linguarum, VIV. I, The Hague: Mouton, 54–82.

James, Mervyn E. (1974), *Family, Lineage and Civil Society*, Oxford: Clarendon Press.

——— (1978), "English Politics and the Concept of Honour 1485–1642," *Past and Present*, Supplement No. 3.

Jefferson, Tony (1975), "Cultural Responses of the Teds: The Defense of Space and Status," in *Resistance Through Rituals*, eds. Stuart Hall and Tony Jefferson, London: Hutchinson and Co., 81–86.

Jones, Paul V. B. (1917), "The Household of a Tudor Nobleman," *University of Illinois Studies in the Social Sciences*, 6 (4), 1–277.

Joseph, Nathan (1986), *Uniform and Nonuniform: Communication through Clothing*, Westport, CT: Greenwood Press.

Kassarjian, Hal (1986), "Consumer Research: Some Recollections and a Commentary," in *Advances in Consumer Research*, Vol. 13, ed. Richard J. Lutz, Provo, UT: Association for Consumer Research, 6–8.

——— and Mary Jane Sheffet (1975), "Personality and Consumer Behavior: One More Time," *1975 AMA Combined Proceedings*, Series No. 37, Chicago: American Marketing Association, 197–201.

Katz, Elihu and Paul F. Lazarsfeld (1955), *Personal Influence*, Glencoe, IL: The Free Press.

Kavanaugh, James V. (1978), "The Artifact in American Culture," in *Material Culture and the Study of American Life*, ed. Ian M. G. Quimby, New York: W. W. Norton and Co., 65–74.

Kehret-Ward, Trudy (1985), "Improving Recall By Manipulating the Syntax of Consumption Rituals," in *Advances in Consumer Research*, Vol. 12, eds. Elizabeth C. Hirschman and Morris B. Holbrook, Provo, UT: Association for Consumer Research, 319–328.

——— and Anya Golden (1986), "Gender and Situational Influences on Ritual Syntax," paper presented at the 1986 Annual Conference of the Association for Consumer Research, Toronto, 17 October, 1986.

—— and Richard Yalch (1984), "To Take or Not to Take the Only One: Effects of Changing the Meaning of a Product Attribute on Choice Behavior," *Journal of Consumer Research*, 10 (4 March), 410–416.

Kelso, Ruth (1929), *The Doctrine of the English Gentleman in the 16th Century*, Urbana: University of Illinois Press.

Kidwell, Claudia B. and Margaret C. Christman (1974), *Suiting Everyone: The Democratization of Clothing in America*, Washington: Smithsonian Institution Press.

King, Charles W. (1963), "Fashion Adoption: A Rebuttal to the 'Trickle-Down' Theory," in *Toward Scientific Marketing*, ed. Stephen A. Greyser, Chicago: American Marketing Association, 108–125.

—— and Lawrence J. Ring (1980), "The Dynamics of Style and Taste Adoption and Diffusion: Contributions from Fashion Theory," in *Advances in Consumer Research*, Vol. 7, ed. Jerry C. Olson, Ann Arbor, MI: Association for Consumer Research, 13–16.

Kluckhohn, Clyde (1962), "Values and Value-Orientations in the Theory of Action," in *Toward a General Theory of Action*, eds. Talcott Parsons and Edward A. Shils, Cambridge: Harvard University Press, 388–433.

Kollat, David T. and Ronald T. Willett (1967), "Customer Impulse Purchasing Behavior," *Journal of Marketing Research*, 4 (1 February), 21–31.

Kron, Joan (1983), *Home-Psych: The Social Psychology of Home and Decoration*, New York: Clarkson N. Potter, Inc.

Krampen, Martin (1979), "Survey of Current Work on the Semiology of Objects," in *A Semiotic Landscape: Proceedings of the First Congress of the International Association for Semiotic Studies*, eds. Seymour Chatman et al., The Hague: Mouton, 158–168.

Kuper, Hilda (1972), "The Language of Sites in the Politics of Space," *American Anthropologist*, 74, 411–425.

—— (1973a), "Costume and Identity," *Comparative Studies in Society and History*, 15 (3), 348–367.

—— (1973b), "Costume and Cosmology: The Animal Symbolism of the Ncwala," *Man*, 8, new series (4 December), 613–630.

Lasch, Christopher (1979), *The Culture of Narcissism*, New York: W. W. Norton and Co.

Laslett, Peter (1971), *The World We Have Lost: England Before the Industrial Age*, second ed., New York: Charles Scribner's Sons.

Laumann, Edward O. and James S. House (1970), "Living Room Styles and Social Attributes: The Patterning of Material Artifacts in a Modern Urban Community," *Sociology and Social Research*, 54 (3 April), 321–342.

Lawrence, Roderick J. (1981), "The Social Classification of Domestic Space: A Cross-Cultural Case Study," *Anthropos*, 76, 649–664.

—— (1982), "Domestic Space and Society: A Cross-Cultural Study," *Comparative Studies in Society and History*, 24 (1), 104–130.

—— (1984), "Transition Spaces and Dwelling Design," *Journal of Architectural and Planning Research*, 1, 261–271.

Lazer, William (1963), "Life Style Concepts and Marketing," in *Toward Scientific Marketing*, ed. Stephen A. Greyser, Chicago: American Marketing Association, 130–139.

Leach, Edmund R. (1961), "Time and False Noses," in *Rethinking Anthropology*, ed. R. Edmund Leach, London: Athlone Press, 132–136.

Leach, William R. (1984), "Transformations in a Culture of Consumption: Women and Department Stores, 1890–1925," *The Journal of American History*, 71 (September), 319–342.

Lears, T. J. Jackson (1981), *No Place of Grace: Antimodernism and the Transformation of American Culture 1880–1920*, New York: Pantheon Books.

Lechtman, Heather and Robert S. Merrill, eds. (1977), *Material Culture: Styles, Organization, and Dynamics of Technology*, St. Paul: West Publishing Co.

Leiss, William (1983), "Things Come Alive: Economy and Technology as Modes of Social Representation in Modern Society," paper presented at Table Ronde Internationale sur les Representations, Montreal, October, 1983.

———, Stephen Kline, and Sut Jhally (1986), *Social Communication in Advertising*, New York: Methuen.

Lévi-Strauss, Claude (1963), "Structural Analysis in Linguistics and Anthropology," in *Structural Anthropology I*, trans. Claire Jacobson and Brooke Grundfest Schoepf, Harmondsworth: Penguin Books, 31–54.

——— (1966), *The Savage Mind*, Chicago: University of Chicago Press.

Levy, Sidney J. (1959), "Symbols for Sale," *Harvard Business Review*, 37 (4 July/August), 117–124.

——— (1963), "Symbolism and Life Style," in *Toward Scientific Marketing*, ed. Stephen A. Greyser, Chicago: American Marketing Association, 140–150.

——— (1978), "Hunger and Work in a Civilized Tribe," *American Behavioral Scientist*, 21 (4 March/April), 557–570.

——— (1981), "Interpreting Consumer Mythology: A Structural Approach to Consumer Behavior," *Journal of Marketing*, 45 (Summer), 49–61.

Lewis, David L. and Laurence Goldstein, eds., (1983), *The Automobile and American Culture*, Ann Arbor: University of Michigan Press.

Lewis, Oscar (1969), "The Possessions of the Poor," *Scientific American*, 221 (4), 114–124.

Linthicum, Marie Channing (1936), *Costume in the Drama of Shakespeare and His Contemporaries*, Oxford: Clarendon Press.

Lohof, Bruce A. (1969), "The Higher Meaning of Marlboro Cigarettes," *Journal of Popular Culture*, 3 (3), 441–450.

Lurie, Alison (1981), *The Language of Clothes*, New York: Random House.

Macfarlane, Alan (1978), *The Origins of English Individualism: The Family, Property, and Social Transition*, Oxford: Basil Blackwell.

Manuel, Frank Edward and Fritzie Prigohzy Manuel (1979), *Utopian Thought in the Western World*, Cambridge, MA: Belknap Press.

Maranda, Pierre (1972), "Structuralism in Cultural Anthropology," *Annual Review of Anthropology*, 1, 329–348.

Marchand, Roland (1985), *Advertising the American Dream: Making Way for Modernity, 1920–1940*, Berkeley: University of California Press.

Marcus, George E. (1985), "Spending: the Hunts, Silver, and Dynastic families in America," *Archives Européennes de Sociologie*, 26 (2), 224–259.

Marshall, Gordon (1980), *Presbyteries and Profits: Calvinism and the Development of Capitalism in Scotland, 1560–1707*, New York: Oxford University Press.

——— (1982), *In Search of the Spirit of Capitalism: An Essay on Max Weber's Protestant Ethic Thesis*, New York: Columbia University Press.

Marston, Jerrilyn Greene (1973), "Gentry Honor and Royalism in Early Stuart England," *The Journal of British Studies*, 13 (1 November), 21–43.

Martin, Bernice (1981), *A Sociology of Contemporary Cultural Change*, Oxford: Basil Blackwell.

Mason, Roger S. (1981), *Conspicuous Consumption*, New York: St. Martin's Press.

——— (1984), "Conspicuous Consumption: A Literature Review," *European Journal of Marketing*, 18 (3), 26–39.

Mauss, Marcel (1970), *The Gift*, London: Routledge and Kegan Paul.

——— (1985), "A Category of the Human Mind: the notion of the person; the notion of self," in *The Category of the Person*, eds. Michael Carrithers, Steven Collins, and Steven Lukes, Cambridge: Cambridge University Press, 1–25.

Mayer, Robert (1978), "Exploring Sociological Theories By Studying Consumers," *American Behavioral Scientist*, 21 (March/April), 600–613.

Mazuri, Ali A. (1970), "The Robes of Rebellion," *Encounter*, 34 (2), 19–30.

McCracken, Grant (1980), "Anthropology and the Study of Advertising: A Critical Review of Selected Literature," Working Paper 84–103 in the University of Guelph, Department of Consumer Studies, Working Paper Series.

—— (1982a), "Rank and Two Aspects of Dress in Elizabethan England," *Culture*, 2 (2), 53–62.

—— (1982b), "Politics and Ritual Sotto Voce: The Use of Demeanor as an Instrument of Politics in Elizabethan England," *Canadian Journal of Anthropology*, 3 (1 Fall), 85–100.

—— (1983a), "The Exchange of Tudor Children," *Journal of Family History*, 8 (4 Winter), 303–313.

—— (1983b), "History and Symbolic Anthropology: a Review and Critique of Four New Contributions to their Rapprochement," *Culture*, 3 (2), 3–14.

—— (1984a), "The Cultural and Communicative Properties of Houses and Home Furnishings in Contemporary North America," Working Paper 84–402 in the University of Guelph, Department of Consumer Studies, Working Paper Series.

—— (1984b), Review of *From Graven Images: Patterns of Modern Materialism* by Chandra Mukerji, *International Journal of Comparative Sociology*, 25 (3–4), 283–284.

—— (1984c), "The Pre-Coronation Passage of Elizabeth I: Political Theatre or the Rehearsal of Politics?" *Canadian Review of Sociology and Anthropology*, 21 (1 February), 47–61.

—— (1985a), "Dress Colour at the Court of Elizabeth I: An Essay in Historical Anthropology," *Canadian Review of Sociology and Anthropology*, 22 (4 November), 515–533.

—— (1985b), "The Trickle-Down Theory Rehabilitated," in *The Psychology of Fashion*, ed. Michael R. Solomon, Lexington, MA: Lexington Books, 39–54.

—— (1985c), "Clio in the Marketplace: Theoretical and Methodological Issues in the History of Consumption," in *Historical Perspectives in Consumer Research: National and International Perspectives*, eds. Chin Tiong Tan and Jagdish N. Sheth, Singapore: National University of Singapore, 151–154.

—— (1986a), "Culture and Consumption: A Theoretical Account of the Structure and Movement of the Cultural Meaning of Consumer Goods," *Journal of Consumer Research* 13 (1 June): 71–84.

—— (1986b), "Upstairs/Downstairs: The Canadian Production," *Purposes in Built Form and Culture Research, Proceedings of the 1986 Conference on Built Form and Culture Research*, eds. J. William Carswell and David G. Saile, Lawrence: University of Kansas, 68–71.

—— (1987a), "Advertising: Meaning or Information?" in *Advances in Consumer Research*, Vol. 14, eds. Paul F. Anderson and Melanie Wallendorf, Provo, UT: Association for Consumer Research, 121–124.

—— (1987b), "The History of Consumption: A Research and Consumer Guide," *Journal of Consumer Policy*, 12, 10 (2 June), 139–166.

—— (1987c), "Culture and Consumption Among the Elderly: Research Objectives for the Study of Person-Object Relations in An Aging Population," *Ageing and Society*, 7 (2 June), forthcoming.

—— (1987d), "Qualitative Methods and the Study of Consumer Behavior: A Model of and for Inquiry." Working Paper 87–103, University of Guelph, Department of Consumer Studies, University of Guelph, Working Paper Series.

—— and Victor J. Roth (1986), "Does Clothing Have a Code? Empirical Findings and Theoretical Implications in the Study of Clothing as a Means of Communication,"

Working Paper 86–101, University of Guelph, Department of Consumer Studies, Working Paper Series.

McKendrick, Neil, John Brewer, and J. H. Plumb (1982), *The Birth of a Consumer Society: The Commercialization of Eighteenth-Century England*, Bloomington: Indiana University Press.

Meikle, Jeffrey L. (1979), *Twentieth Century Limited: Industrial Design In America, 1925–1939*, Philadelphia: Temple University Press.

Mertz, Elizabeth and Richard J. Parmentier, eds. (1985), *Semiotic Mediation: Sociocultural and Psychological Perspectives*, Orlando: Academic Press.

Messerschmidt, Donald A., ed. (1981), *Anthropologists at Home in North America*, New York: Cambridge University Press.

Messing, S. (1960), "The Nonverbal Language of the Ethiopian Toga," *Anthropos*, 55, 558–561.

Meyersohn, Rolf and Elihu Katz (1957), "Notes on a Natural History of Fads," *American Journal of Sociology*, 62 (May), 594–601.

Mick, David Glen (1986), "Consumer Research and Semiotics: Exploring the Morphology of Signs, Symbols and Significance," *Journal of Consumer Research*, 13 (2 September), 196–213.

Miller, Michael B. (1981), *The Bon Marché: Bougeois Culture and the Department Store, 1869–1920*, Princeton: Princeton University Press.

Miner, Horace (1956), "Body Ritual among the Nacirema," *American Anthropologist*, 58, 503–507.

Mitchell, Arnold (1983), *The Nine American Lifestyles*, New York: Warner Books.

Moeran, Brian (1985), "When the Poetics of Advertising Becomes the Advertising of Poetics: Syntactical and Semantic Parallelism in English and Japanese Advertising," *Language and Communication*, 5 (1), 29–44.

Moers, Ellen (1960), *The Dandy: Brummel to Beerbohm*, London: Secker and Warburg.

Molloy, John T. (1977), *The Woman's Dress for Success Book*, New York: Warner Books.

Montrose, Louis (1980), " 'Eliza, Queene of Shepheardes,' and the Pastoral of Power," *English Literary Renaissance*, 10, 153–182.

Moorhouse, H. F. (1983), "American Automobiles and Workers' Dreams," *The Sociological Review*, 31 (3 August), 403–426.

Moore, D.G. (1963), "Life Styles in Mobile Suburbia," in *Toward Scientific Marketing*, ed. Stephen A. Greyser, Chicago: American Marketing Association, 151–163.

Mukerji, Chandra (1983), *From Graven Images: Patterns of Modern Materialism*, New York: Columbia University Press.

Muncy, James A. and Shelby D. Hunt (1984), "Consumer Involvement: Definitional Issues and Research Directions," in *Advances in Consumer Research*, Vol. 11, ed. Thomas C. Kinnear, Provo, UT: Association for Consumer Research, 193–196.

Munn, Nancy (1973), "Symbolism in a Ritual Context: Aspects of Symbolic Action," in *Handbook of Social and Cultural Anthropology*, ed. John L. Honigmann, Chicago: Rand McNally, 579–612.

Murphy, Robert F. (1964), "Social Distance and the Veil," *American Anthropologist*, 66, 1257–1274.

Myers, Elizabeth (1985), "Phenomenological Analysis of the Importance of Special Possessions: An Exploratory Study," in *Advances in Consumer Research*, Vol. 12, eds. Elizabeth C. Hirschman and Morris B. Holbrook, Provo, UT: Association for Consumer Research, 560–565.

Myers, James H. and Jonathan Gutman (1974), "Life Style: The Essence of Social Class," in *Life Style and Psychographics*, ed. William D. Wells, Chicago: American Marketing Association, 235–256.

Naisbitt, John (1982), *Megatrends*, New York: Warner Books.

Nash, Jeffrey E. (1977), "Decoding the Runner's Wardrobe," in *Conformity and Conflict:*

Readings in Cultural Anthropology, third ed., eds. James P. Spradley and David W. McCurdy, Boston: Little, Brown, and Co., 172–185.

Neich, Roger (1982), "A Semiological Analysis of Self-Decoration in Mount Hagen, New Guinea," in *The Logic of Culture*, ed. Ino Rossi, South Hadley, MA: J. F. Bergin, 214–231.

Nicosia, Francesco M. and Robert N. Mayer (1976), "Toward a Sociology of Consumption," *Journal of Consumer Research*, 3 (2 September), 65–75.

Nisbet, Robert A. (1969), *Social Change and History*, New York: Oxford University Press.

Norris, Herbert (1938), *The Tudors*, London: J. M. Dent and Sons.

O'Guinn, Thomas C., Ronald J. Faber, and Marshall Rice (1985), "Popular Film and Television as Consumer Acculturation Agents: America 1900 to Present," in *Historical Perspective in Consumer Research: National and International Perspectives*, eds. Chin Tiong Tan and Jagdish N. Sheth, Singapore: National University of Singapore, 297–301.

――――, Ronald J. Faber, and Raymond Krych (1987), "Compulsive Consumption," in *Advances in Consumer Research*, Vol. 14, eds. Paul F. Anderson and Melanie Wallendorf, Provo, UT: Association for Consumer Research, forthcoming.

Olson, Clark D. (1985), "Materialism in the Home: The Impact of Artifacts on Dyadic Communication," in *Advances in Consumer Research*, Vol. 12, eds. Elizabeth C. Hirschman and Morris B. Holbrook, Provo, UT: Association for Consumer Research, 388–393.

O'Neill, John (1978), "The Productive Body: An Essay on the Work of Consumption," *Queen's Quarterly*, 85 (2 Summer), 221–230.

Ortner, Sherry (1978), *Sherpas through their Rituals*, Cambridge: Cambridge University Press.

Ovidus Naso, Publius (1960), *Metamorphoses*, trans. F. J. Miller, Cambridge: Harvard University Press.

Peirce, Charles S. (1932), *Collected Papers of Charles Sanders Peirce*, Vol. 2, eds. Charles Hartshorne and Paul Weiss, 3 vols. Cambridge: Harvard University Press.

Phillips, Joanna W. and Helen K. Staley (1961), "Sumptuary Legislation in Four Centuries," *Journal of Home Economics*, 53 (8 October): 673–677.

Pittman, Frank S. (1985), "Children of the Rich," *Family Process*, 24 (December), 461–472.

Pitt-Rivers, A. Lane-Fox (1906), "On the Evolution of Culture," in *The Evolution of Culture and Other Essays*, ed. J. L. Myers, Oxford: Clarendon Press, 20–44.

Plummer, Joseph T. (1971), "Life Style Patterns and Commercial Bank Credit Card Usage," *Journal of Marketing*, 35 (April), 35–41.

Poggi, Gianfranco (1983), *Calvinism and the Capitalist Spirit, Max Weber's Protestant Ethic*, Amherst: University of Massachusetts Press.

Polanyi, Karl (1957), *The Great Transformation: The Political and Economic Origins of Our Time*, Boston: Beacon Press.

Polegato, Rosemary and Marjorie Wall (1980), "Information Seeking by Fashion Opinion Leaders and Followers," *Home Economics Research Journal*, 8 (5 May), 327–338.

Pollay, Richard W. (1984), "The Identification and Distribution of Values Manifest in Print Advertising, 1900–1980," in *Personal Values and Consumer Behavior*, eds. Robert E. Pitts, Jr. and Arch G. Woodside, Lexington, MA: Lexington Books, 111–135.

―――― (1985), "American Advertising and Societal Values During the Twentieth Century," in *Historical Perspective in Consumer Research: National and International Perspectives*, eds. Chin Tiong Tan and Jagdish N. Sheth, Singapore: National University of Singapore, 60–71.

―――― (1986), "The Distorted Mirror: Reflections on the Unintended Consequences of Advertising," *Journal of Marketing*, 50 (2 April), 18–36.

Pope, Daniel (1983), *The Making of Modern Advertising*, New York: Basic Books.

Pratt, Gerry (1981), "The House as an Expression of Social Worlds," in *Housing and Identity: Cross-Cultural Perspectives*, ed. James S. Duncan, London: Croom Helm, 135–180.

Presbry, Frank S. (1968), *The History and Development of Advertising*, New York: Greenwood Press.

Prown, Jules D. (1980), "Style as Evidence," *Winterthur Portfolio*, 15 (3 Autumn), 197–210.

——— (1982), "Mind in Matter: An Introduction to Material Culture Theory and Method," *Winterthur Portfolio*, 17 (1 Spring), 1–19.

Pulos, Arthur J. (1983), *American Design Ethic: A History of Industrial Design to 1940*, Cambridge: M.I.T. Press.

Quimby, Ian, ed. (1978), *Material Culture and the Study of Material Life*, New York: W. W. Norton and Co.

Rae, John B. (1971), *The Road and Car in American Life*, Cambridge: M.I.T. Press.

Rainwater, Lee, Richard P. Coleman, and Gerald Handel (1959), *Workingman's Wife: Her Personality, World and Life Style*, New York: Macfadden Books.

Rapoport, Amos (1968), "The Personal Element in Housing—an argument for open-ended design," *Journal of the Royal Institute of British Architects*, 75 (July), 300–307.

——— (1982), *The Meaning of the Built Environment*, Beverly Hills: Sage Publications.

Rathje, William (1978), "Archaeological Ethnography," in *Explorations in Ethnoarchaeology*, ed. Richard A. Gould, Albuquerque: University of New Mexico Press, 49–76.

Reynolds, Barrie and Margaret Stott, eds. (1986), *Material Anthropology: Contemporary Approaches in Material Cuture*, New York: University Press of America.

Richardson, J. and A. L. Kroeber (1940), "Three Centuries of Women's Dress Fashions: A Quantitative Analysis," *Anthropological Records*, 2, 111–153.

Richardson, Miles (1974), "Images, Objects and the Human Story," in *The Human Mirror: Material and Spatial Images of Man*, ed. Miles Richardson, Baton Rouge: Louisiana State University Press, 3–14

Richwood, Peter (1984), "Lottery Win Not All Roses, Woman Finds," *The Toronto Sunday Star*, 29 April 1984, p. A14.

Roach, Mary Ellen (1979), "The Social Symbolism of Women's Dress," in *The Fabrics of Culture*, eds. Justine M. Cordwell and Ronald A. Schwarz, The Hague: Mouton, 415–422.

——— and Joanne Bubolz Eicher, eds. (1965), *Dress, Adornment and the Social Order*, New York: Wiley.

——— and J. B. Eicher (1979), "The Language of Personal Adornment," in *The Fabrics of Culture*, eds. Justine Cordwell and Ronald A. Schwarz, The Hague: Mouton, 7–22.

Roberts, Helene E. (1977), "The Exquisite Slave: The Role of Clothes in the Making of the Victorian Woman," *Signs*, 2 (3 Spring), 554–567.

Rodman, Margaret C. and Jean-Marc Philibert (1985), "Rethinking Consumption: Some Problems Concerning The Practice of Objects in the Third World," paper presented at the Canadian Ethnological Society Meetings, University of Toronto, 11 May 1985.

Rogers, Everett M. (1983), *Diffusion of Innovations*, third ed. New York: The Free Press.

Rokeach, Milton, ed. (1979), *Understanding Human Values*, New York: The Free Press.

Rook, Dennis W. (1984), "Ritual Behavior and Consumer Symbolism," in *Advances in Consumer Research*, Vol. 11, ed. Thomas C. Kinnear, Provo, UT: Association for Consumer Research, 279–284.

——— (1985), "The Ritual Dimension of Consumer Behavior," *Journal of Consumer Research*, 12 (3 December), 251–264.

——— and Stephen J. Hoch (1985), "Consuming Impulses," in *Advances in Consumer Research*, Vol. 12, eds. Elizabeth C. Hirschman and Morris B. Holbrook, Provo, UT: Association for Consumer Research, 23–27.

——— and Sidney J. Levy (1983), "Psychosocial Themes in Consumer Grooming Rituals," in *Advances in Consumer Research*, Vol. 10, eds. Richard P. Bagozzi and Alice M. Tybout, Ann Arbor, MI: Association for Consumer Research, 329–333b.

Rosenfeld, Lawrence B. and Timothy G. Plax (1977), "Clothing as Communication," *Journal of Communication*, 27 (2 Spring), 24–31.

Rubenstein, Harry R. (1985), "Collecting for Tomorrow: Sweden's Contemporary Documentation Program," *Museum News*, August, 55–60.

Sahlins, Marshall (1972), "The Spirit of the Gift," in *Stone Age Economics*, by Marshall Sahlins, Chicago: Aldine, 149–183.

——— (1976), *Culture and Practical Reason*, Chicago: University of Chicago Press.

——— (1977), "The State of the Art in Social/Cultural Anthropology: Search for an Object," in *Perspectives on Anthropology 1976*, eds. A. F. C. Wallace et al., Special Publication of the American Anthropological Association, No. 10, 14–32.

——— (1981), *Historical Metaphors and Mythical Realities: Structure in the Early History of the Sandwich Islands Kingdom*, Ann Arbor: University of Michigan Press.

Sapir, Edward (1931), "Communication," *Encyclopedia of the Social Sciences*, first ed. 78–80.

Sapir, J. David (1977), "The Anatomy of Metaphor," in *The Social Use Of Metaphor*, eds. J. David Sapir and J. Christopher Crocker, Philadelphia: University of Pennsylvania Press, 3–32.

de Saussure, Ferdinand (1966), *Course in General Linguistics*, New York: McGraw-Hill.

Schlereth, Thomas J. (1982), "Material Culture Studies in America, 1876–1976," in *Material Culture Studies in America*, ed. Thomas J. Schlereth, Nashville, TN: The American Association for State and Local History, 1–75.

——— (1983), "Material Culture Studies and Social History Research," *Journal of Social History*, 16 (4), 111–143.

——— (1984), "Contemporary Collecting for Future Recollecting," *Museum Studies Journal*, 2 (Spring), 23–30.

——— (1985), "The Material Culture of Childhood: Problems and Potential in Historical Explanation," *Material History Bulletin*, 21 (Spring), 1–14.

Schneider, David M. (1968), *American Kinship: A Cultural Account*, Englewood Cliffs, NJ: Prentice-Hall.

Schudson, Michael (1984), *Advertising, The Uneasy Persuasion*, New York: Basic Books.

Schwartz, Barry (1967), "The Social Psychology of the Gift," *American Journal of Sociology*, 73 (July), 1–11.

Schwartz, Jack (1963), "Men's Clothing and the Negro," *Phylon*, 24 (3), 224–231.

Schwarz, Ronald A. (1979), "Uncovering the Secret Vice: Toward an Anthropology of Clothing and Adornment," in *The Fabrics of Culture*, eds. Justine Cordwell and Ronald A. Schwarz, The Hague: Mouton, 23–45.

Scitovsky, Tibor (1976), *The Joyless Economy: An Inquiry into Human Satisfaction and Consumer Dissatisfaction*, New York: Oxford University Press.

Sellerberg, Ann-Mari (1976), "On Differing Social Meanings of Consumption," *Journal of the Market Research Society*, 18 (4), 211–213.

Shell, Marc (1978), *The Economy of Literature*, Baltimore: Johns Hopkins University Press.

——— (1982), *Money, Language, and Thought: Literary and Philosophical Economies from the Medieval to the Modern Era*, Berkeley: University of California Press.

Sherman, Edmund and Evelyn S. Newman (1977–78), "The Meaning of Cherished Possessions for the Elderly," *International Journal of Aging and Human Development*, 8 (2), 181–192.

Sherry, John F., Jr. (1983), "Gift-Giving in Anthropological Perspective," *Journal of Consumer Research*, 10 (2 September), 157–168.

——— (1985), "Advertising as a Cultural System," paper presented at the 1985 American Marketing Association Educators' Conference, Phoenix, Arizona.

Shi, David E. (1985), *The Simple Life: Plain Living and High Thinking in American Culture*, New York: Oxford University Press.

Shweder, Richard A. and Robert A. LeVine, eds. (1984), *Culture Theory: Essays on Mind, Self and Emotion*, Cambridge: Cambridge University Press.

Silverman, Martin G. (1969), "Maximize Your Options: A Study in Values, Symbols, and Social Structure," in *Forms of Symbolic Action*, ed. Robert F. Spencer, Seattle: University of Washington Press, 97–115.

Silverstein, Michael (1976), "Shifters, Linguistic Categories, and Cultural Description," in *Meaning in Anthropology*, eds. Keith H. Basso and Henry A. Selby, Albuquerque: University of New Mexico Press, 11–55.

Simmel, G. (1904), "Fashion," *International Quarterly*, 10, 130–155.

Simmons, Roberta G., Susan D. Klein, and Richard L. Simmons (1977), *Gift of Life: The Social and Psychological Impact of Organ Transplantation*, New York: John Wiley and Sons.

Singer, Benjamin D. (1986), *Advertising and Society*, Don Mills, Ontario: Addison-Wesley.

Singer, Milton B. (1984), *Man's Glassy Essence: Explorations in Semiotic Anthropology*, Bloomington: Indiana University Press.

Smith, Thomas Spence (1974), "Aestheticism and Social Structure: Style and Social Network in the Dandy Life," *American Sociological Review*, 39 (5 October), 725–743.

Solomon, Michael R. (1983), "The Role of Products as Social Stimuli: A Symbolic Interactionism Perspective," *Journal of Consumer Research*, 10 (December), 319–329.

——— ed. (1985), *The Psychology of Fashion*, Lexington, MA: Lexington Books.

——— and Henry Assael (1986), "The Product Constellation: A Gestalt Approach to Symbolic Consumption," unpublished manuscript, Graduate School of Business Administration, New York University.

Sombart, Werner (1967), *Luxury and Capitalism*, trans. W. R. Dittmar, Ann Arbor: University of Michigan Press.

Sommers, Montrose (1963), "Product Symbolism and the Perception of Social Strata," in *Toward Scientific Marketing*, ed. Stephen A. Greyser, Chicago: American Marketing Association, 200–216.

——— (1983), "Evolution of Marketing Thought and Its Implications for the Study of Advertising," paper given at Session 26 ("Research in Advertising"), Joint meetings of the Canadian Communication Association and the Canadian Sociology and Anthropology Association, Vancouver, British Columbia, 4 June 1983.

Spencer, Herbert (1897), *Principles of Sociology*, Vol. 2, part 1, New York: D. Appleton.

Sproles, George B. (1981), "Analyzing Fashion Life Cycles—Principles and Perspectives," *Journal of Marketing*, 45 (Fall), 116–124.

Spufford, Margaret (1984), *The Great Reclothing of Rural England*, London: The Hambledon Press.

Steele, Valerie (1985), *Fashion and Eroticism: Ideals of Feminine Beauty from the Victorian Era to the Jazz Age*, New York: Oxford University Press.

Steiner, Robert L. and Joseph Weiss (1951), "Veblen Revised in the Light of Counter-Snobbery," *Journal of Aesthetics and Art Criticism*, 9 (3 March), 263–268.

Stone, Lawrence (1965), *The Crisis of the Aristocracy 1558–1641*, London: Oxford University Press.

——— (1977), *Family, Sex, and Marriage 1500–1800*, New York: Harper and Row.

——— (1984), "The New Eighteenth Century," *The New York Review of Books*, 31 (5), 42–48.

——— and Jeanne C. Fawtier Stone (1984), *An Open Elite? England 1540–1880*, Oxford: Clarendon Press.

Strong, Roy C. (1973), *Splendour at Court: Renaissance Spectacle and Illusion*, London: Weidenfeld and Nicolson.

—— (1977), *The Cult of Elizabeth. Elizabethan Portraiture and Pageantry,* London: Thames and Hudson.

Summers, John D. (1970), "The Identity of Women's Clothing Fashion Opinion Leaders," *Journal of Marketing Research,* 7, 178–185.

Tambiah, S. J. (1969), "Animals are good to think and good to prohibit," *Ethnology,* 8 (4 October), 424–459.

—— (1977), "The Cosmological and Performative Significance of a Thai Cult of Healing Through Mediation," *Culture, Medicine, and Psychiatry,* 1, 97–132.

Tarde, Gabriel de (1962), *The Laws of Imitation,* Gloucester, MA: P. Smith.

Thirsk, Joan (1978), *Economic Policy and Projects: The Development of a Consumer Society in Early Modern England,* Oxford: Clarendon Press.

Thompson, E. P. (1967), "Time, Work-Discipline, and Industrial Capitalism," *Past and Present,* 38 (December), 56–97.

—— (1974), "Patrician Society, plebeian culture," *Journal of Social History,* 7, 277–304.

Thrupp, Sylvia L. (1948), *The Merchant Class of Medieval London,* Ann Arbor, MI: University of Michigan Press.

Tigert, Douglas, C. W. King, and L. Ring (1980), "Fashion Involvement: A Cross-Cultural Comparative Analysis," in *Advances in Consumer Research,* Vol. 7, ed. Jerry Olson, Ann Arbor, MI: Association for Consumer Research, 17–21.

Tuan, Yi-Fu (1982), *Segmented Worlds and Self,* Minneapolis: University of Minnesota Press.

Turner, Terence (1969), "Tchikrin, A Central Brazilian Tribe and Its Symbolic Language of Bodily Adornment," *Natural History,* 78 (October), 50–59, 80.

Turner, Victor (1967), "Betwixt and Between: the Liminal Period in Rites of Passage," in *The Forest of Symbols,* ed. V. Turner, Ithaca: Cornell University Press, 93–111.

—— (1969), "Forms of Symbolic Action: Introduction," in *Forms of Symbolic Action,* ed. Robert F. Spencer, Seattle: American Ethnological Society, 3–25.

Unruh, David R. (1983), "Death and Personal History: Strategies of Identity Preservation," *Social Problems,* 30 (3 February), 340–351.

Veblen, Thorstein (1912), *The Theory of the Leisure Class,* New York: Macmillan.

Vershure, Beth, Stephen Magel and Edward K. Sadalla (1977), "House Form and Social Identity" in *The Behavioral Basis of Design,* Book 2, eds. Peter Suedfeld, James A. Russell, Lawrence M. Ward, Francoise Szigeti, and Gerald Davis, Stroudsburg, PA: Dowden, Hutchinson and Ross, 273–278.

Vichert, Gordon (1971), "The Theory of Conspicuous Consumption in the 18th Century," in *The Varied Pattern: Studies in the 18th Century,* eds. Peter Hughes and David Williams, Toronto: A. M. Hakkert, 253–267.

Wallendorf, Melanie and Michael D. Reilly (1983), "Ethnic Migration, Assimilation, and Consumption," *Journal of Consumer Research,* 10 (3 December), 292–302.

Warner, W. Lloyd and Paul S. Lunt (1941), *The Social Life of a Modern Community,* New Haven: Yale University Press.

Welch, Barbara (1986), "American Trade Cards: Peering into the Pre-History of the Consumption Culture," paper presented at the 6th International Conference on Culture and Communication, Philadelphia, 9 October 1986.

Wells, William D. (1974), Life Style and Psychographics: Definitions, Uses and Problems," in *Life Style and Psychographics,* ed. William D. Wells, Chicago: American Marketing Association, 317–363.

—— (1986), "Three Useful Ideas," in *Advances in Consumer Research,* Vol. 13, ed. Richard J. Lutz, Provo, UT: Association for Consumer Research, 9–11.

—— and Stephen C. Cosmas (1977), "Lifestyles," in *Selected Aspects of Consumer Behavior,* Washington: National Science Foundation, 299–316.

Wernick, Andrew (1984), "Sign and Commodity: Aspects of the Cultural Dynamic of Advanced Capitalism," *Canadian Journal of Political and Social Theory,* 8 (1–2 Winter), 17–32.

West, Pamela (1976), "The Rise and Fall of the American Porch," *Landscape,* 20 (3 Spring), 42–47.

Wiener, Martin J. (1981), *English Culture and the Decline of the Industrial Spirit, 1850–1980,* Cambridge: Cambridge University Press.

Williams, Rosalind H. (1982), *Dream Worlds: Mass Consumption in Late Nineteenth Century France,* Berkeley: University of California Press.

Williamson, Judith (1978), *Decoding Advertising,* New York: Marion Boyars.

Wills, Gordon and David Midgley, eds. (1973), *Fashion Marketing: An Anthology of Viewpoints and Perspectives,* London: George Allen and Unwin.

Winick, Charles (1961), Anthropology's Contributions to Marketing," *Journal of Marketing,* 25 (5 July), 53–60.

Wolf, Arthur P. (1970), "Chinese Kinship and Mourning Dress," in *Family and Kinship in Chinese Society,* ed. Maurice Freedman, Stanford, CA: Stanford University Press, 189–207.

Wolfe, Tom (1970), *Radical Chic and Mau-Mauing the Flak Catchers,* New York: Farrar, Straus and Giroux.

Wright, Gwendolyn (1980), *Moralism and the Model Home: Domestic Architecture and Cultural Conflict in Chicago, 1873–1913,* Chicago: University of Chicago Press.

York, Peter (1980), *Style Wars,* London: Sidgwick and Jackson.

INDEX